Order In The Court

Order In The Court

A writer's guide to the legal system

David S. Mullally

WRITER'S DIGEST BOOKS
CINCINNATI, OHIO

www.writersdigest.com

Order in the Court. Copyright © 2000 by David S. Mullally. Manufactured in the United States of America. All rights reserved. No part of this book may be reproduced in any form or by any electronic or mechanical means including information storage and retrieval systems without permission in writing from the publisher, except by a reviewer, who may quote brief passages in a review. Published by Writer's Digest Books, an imprint of F&W Publications, Inc., 1507 Dana Avenue, Cincinnati, Ohio 45207. (800) 289-0963. First edition.

Visit our Web site at www.writersdigest.com for information on more resources for writers.

To receive a free weekly E-mail newsletter delivering tips and updates about writing and about Writer's Digest products, send an E-mail with "Subscribe Newsletter" in the body of the message to newsletter-request@writersdigest.com, or register directly at our Web site at www.writersdigest.com.

04   03   02   01   00   5   4   3   2   1

Library of Congress Cataloging-in-Publication Data

Mullally, David S.
    Order in the court: a writer's guide to the legal system / by David S. Mullally.
        p.   cm.
    Includes bibliographical references and index.
    ISBN 0-89879-858-2 (pbk.: alk. paper)
    1. Law—United States. I. Title.
KF385.M85   1999
349.73—dc21   90-046123
                                                                                    CIP

Editor: Jack Heffron
Production editor: Bob Beckstead
Interior designer: Sandy Conopeotis Kent
Cover illustration: © Superstock
Production coordinator: Rachel Vater

This book is dedicated to all the people in the legal profession
who work tirelessly to assure us of our legal rights and protections.

Acknowledgments

For providing me with their time, knowledge and experience: Judges Robert M. Hinrichs, John Anton and William Curtis; Terry L. Spitz, Deputy District Attorney; Fred Herro, Assistant Public Defender; Thomas S. Worthington, Criminal Law Specialist; Larry Hayes, Civil Law Litigator; Karen Johnson-McKewan, Partner with Brobeck, Phleger & Harrison; Michelle Leetham, Senior Counsel with Bechtel Corporation; Matthew E. Williamson, Attorney; Sherri L. Pedersen, Executive Officer and Jury Commissioner; Sue Walker and Chris Orlis, Family Court Mediators; Shelly Ryder Smith, Supervising Probation Officer; Eva Santos, Court Clerk; Marjory Lord, Court Reporter; Jennifer Jones, Bailiff; Rosemary Rovick, Legal Research Attorney.

For passing on creativity and imagination, my mom: Jeanne. For providing me with suggestions and support, my wife: Linda. For his interest in this project, my son: Christopher.

A special thank you to Writer's Digest Books for publishing this book and to senior editor Jack Heffron for his direction, editing and assistance.

About the Author

David S. Mullally has practiced law since 1976 and is licensed in California, Hawaii and Washington , D.C. He has worked with public defenders and district attorneys, in law firms and as a sole practitioner, trying criminal and civil cases. He has represented adults and minors, individuals and insurance companies, plaintiffs and defendants. He has served as judge pro tem, arbitrator, mediator, lecturer at state bar meetings and professor of law. He started writing in high school, working as a reporter for the local newspaper, and contributed articles while at UCLA and law school. Since 1992 he has worked part-time as an attorney, devoting the balance of his time to writing both legal and general-interest articles for newspapers and magazines. This is his first book. He resides in Monterey, California, is married and has a son.

— TABLE OF CONTENTS —

CHAPTER ONE
The Origin and Structure of the Legal System 1
The First Written Laws; A Brief History of Western Law; A Brief History of
Common Law; A Brief History of American Law; Elements of the Common
Law; Organization of the American Legal System; The Federal Court System;
The State Court System; General Principles

CHAPTER TWO
People of the Legal System 14
Lawyers; Law Firms; Sole Practitioners; Tools of the Trade; Personalities; Law
Office Personnel; Judges; Court Personnel; Expert Witnesses; Jury; Criminals;
Victims of Crime; Plaintiff; Defendant; Alternative Dispute Resolution; In Pro
Pers; A Typical Day in a Courthouse

CHAPTER THREE
Crimes, Defenses and Punishments......................................58
Categories of Crimes; Elements of a Crime; Corpus Delicti; Preliminary
Crimes; Crimes Against the Person; Crimes Against Property; Crimes Against
Public Health, Safety and Morals; Controlled Substance Offenses; Crimes
Involving Minors; Miscellaneous Crimes; Federal Crimes; Accomplices and
Accessories; Multiple Offenses; Multiple Prosecutions; Defenses; Punishments

CHAPTER FOUR
Search and Seizure, Arrest and Confession................................85
Search and Seizure; Search Warrants; Execution of Warrant; Exceptions to
Warrant Requirement; Searches of People; Searches of Places; Searches of
Things; Search Methods; Searches by Private Parties; Receipt, Return and
Inventory of Items Seized; The Exclusionary Rule; Stop, Search and Arrest;
Confessions

CHAPTER FIVE
Outline of a Criminal Trial 130
People vs. Ramon Valdez; Here Comes the Attorney; Bail; Postarrest
Appearance; Arraignment; Grand Jury Indictment vs. Criminal Complaint;
Preliminary Hearing; Gathering Evidence; Experts; Pretrial Discovery; Theory
of the Case; Mental Competence and Mental Defenses; Defendant Acting as
His Own Attorney; Pretrial Motions to Suppress Evidence; Change of Venue;
Let's Make a Deal—Plea Bargaining; Pretrial Conference; Right to Speedy
Trial; Preparing Witnesses for Trial; Witnesses' Obligation to Testify; There
Goes the Judge; Trial; Jury Selection; Ideal Juror; Assistance in Jury Selection;

Voir Dire; Challenges for Cause; Peremptory Challenges; Death-Qualification Process; Preparing the Jurors for the Case; Swearing In the Jury; Opening Statements; Direct Examination; Cross-Examination; Re-Direct and Re-Cross Examination; Jurors' Questions; Judge's Questions; Objections; Defense Motions; Defense's Case; Should the Defendant Testify?; Rebuttal and Surrebuttal; Closing Argument; Jury Instructions; Jury Deliberations and Verdict; Communications Between Judge and Jury; Motion for Mistrial; Prejudgment Motions; Death-Penalty Cases; Prior Convictions; Sentencing Hearing—Nondeath Cases; Probation; Appeal; Federal Habeas Corpus Review of State-Court Convictions; Juvenile Proceedings

CHAPTER SIX
Civil Law...175
Personal Injury and Property Damage; Intentional Misconduct; Negligence; Strict Liability; Contracts; Business Law; Intellectual Property Law; Commercial Law; Labor Law; Antitrust Law; Types of Damages; Debtor-Creditor; Bankruptcy; Real Property; Family Law; Estate Planning; Taxation Law; Environmental Law; Immigration; International Law; Air and Space Law; Administrative Law; Admiralty/Maritime Law; Appellate Law; Insurance Law

CHAPTER SEVEN
Outline of a Civil Trial...208
Facts of the Case; Evaluating the Client; Evaluating the Case; Attorney Fees; Managing the Case; Settlement Efforts With an Insurance Company; Litigation; Discovery; Alternative Dispute Resolution; Jury Trial vs. Bench Trial; Preparing for Trial; Settlement Conference; Pretrial Conference in Chambers; Jury Selection; Opening Statements; Rules of Evidence; Form of Question; Plaintiff's Case; Defendant's Case; Expedited Methods of Introducing Evidence; Motions During Trial; Closing Argument; Jury Instructions; Jury Deliberations; Verdicts; Judgments; Motions After Trial; Appeal

APPENDIX A
Glossary of Legal Terms...249
Common Legal Terms; Abbreviations and Acronyms; Common Legal Slang

APPENDIX B
Research Resources...265
The Federal Court System; The State Court System; Finding the Law in a Law Library; Internet Resources; Legal Organizations; Reference Books

Index...272

CHAPTER ONE

The Origin and Structure of the Legal System

> "Society has had to enforce from without rules meant to subdue tides of emotional excess that surge too freely within."
>
> —Sigmund Freud, *Civilization and Its Discontents*

O ur modern world is so intertwined with laws, rules and regulations that it's hard to conceive of society before there were laws. But let's imagine for a minute what could happen if there were no laws limiting people's conduct. Someone could enter your home, take your valuable possessions, load them into your car, hit you with a club when you tried to stop them and speed away, jeopardizing the lives of your neighbors. Wait a minute! There are laws against all this, and it still goes on. So it's not just the presence or absence of the law that's important. There has to be a system to enforce the law. Otherwise your only recourse would be to get your family and friends to assist you in recovering your stuff or seek revenge against your attacker. Vigilante justice.

Laws are meant to provide us with guidance in our own conduct and to protect us from the inappropriate actions of others. But laws only have value if they are enforced. The courts (judges) apply the law and if it's decided the law's been broken, they impose fines or penalties. Together, the law and the courts make up our legal system.

The First Written Laws

The earliest written laws are the Code of Hammurabi, written in ancient Babylonia about 1800 B.C.; the Ten Commandments of the Hebrews handed down to Moses in about 1300 B.C.; and the Edicts of Emperor Asoka, written in Ancient India about 250 B.C.. These were guidelines for proper human behavior, e.g., "the strong should not oppress the weak; wrongs should be set right; obedience should be shown to your mother and father, and respect should be shown to other people and their property; ferocity, cruelty, anger, arrogance and jealousy should be avoided; tolerance, truthfulness, compassion, purity, kindness, gentleness, goodness and forgiveness should be practiced; and the supreme value and sacredness of all living creatures should be respected."

Some of these early laws include the penalties for their violations:

> "If a man brings an accusation against a man and charges him with a capital crime but cannot prove it, he, the accuser, shall be put to death";
> "If a man destroy the eye of another man, they shall destroy his eye";
> "If the wife of a man be taken in lying with another man, they shall bind them and throw them into the water."

The blending of these fundamental religious and moral principles became the underlying basis for future legal systems. Over the centuries, as states grew into nations and developed socially, economically and politically, their legal systems grew and developed too, molded by local traditions, values and needs and often borrowing from other countries' laws and justice systems.

A Brief History of Western Law

Western law originated from the Roman Empire and England. Emperor Justinian, in the sixth century, created a written summary of the laws used during the height of the Roman Empire:

> "It is an affront contrary to sound morals when a person showers another with excrement, smears him with mud and filth, defiles waters, water pipes, or a lake, or contaminates anything to the detriment of the public; against such persons, stern action is taken."

This "Justinian Code," as it became known, was kept alive after the fall of Rome through the laws of the early Christian Church, called canon law:

"Between the abductor and the woman abducted with a view to marriage there can be no marriage as long as the abducted person is in the abductor's power."

In the twelfth century the Code was revived by Renaissance scholars in northern Italy and used for nonreligious legal matters. Soon scholars from around Europe were traveling to Italy to learn this revived legal system for application in their own developing countries. Following the French Revolution in the early 1800s, the Code was adapted to the needs of modern life and formulated into the "Civil Code," also called the Napoleonic Code, and has been used throughout continental Europe since.

A Brief History of Common Law

English common law began with King Henry II during the twelfth century. He wanted to create a national legal system and consolidate his royal power. He ordered his representatives to develop and extend his court system (King's Court) to take precedence over local rules and customs administered by village or church courts. The king's judges traveled the country deciding disputes based on their interpretation of customs "common" to the whole kingdom. Thus the law the King's Courts applied became known as the "common law."

A Brief History of American Law

When English colonists came to the New World in the seventeenth and eighteenth centuries, they brought with them the law they were familiar with in England. In fact, when the colonies broke away from England in the War of Independence, the revolutionaries developed their arguments about their rights to freedom and liberty straight from *Blackstone's Commentaries*, a four-volume summary of English common law written in the 1760s by Sir William Blackstone, a British jurist and lecturer at Oxford.

The Revolution freed the colonies from English control, but the common-law system continued. However, now it was free to evolve with the rapidly developing new nation based on local requirements and conditions.

The common law was officially adopted by all thirteen colonies and by the new national government, and for decades American lawyers continued to read and rely on *Blackstone's Commentaries* as their preparation for legal practice.

French and Spanish colonial activity in America brought laws derived from Roman law (civil law). However, the pattern of territorial expansion of the

United States resulted in the predominance of English common law. Today the common law exists in forty-nine states and nine of ten Canadian provinces. Louisiana, Quebec and Mexico use the civil law, though over the centuries many common law principles have been adopted into their systems.

Elements of the Common Law

The common law evolved to get away from rule by local custom or the dictates of barons, lords or churches. Under those systems the law depended on the benevolence, mood or personal interest of the ruler, church official or community. As the common law developed, the decisions of the judges gained greater strength, and eventually even the king was subject to the law.

The overriding principle established by the common law that we have today is that the law is supreme. Society is ruled by law, not by individuals. The highest government officials, be they presidents, congressmen or governors, are subject to the law. They are not permitted to act arbitrarily. And all government agencies, e.g., the IRS, FBI and CIA, are subject to examination in the courts.

Individuals or private organizations, whether rich or poor, influential or downtrodden, are subject to court process. And the courts and judges themselves are required to follow established procedures and to reach decisions based not on whim, but on generally accepted principles and sound reasoning.

Due Process

The fair, established and accepted procedures for enforcement of the law became known as due process. The right to due process was first written in the Magna Carta in A.D. 1215:

> "No free man shall be taken or imprisoned or dispossessed, or outlawed, or banished, or in any way destroyed, nor will we go upon him, nor send upon him, except by the legal judgment of his peers or by the law of the land."

These rights were extended in 1791 and placed in the first ten amendments, the Bill of Rights, to the U.S. Constitution:

Freedom from unreasonable search and seizure

Trial only after indictment by a grand jury

Prohibition against double jeopardy

Prohibition against witnesses being forced to testify against themselves

No punishment except by due process of law
Speedy, public trial in the state where the offense was committed
Trial by jury in civil suits
Excessive bail and cruel and unusual punishments prohibited

These rights, which limited federal action, were extended to limit state action in 1868 by the Fourteenth Amendment to the U.S. Constitution:

". . . (N)or shall any state deprive any person of life, liberty, or property, without due process of law . . ."

The Use of Precedent

Another protection against arbitrariness or the whim of those in power is the requirement that the law be based on established principles. The common law looks first to the basic principles of previous court decisions for guidance in resolving present conflicts. These decisions provide the court and the public with established rules to follow to make life and activities predictable. It also lets people determine if they are being treated equally and fairly based on how others in the same situation were treated.

Developed From Actual Legal Controversies

The common law arose from actual legal controversies. Disputing parties brought their grievances before a common-law judge, who heard each side's case and resolved the dispute in a practical and efficient manner. The judge looked to past decisions for guidance but retained the flexibility to interpret and adapt past decisions as conditions changed and society evolved. Basically, the common law applies established legal principles and judicial precedents to new combinations of circumstances.

The Adversary System

The theory of the adversary system is that through observing the presentation of evidence and argument favorable to each party, the truth will become apparent to the judge or jury making the decision.

The Judge's Role

In the common-law system, the judge has a relatively passive role. He is more a manager of the courtroom and an umpire of the advocates. If sitting without a jury, the judge decides questions of law and fact. If sitting with a jury, the judge still decides questions of law but the jury decides questions of fact.

The Role of Attorneys

In early common-law courts, the disputing parties were usually from the upper echelons of society: lords, dukes and barons. They had the sophistication and ability to function within the legal system and to present their claim or dispute to the court themselves. Even so, litigants found it convenient to have advice from court attendants familiar with the court's procedures. Those who made such appearances with the parties were called attorneys, meaning "party agents." Use of an attorney was convenient but not legally required. However, as the complexity of the legal system increased and as access to the courts was sought by a broader section of the population, the use of attorneys who knew the law and procedure became common.

Today attorneys have come to play a dominant role. They choose what evidence to present, what questions to ask and what tactics and strategies to use. They are the actors. The judge and jury are the audience.

Trial by Jury

Jury trials have become such an integral part of our system (more so than any other legal system in the world) that a brief history of their origins is valuable.

The Athenians were the first people to use juries, about 400 B.C. The accused were allowed to argue their cases before a tribunal of peers, numbering 201 in civil cases and 501 to 1,501 in criminal cases. These juries applied their understanding of general justice. As soon as the parties finished arguing their cases, the jurors voted. There were no deliberations.

In England, after Rome's governors departed in A.D. 407, families usually sought their own justice against the family of the perpetrator, called family vendettas, or blood feuds. Eventually, when a crime was committed that could cause a blood feud, there developed a process known as "hue and cry." A witness would call out that a crime had been committed and by whom. The people of the village would then join together, hunt down the accused and kill him on the spot.

This system was replaced with trial by ordeal administered by church clerics. It was practiced in England and throughout Europe until about 1480. One common procedure was to have the accused hold hot irons in his bare hands or plunge his hands or arms in boiling water. If, after several days, the local priest, following inspection of the person's hands and arms, declared the wounds healed, the accused was found innocent.

When William the Conqueror defeated the English in 1066, he brought with him from Normandy another form of trial: battle. The accused and accuser would whack at each other with axes or fists, and the victor or survivor would be declared the innocent party.

Evolution of the Modern Jury

Henry II, the originator of the common law, also initiated the modern jury system. He did this for two reasons. First, it would give people a chance to help decide their own affairs, so its use added to the popular support he was seeking for his royal courts over the baronial ones. Second, the jury would provide a method of justice that the church could not readily control. Henry did not abolish either the ordeal or the battle as a trial method. Both remained options that the defendant could choose instead of the jury.

For the first time since the height of Athens, those seeking redress for their grievances could have their cases settled not by royalty, clergy or by the king's judge or commissioners, but by their own peers.

Criminal cases, including capital cases, increasingly were submitted to juries because judges were afraid to find a defendant guilty, fearing the defendant's family would murder them. By the end of the thirteenth century, virtually every contested felony and civil case was being resolved by juries.

STORY IDEAS

News reported in local, state and national newspapers and magazines can provide background information and story ideas. I have sprinkled such news bits, like the following, throughout this book.

A U.S. district judge testified that a defendant threatened to kill him for foreclosing on the man's property. The judge said he was so shaken by the threats that he armed himself in self-defense. He also disqualified himself from hearing the criminal trial against the man. The man is accused of crimes ranging from bank robbery and wire fraud to threatening a federal judge.

Initially jurors were chosen for their knowledge of the facts of the case. There were no lawyers and no presentation of evidence. The jurors would discuss what they each knew about the case and reach a unanimous decision. If twelve knowledgeable jurors could not be found then jurors who were on hand for other cases were chosen to serve with the knowledgeable jurors. The facts were explained to the newcomers and a decision was made.

The practice of calling witnesses became common in the fifteenth and early sixteenth centuries, and by the seventeenth century jurors were chosen on the basis of their impartiality. Because the jurors had no knowledge of the events, they relied on evidence provided by the parties. As this transition occurred during the late seventeenth and early eighteenth centuries, defendants increasingly used advocates in jury trials.

Trial by jury has become a cornerstone of American justice. More than 90 percent of all jury trials in the world occur in the United States.

The Dynamic Nature of the Common Law

The common law has survived for almost eight hundred years because judges have a certain degree of flexibility in interpreting, applying and modifying established law to fit the needs of a current situation. For example, in the precedent-setting case of *Brown vs. The Board of Education*, the U.S. Supreme Court, which previously allowed racial segregation under the principle of "separate but equal," acknowledged that separation precludes equality and ruled that the law required racial integration.

As a famous judge observed:

> "The life of the law is not logic but experience."
> —Oliver Wendell Holmes

Organization of the American Legal System

The colonists came from a land where power was concentrated in the king. They saw the abuse of that unchecked power, so when establishing their new government after the war of independence, they dispersed power as a method of checking and balancing the use of authority. They established two sovereign structures of government, the federal (national) system and the state system. Then they divided those two systems into three bodies: the legislative branch, which makes the laws; the judicial branch, which interprets the law; and the executive branch, which enforces the law.

Today we have the federal government and fifty state governments, each with its own executive, legislative and judicial branches. Though separate, these fifty-one systems often borrow from each other and therefore are similar in many ways. Each has its own constitution, set of laws and court system.

The Federal Court System

To further prevent concentration of power at the national or federal level, the early colonists made the federal government a government of limited powers, having only those powers expressly granted to it in the federal constitution. Any powers not explicitly given to the federal government by the Constitution are reserved to the states, or to the people (Tenth Amendment).

In addition to dispersing and limiting government power, the U.S. Constitution and state constitutions specifically guarantee individual liberties, many of which are stated in the Bill of Rights. These rights have been interpreted and extended through case law and legislation.

The federal system, which includes a separate system for military justice, has exclusive jurisdiction over certain matters, such as bankruptcy, copyright and patent infringements, and crimes committed on federal property. It has three levels. The lowest level is the trial courts. This includes the U.S. District Courts, where most federal cases are filed and tried; Bankruptcy Courts, which handle all bankruptcy matters; Tax Courts, which handle disputes involving federal taxes; the Court of Federal Claims, which handles certain types of cases against the U.S.; and the Court of International Trade, which handles disputes involving customs tariffs. (See page 10.)

The federal District Courts (with more than 90 districts and 630 judges) adjudicate all civil and criminal matters within the authority of the federal-courts system. They are established throughout the country and organized along the territorial boundaries of the states. Each state consists of at least one district, and the larger states have several districts. Almost every district has at least five judges, and some have twenty. The chief judge is responsible for general administration of the court but has no greater judicial authority than the other judges. Cases are assigned to judges randomly and a single judge decides each case.

Parties that are unhappy with the decision of the district court can appeal to the second level of federal courts, the U.S. Circuit Court of Appeals or the Court of Customs and Patent Appeals. (In rare cases an appeal may proceed from a district court directly to the Supreme Court.) Appellate courts accept no new evidence. They base their decisions on the transcript from the trial court and sometimes a short oral argument from each side's attorney. The U.S. Court of Appeals is organized in circuits, or groups of states, and it hears appeals from

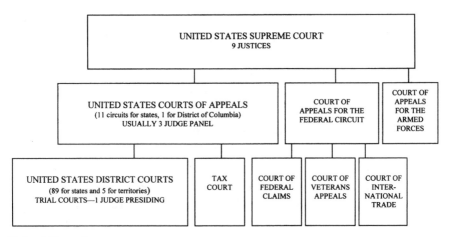

Federal Court Structure

District Courts within its circuit. A three-judge panel considers appeals. However, in cases of exceptional importance, usually involving constitutional issues or cases in which panels of the court have reached inconsistent results, all the judges of the circuit may hear and decide the matter, a procedure called an "en banc" hearing.

Parties unhappy with the decision of the Circuit Court of Appeal can petition the U.S. Supreme Court to review the case. The Supreme Court has discretion to accept or reject the case for hearing. The Supreme Court usually considers only cases that will affect many more people than just the parties involved.

The Supreme Court has nine justices (trial judges are usually called judges, appellate judges are usually called justices) who are appointed by the president with the advice and consent of the Senate. They hold office during good behavior. Impeachment and conviction of treason, bribery or other serious crimes can remove them. The chief justice presides and has general supervisory responsibility.

The Supreme Court has appellate jurisdiction over the U.S. Court of Appeals and state courts in cases involving federal law or the U.S. Constitution. It receives thousands of applications for appeals each year, called petitions for certiorari. Of these, about 120-150 cases per year are accepted (granted "cert.") for full consideration. The Court also takes judicial action in several hundred additional cases from lower federal courts.

The military justice system deals with violations of the Uniform Code of Military Justice by service people. When an offense is charged, a court-martial is ordered by the commanding officer. The accused can have a military lawyer for defense or hire a civilian lawyer with private funds. The jury is composed of military officers. An enlisted person who is accused has the right to have enlisted people on the jury. If the jury convicts, the accused can appeal to the commanding officer, then to the Military Court of Review or the Judge Advocate General, then to the U.S. Court of Military Appeals, and finally to the president as commander in chief.

The State Court System

The states have exclusive jurisdiction over certain matters, such as divorce, probate and most personal-injury cases. Most states, just like the federal court sys-

---

COURT OF LAST RESORT
CALLED "SUPREME COURT" IN MOST STATES
CALLED "COURT OF APPEALS" IN A FEW STATES
5-9 JUSTICES——7 IN MOST STATES

INTERMEDIATE APPELLATE COURT
CALLED "COURT OF APPEALS" OR
"APPELLATE DIVISION" OR "APPELLATE COURT"
USUALLY 3 JUDGE PANEL

TRIAL COURT
COURT OF GENERAL JURISDICTION
DEPENDING ON THE STATE, CALLED "SUPERIOR COURT",
"DISTRICT COURT", "CIRCUIT COURT", "COURT OF COMMON PLEAS"
"COUNTY COURT", "CHANCERY COURT" OR "SUPREME COURT"

TRIAL COURT
COURT OF LIMITED JURISDICTION
DEPENDING ON THE STATE AND DEPENDING ON THE SUBJECT MATTER DEALT WITH,
CALLED "MUNICIPAL COURT", JUSTICE COURT", "DISTRICT COURT",
"COURT OF COMMON PLEAS", "COUNTY COURT", "POLICE COURT", "CITY COURT",
"PROBATE COURT", "FAMILY COURT", MAGISTRATE COURT", OR "JUVENILE COURT"

State Court Structure

tem, have a three-level court system. The lowest level is the trial courts, the second level is the intermediate appellate courts and the third level is the state supreme court. The names of the courts vary in some states, e.g., in New York, the trial court is called the Supreme Court (the equivalent of a superior court or district court in other states), the intermediate appellate court is called the Supreme Court, Appellate Division, and New York's highest court is called the Court of Appeals.

In many states, the lowest level of courts, the trial courts, is organized along county lines and has two levels. One level (called in various states, superior court, county court, chancery court, circuit court, district court or court of common pleas) handles more serious matters, such as felonies and civil disputes involving more than a certain dollar amount, usually $25,000. Some courts, such as criminal court, family court, probate court and juvenile court, deal with specific controversies. The other level (called in various states municipal, county, district, justice, justice of the peace, magistrate or police courts) handles minor civil disputes (usually under $25,000) and the preliminary stage of criminal prosecutions and misdemeanors. Some courts on this level, such as small claims, landlord-tenant and traffic courts, handle specific matters. (See diagram page 11.)

Disputing parties can appeal the trial-court decision to the state court of appeals, made up of three-judge panels, and then to the state supreme court, which can choose whether to hear the case. The number of justices on state supreme courts varies from five to nine, with most states having seven. They act together when hearing and deciding cases. The presiding judge of each court is responsible for the court's administration. In deciding cases, they have authority equal to the other judges.

General Principles
Jurisdiction

State courts and federal courts may have "concurrent" jurisdiction, which means the case could be heard by either court, e.g., blowing up a federal building in a state can be both a federal crime and a state crime. Federal courts hear disputes between citizens of different states, called "diversity" jurisdiction, so that one party doesn't feel like the other party has a "home court" advantage. Courts of general jurisdiction usually hear felony criminal cases and high-stakes civil suits, while courts of limited jurisdiction hear specific matters, i.e., family law cases, misdemeanor cases or small-stakes civil cases.

Venue

Venue is the proper place for the case to be heard. Although a court might have jurisdiction over a case, it may be more appropriate and convenient for the parties if the trial were held somewhere else. The court can, on a party's motion, order a change of venue to a more appropriate location.

Application of the Law by Judges

Theoretically, when deciding cases, judges look first to the respective federal or state constitution, then respective statutory law, then established case law.

Case Law

The appellate and supreme courts review the facts and laws applied in trial courts and decide if the trial court's decision was proper. They then give their written opinion, and if the decision is considered important enough to be used as precedent for future decisions, it is "certified" by the court for publication. These decisions, or cases, are printed in state appellate court and supreme court reports, and the federal court and U.S. Supreme Court reports. They then line law office and library walls. They are a great source of fact situations and idea stimulators for stories.

Statutory Law (Codes)

Laws passed by state legislatures become state codes or statutes, and laws passed by Congress are federal codes. These are the black-letter laws that judges are supposed to apply in the day-to-day activities in the courtroom. Their meaning and application are subject to interpretation by trial judges, who must tailor the law to reach a just result in each situation.

Constitutional Law

Recognizing the need to limit conflict between federal and state laws, the founding fathers made the U.S. Constitution and the federal laws the supreme laws of the land. Neither state statutes nor state constitutions may conflict with the U.S. Constitution. This concept is stated in the supremacy clause of the U.S. Constitution. No state law can conflict with that state's constitution.

CHAPTER TWO

People of the Legal System

"Whenever I try a case, I suffer all the ailments, pains and agony, all the ridicule, humiliation and embarrassment of my client. I have been a sick pregnant woman, a man with one leg, a blind man, a woman about to be committed to Bedlam, a man with a burst appendix, a woman with quadriplegia, a chorus girl with diarrhea . . ."

—Melvin Belli, *My Life on Trial*

Lawyers

Most lawyers receive a bachelor's degree prior to entering a three-year course of study in law school. Some attend night law school for four years, usually holding down day jobs. Some states allow would-be lawyers to "read the law" with an attorney or judge for three to four years rather than attend classes, and one state (California) allows students to study law through correspondence school, though only a tiny percentage qualify as lawyers through these two methods.

Whatever their education, each potential lawyer must pass his state's bar examination on law and ethics (usually two to three days of testing), pass a character and fitness review (no serious criminal background), and take an oath to uphold the laws and the state and federal constitutions. They can then practice before the state courts and the federal courts in that state. However, an attorney licensed in one state cannot automatically practice in another state. He has to meet each state's requirements for practice or work under the license of a local law firm and request permission of the local court to make appearances on a specific case.

Duties and Behavior

Lawyers owe certain duties to their clients. Loyalty to the client means that the lawyer must put the client's interests first. If a client tells his lawyer he is thinking of buying a piece of property because it is a super deal, the lawyer cannot go

In the courtroom, the railing between the spectators and the lawyers' tables is "the bar." "Passing the bar" means that the attorney can legally pass through that bar (the little swinging gate) to the judge's side and practice law. A nonlawyer, unless he is a witness or party to a case, cannot address the court from the judge's side of the bar. Recently, when the judge called a case, I witnessed a woman stand and walk past the bar to the counsel table, and say she was there to help the defendant who could not make it to court. The judge asked her if she was an attorney and the woman said no, she was just there to help. The judge proceeded to give her a lecture about passing onto his side of the bar without a license to practice law and that she had better withdraw behind the bar, for she was in violation of the law. The woman became somewhat confused, but from the judge's tone she realized she had better excuse herself and make a hasty retreat. She hadn't obtained the right to "pass the bar."

Courtroom

out, or send his cousin out, to snap up the bargain. He must help his client obtain the deal.

Avoiding conflicts of interest means that a lawyer cannot represent adverse interests, i.e., both the husband and wife in a divorce. Usually the husband and wife have conflicting interests regarding division of property or support or custody, and both need to be represented by their own attorneys.

Lawyers must maintain the secrecy of confidential information obtained from their clients. If a client tells his attorney he committed a robbery, the attorney cannot disclose this information to the police or anyone else (not even his wife). However, if a client tells his attorney he is going to commit a murder, if the attorney cannot talk the client out of it, some courts allow him and others require him to disclose this information to the authorities to prevent a crime and protect the intended victim. If a client makes a false statement in court and the lawyer knows it is false, most states require the lawyer to break confidentiality and reveal the lie if he cannot convince his client to correct the lie first.

Lawyers are "officers of the court" and must maintain respect and deal fairly and honestly with the court and other lawyers. A lawyer cannot misrepresent the law or facts to the court. He must dress properly and meet a certain level of behavior and respect while in court. Even when a judge rules against an attorney and his client, court etiquette requires him to say, "thank you, your honor." What he says under his breath he better keep to himself.

I tested the limits of judicial tolerance once at a hearing to obtain attorney fees. The judge cut my requested fees in half. That meant I had worked for less than my overhead. In frustration, I said something to the effect: "Well, I am not going to take any more cases like that if you're going to reduce my fees." The judge pointed his finger at me and said, "Watch it, counsel," and all eyes in the courtroom turned to me for my next move. I knew that if I expressed my frustration any further, I would be hit with monetary sanctions or spend the night in jail for contempt of court. I quickly changed my tune, said, "Thank you, your honor," and snailed out of the courtroom.

Counselors, Advocates and Litigators
Some attorneys act primarily or exclusively as counselors and advisors to their clients, helping them keep their behavior and actions within the bounds of the law (setting up corporations, writing wills and trusts), or helping them prevent or forestall controversy and courtroom conflicts (counseling a client on settling a dispute). Other attorneys act as advocates, furthering their clients' positions

in dealings with others (negotiating the purchase of a company). Other attorneys act as litigators (these are the ones we usually see in movies and television) by taking their clients' cases through the judicial process and attempting to convince a judge or jury of the rightness of their clients' actions or position.

Prosecutors and Public Defenders

Prosecutors (called district attorneys or DAs in state court and U.S. attorneys in federal court) and public defenders are employed by the government. Prosecutors file charges with the court against suspected criminals and prosecute the offenders. Public defenders are assigned to low-income suspects and defend them in the criminal proceedings by ensuring that their constitutional rights are protected.

Attorneys are often hired out of law school into these positions. Typically, their first day on the job they are in court, sitting with an experienced attorney learning how to handle a case load (anywhere from twenty-five to one hundred or more cases) that they will take over after several weeks. They get to know the local judges, court personnel, private attorneys, and the policies of their prosecuting or defending office in handling arraignments, plea-bargaining, discovery, evidence-suppression hearings, pretrials and trials. They will initially handle lower-court misdemeanor arraignments, hearings and trials, often handling their first minor criminal trial within a few weeks of hire. They will receive one to two weeks' orientation in their office, but the experience is more of being thrown into the thick of it and having to learn by doing. Depending on their abilities and the needs of their office, they will be promoted up the levels and may be trying serious felony cases and even capital (murder) cases within two to five years.

The prosecutor's office is brought into a criminal case usually after the police department has completed its investigation and turns its report over to the district attorney. The DA's office typically has a "charging attorney" who reviews crime reports and determines if there is sufficient evidence to file charges, if further police investigation is required before charges can be filed, and what charges should be filed. Although the more crimes they can charge the more they have to negotiate with in plea-bargaining, a charging attorney's obligation is to file charges for only what the evidence will support. They cannot charge indiscriminately.

The public defender's office is appointed to represent a criminal defendant by the court. Typically the accused appears in court for his arraignment (his first appearance in court), and the judge asks if he can afford an attorney. If he can't, the judge appoints the public defender's office to represent him. The suspect must complete a financial statement and if he does have sufficient funds he may have to retain a private attorney or reimburse the public defender's office part or all of the cost of representation. Once the public defender's office is appointed, the office assigns the case to a specific attorney. If the accused is in custody, the PD will interview him in jail to prepare for later hearings. If the accused is not in custody, the interview will be in the PD's office. The PD's office has investigators who will interview witnesses and visit the crime scene, if necessary. The PD's office usually contracts with private forensic labs and expert witnesses to assist in the analysis of evidence. Capital cases usually have two attorneys assigned to the case. One attorney might try the guilt phase and the other will try the penalty phase.

Over 90 percent of criminal cases are settled by plea bargaining prior to trial. About 80 percent of those that go to trial result in convictions. Convicted defendants are entitled to one appeal as a matter of right. Their appeals, if not handled by a private attorney (few are because of the cost), are usually handled by nonprofit agencies that contract with appellate attorneys.

On a typical day, prosecutors and public defenders are in court for the morning calendar, which includes arraignments, sentencing and probation violations. For the balance of the day, they are meeting clients, appearing at preliminary hearings, or handling court or jury trials.

They use computers for tracking cases, preparing pleadings and research. They spend a lot of time on the telephone with clients, witnesses and investigators. In court they use chalkboards, large paper pads on easels and overhead projectors, with the better-funded offices using computers and large screens to display exhibits and documents. They may dress less formally for daily routine court appearances, but typically a jury trial brings out the business suit or comparable clothing.

Comments From Prosecutors

Hiring: "New attorneys are hired based on their speaking ability, ability to get along with a wide variety of people they may not particularly like, energy and aggressiveness. Someone who just wants to occupy an office need not apply."

Training: "Depending on our office budget, a new attorney may receive one to two weeks' formal training at a statewide program during his first few months in the office."

Investigation: "The district attorney generally tries to stay out of investigations. We let the police do it. We do have some investigators, but they usually work only specific types of crimes, such as insurance fraud. On occasion they are available for supplemental investigation, to track down witnesses and locate specific evidence."

"If a police detective brought the case in, I might request him to perform further investigation. If a patrol officer brought the case in, I will not ask him to perform further investigation since he is usually going from call to call and doesn't have time to follow up one particular case. A detective's time is freer and it's easier for him to conduct witness interviews and locate further evidence."

Storing of Evidence: "Physical evidence is usually stored with the investigating police agency. The police report will refer to every item placed into evidence. We learn about evidence from the report. I may go to the police agency and with the evidence custodian view evidence. If the case is going to trial, our office may generate our own evidence, i.e., a diagram of the street where the crime occurred or aerial photos to show the location of the scene and the surrounding area or path of a chase."

Use of Grand Jury: "When I am considering taking a case before the grand jury for an indictment rather than just filing a criminal complaint, I look for cases that can be presented briefly and that we want to get into the court fast. We use the grand jury for gang cases, especially if we want to keep a witness's identification secret longer."

Arrest Warrants: "Arrest warrants are seldom used because usually, shortly after the crime is committed, the police have probable cause to arrest the suspect in a public place without a warrant. If more extensive investigation is required before determining a suspect, the police bring the evidence to us, a formal complaint is filed against the suspect, and we have the judge issue an arrest warrant. If the case is a misdemeanor or infraction we usually send out a citing letter that says Dear X, you have been accused of thus-and-so. Please show up on a certain date, which is the time for your arraignment on this charge. If the person doesn't show, the judge will drop the case. Then if we want to pursue the case, we will request the judge issue an arrest warrant. We give people the opportunity to appear in court without formal arrest. They will still be booked, photographed and fingerprinted but they won't have to go through a formal booking where they will be in custody and have to post bail."

Socializing: "We usually don't socialize with the public defenders or defense attorneys."

Clothing: "We usually wear a sport coat and tie, something comparable for women. There is no real dress code but if we have a jury trial there is an expectation we will wear a business suit—professional clothing. There is not a relaxed mode of dress in a jury trial."

Defense Firms: "A good criminal defense firm has six support staff, including paralegals, investigators and secretaries for each attorney. The district attorney's office has one-point-three support staff for each attorney, except the district attorney has the police department to help with investigations. But overall a top defense office has much more to work with than the district attorney."

Rewards of Job: "I enjoy the public service nature of my job. I went through school on scholarships, and this job allows me to give back for what I received. Plus I have a good chance of being appointed a judge someday."

Comments From Public Defenders

Hiring: "We look to hire attorneys who are able to handle a lot of intense work in a pressure situation."

Organization: "We have vertical representation. A PD picks up a client at the beginning of the case and stays with the client until the end."

Plea Bargaining: "Plea bargaining can occur at any point in a case. The DA might make an offer or the PD might seek a settlement. We don't necessarily wait until the pretrial conference."

Jury Selection: "In jury selection I use my intuition. I don't generalize about how a person is going to think or act based on their age, gender, race or occupation."

"In a capital case we may have outside experts help us with jury selection."

Opening Statements: "The theory of our defense determines our opening statement."

Motions: "I only make a motion if it's called for. I'm not going to make a frivolous motion. That will only aggravate the judge for taking up his time."

Rewards of Job: "The primary reward of the job is assisting people during a crucial part of their lives. The worst frustration is there is so much to do and so little time to do it in."

Corporate Attorneys

Attorneys working for corporations advise management on copyrights, trademarks, contracts, antitrust issues, buying and selling assets, issuance of stock and other securities, product liability matters, mergers and acquisitions, and legal procedures in corporate operation. Small corporations may have one or two attorneys, while large ones may have ten to twenty or more. The attorneys are usually seen as part of the corporate team, and sometimes their allegiance to the law is strained or compromised by allegiance to the corporation. In the worst-case scenario, they advise management how to hide or destroy potentially damaging documentation, and they may advise how to engage in illegal activity while making it appear legal. About one-third of all attorneys work for the government or corporations.

Law Firms
Large Law Firms
Law firms are usually organized as partnerships or professional corporations. The largest may have 1,700 or more lawyers with offices in several states and countries. They usually recruit recent graduates from the top law schools, such as Harvard, Yale, Princeton, Stanford or Boalt.

STORY IDEAS

An attorney was banned from practicing law after a state bar court determined that he had overbilled an insurance company. Records showed that he billed the company for work he had not performed and that he charged for more than twenty-four hours on some days and for more than one hundred hours on other days. The attorney denied any wrongdoing.

A new lawyer in a large law firm will be given a small office and assigned to work with one or two senior attorneys who will oversee his training and productivity (how many hours he can bill to clients, typically 2,200 to 2,400 hours a year). He will usually dress in a black or blue or gray suit, white or blue shirt and a bland tie. He may spend the first year or two in the firm's law library researching and preparing points and authorities on the supervising attorney's cases. The firm's clients will include large corporations, insurance companies and sometimes foreign governments. If he is in litigation, he may accompany the senior attorney to court and watch him argue a law and motion matter, and if he is aggressive or articulate or lucky, he may get to argue a minor matter himself. As his training and experience progress, he will be given more responsibility, eventually assisting a senior attorney at trial, and maybe even trying a minor case himself.

Beginning lawyers are usually paid a salary of $50,000 to $75,000 or more and after four to five years of long hours they may be made a partner, allowing them to receive a share of the firm's profits, usually several hundred thousand dollars or more a year. The partner-to-associate ratio may be one partner for each five or ten associates.

These firms are usually very computer literate, with each attorney having a desktop and probably a laptop. These firms usually have a large conference room with a custom-made hardwood table, chairs, original artwork and Persian rugs. They usually also have a marketing department to keep the clients coming in.

Medium Law Firms

Medium-size law firms typically have twenty to fifty attorneys and they tend to specialize in a few areas of the law. They may have several attorneys who handle insurance defense, others who handle estate planning and others who handle commercial transactions or family-law matters. Several attorneys may handle personal-injury cases (they cannot conflict with the insurance companies the firm defends), minor criminal matters (drunk driving and misdemeanors), and others who handle land-use planning and development. Salaries tend to be less than the large law firms, but working conditions are usually less formal and attorneys assume greater responsibility earlier in their careers. They are usually expected to bill between 1,700 to 2,000 hours a year at $200–$300 per hour. New attorneys (associates) are usually hired straight out of law school from the top 10 percent of their class, and some firms prefer the new attorney have some experience in the practical side of life and dealing with people, such as part-time or volunteer work, rather than just academic experience.

The new attorney either chooses an area of concentration or is assigned one and works under the direction of a partner, though he typically will be assigned his own cases for handling.

Members of the firm usually have weekly meetings, either on Monday or Friday, to plan the week's calendar, court appearances, and to review the status of current cases.

Attorneys rely heavily on desktop computers for word processing, research, scheduling, mail, case management, including deadlines and a reminder system, expert database and billing. Many have laptops for work out of the office and in court. In complex cases they may scan documents and exhibits into their computers for organization and easy retrieval during trial. They also utilize transcription equipment (with secretaries doing the typing), the telephone, and cameras and video equipment to photograph scenes and evidence. The firm law library may be part or all digital or may be books with annual updates. The firm, like the large law firms, probably has an accounting department and law librarian.

Small Law Firms

Small firms usually have between three and twenty attorneys. They may specialize in one area of the law, such as public-interest law or civil rights, or handle cases in three or four areas, such as criminal law, family law and personal injury. They tend to be loosely organized, with each attorney having a fair amount of autonomy and say in the firm's activities. Sometimes these firms are formed by a group of friends from law school, or evolve from friendships or acquaintances of the attorneys. Some draw new members from the same law school the other members attended, while personality or experience may be the basis for hiring for other firms. About one-third of all attorneys are in large, medium or small firms.

Sole Practitioners

Most new lawyers entering sole practice will be hustling for clients. Some may have a following due to prior employment (especially those that went to night law school and worked during the day), friends or family relationships. Joining and volunteering in local service and charitable organizations gives exposure and contacts for referrals. Since 1977, attorneys have been allowed to advertise their services. The most popular and probably the most effective are the yellow pages. Ads that started out as quarter pages have grown to full and double pages, with some attorneys buying the back covers of phone books to display their smiling faces and toll-free phone numbers. Television is probably the second most effective form of lawyer advertising, followed by the newspaper and radio. Some lawyers have pushed advertising into solicitation by sending letters offering their services to people injured in accidents or recently arrested. Most state bar associations require the attorneys to wait for thirty days after the person is injured before sending a letter offering the attorney's services.

Many sole practitioners share office space, libraries, conference rooms and receptionists with other sole practitioners. Some have replaced the receptionist with answering machines, answering services, pagers, cell phones, call waiting and call forwarding. They have replaced the secretary with personal digital assistants, computers, word processing and voice-recognition software. They have replaced the paralegal with digital libraries and on-line research and flatbed scanners to copy and store standard forms and pleadings. These "wired" attorneys function like mobile law offices, able to communicate with and provide services to clients from any location.

The key to success for sole practitioners, more so than any firm, is getting paid for work done, requiring a retainer before commencing work and keeping billing and payments current. They quickly learn that large receivables do not pay the rent or buy food. The benefit for successful sole practitioners is more freedom, for they do not have partners or associates watching over their billing or time out of the office. About one-third of all attorneys are sole practitioners.

Tools of the Trade

When you visit the courthouse, you can usually identify the attorneys going to court for trial vs. those in for just a brief hearing. The trial attorneys are carrying large rectangular "salesmen sample cases" that can hold books (like a copy of the rules of evidence and rules of civil procedure), files, exhibits, laptop computers, cell phones and other materials and equipment used at trial. They may also have cardboard storage boxes with records, exhibits and other items.

Most trial attorneys have a trial notebook, usually a three-ring binder, often black leather (black is taken more seriously than white or blue), with tab dividers to organize materials. Some use file folders, each for a different subject or issue. The size of the notebook or number of files depends on the amount of evidence, number of witnesses and complexity of the case. Common categories for a trial notebook are:

Trial brief

Motions in limine

Questions for voir dire

Opening statement

Exhibit list, in order of planned introduction, with place to check when exhibit is admitted into evidence

Witness list

Issues to be proved and what evidence will prove them

Key discovery documents

Questions for witnesses and deposition summaries (separate section for each witness)

Anticipated objections to admissibility of evidence

Legal points and authorities to support admissibility of evidence or questions of witnesses

Closing argument

Jury instructions
Verdict forms
Costs sheet
Local rules

The term "ambulance chasers" usually refers to personal-injury attorneys who represent people injured in accidents. In reality, there are few attorneys who literally "chase" ambulances. The attorneys who seek personal-injury clients tend to be subtler than this. Some have a system in place that funnels the clients to them. Some employ private investigators that show up at the hospital, allegedly "investigating" the accident, wanting only to interview the victim. During the course of the interview, the investigator will try to route the victim to the attorney the investigator is working for. Other attorneys have relationships with paramedics who are already in the ambulance, or with staff in hospitals, tow-truck drivers and auto-repair garages, doctors, chiropractors and others who just "happen" to have the attorney's card to give to the accident victim.

One enterprising attorney I know opened his office next door to a funeral home. He would dress nicely and regularly attend funeral services of people who died in accidents. He would meet the family members, offer his condolences and suggest they visit his office after the service to discuss the compensation they may be entitled to from the death of their loved one. He was extremely successful.

PERSONALITIES

A study reports that one-third of lawyers suffer from either depression, alcohol or drug abuse, anxiety, obsessive behavior, strong feelings of isolation or social alienation. They feel that people don't understand how they work or how hard, and don't appreciate how important law is to the world. Over one-half say they would not recommend law as a career to their own children. Lawyers complain of feelings of inadequacy and inferiority in relationships. Many are lonely. Here are a few examples I have witnessed:

A defense trial attorney who spends most of his days cross-examining witnesses comes home and subjects his wife and children to the same questioning, making them justify their activities, thoughts and feelings. One child develops a strong mind to deal with him. The other becomes moody and resentful with low self-esteem.

A plaintiff's trial attorney who is sensitive and compassionate works long hours representing his clients, but every few weeks he becomes intoxicated and lies in a drunken stupor in his office, sometimes for three or four days.

A general practice attorney that is a "helper" by nature finds it impossible to say no to clients asking for his assistance. He accepts all cases, even those he has no skill in handling. When clients call to check on case progress, he gives them excuses or has the receptionist say he is not in. He takes many breaks during the day, and walks to local bars for a drink, followed by breath mints to cover the alcohol smell.

An attorney that likes to play the stock market couldn't resist the temptation and decides to "borrow" money from a client's estate account, hoping to invest it successfully and pay it back before the client notices it is missing. His stock market investments go sour, the client notifies the state bar, the attorney is disbarred, his wife divorces him, and he becomes homeless, finally living in a shelter he helped establish before his troubles began.

A district attorney working on a drug- and gang-related case mistakenly calls the wrong number for his informant and provides information about a planned meeting. The person he called tells the gang members and they kill the informant. The district attorney, wracked by guilt, commits suicide.

A family-law attorney hates her work and the stress from dealing with angry and vindictive clients. Her only solace is having affairs with her male clients, but when the wife of one client learns of the affair, she sends an anonymous letter to the attorney's husband, who starts his own divorce proceeding.

Law Office Personnel

Receptionist

Many sole practitioners, with the aid of an answering machine, act as their own receptionist. The most organized update their message daily.

Small firms usually have a full-time receptionist to greet clients, answer and direct calls, and perform various administrative jobs, such as ordering supplies, typing, bookkeeping and opening files. Larger firms will have a full-time receptionist just to answer the constant flow of incoming calls.

Legal Secretary

Legal secretaries generally know legal terminology, proper setup for typing pleadings and other court documents and have good phone skills for conversing with clients. Sole practitioners may have one part-time or full-time secretary, depending on their workload. Some larger firms have secretarial pools, a group of secretaries who are available for typing and word processing for whichever attorney has work. In other firms each attorney has a secretary (or sometimes two) who may help manage the attorney's calendar, make travel arrangements and provide typing and word processing. After gaining sufficient experience, some legal secretaries become paralegals.

Paralegal

Paralegals are more than legal secretaries but less than lawyers. They are trained in basic legal concepts and may specialize in one particular area, such as bankruptcy, probate or family law. They often do all the same work an attorney would do, including interviewing new clients, handling all the legal aspects of the matter such as drafting letters and pleadings. The two exceptions are that paralegals cannot give legal advice (though many do) and they cannot represent a person in court. Many work in established law offices, and some have their own offices, advertising their services to help people complete forms for divorce, bankruptcy, name changes, conservatorship and guardianships, or probate.

Some paralegals bring other specialties to their work. Some personal-injury law firms have nurses serve as paralegals, interviewing clients about their injuries, reviewing and summarizing medical records, and assisting the attorney in preparation for the medical aspects of a case.

Law Clerk

Law clerks are typically second- or third-year law students who work in a lawyer's office providing research and drafting pleadings. Since there is no internship requirement for attorneys, clerking provides practical experience with clients and current controversies, rather than reading case-law decisions for classroom discussion.

Private Investigator

Some firms hire independent private investigators on an as-needed basis. Others employ investigators full time. Investigators locate and interview witnesses, photograph accident scenes and damaged vehicles and obtain accident reports, and sometimes interview and sign up clients. The typical private investigator is a former law enforcement officer.

Judges

Almost all judges, both state and federal, were practicing attorneys prior to appointment or election. A large percentage were prosecuting attorneys, which reflects a strong public preference for those that enforce laws and lock up criminals to preside as judges. Appellate judges often served as trial judges prior to appointment to the appellate bench.

Selection

All federal judges, whether Supreme Court justices, appellate court judges or district court judges, are appointed by the president subject to approval by Congress. They serve for life, but if they fail to exhibit good behavior, they can be impeached if convicted by Congress.

States vary in their methods of selecting judges. In some the governor appoints, and in others judges run for election. One state court judge said:

"A judge is a lawyer who knew the governor. It's unfortunate because we have so many qualified lawyers who would make great judges, much better than what we have on the bench, but it gets to be politics."

Terms for state court judges vary from four to fifteen years, with judges of higher state courts having the longer terms. Some states' judicial elections are nonpartisan while others are partisan, so judges can receive the support of a local party. Some states have a combination method where judges are appointed, then after a period of years, they must run in a retention election. They usually run unopposed though once in a while an attorney has the temerity to run against an incumbent judge, a move that is certain to raise hackles in the legal community. Reelection is almost a slam-dunk for sitting judges. Voters don't want to change judges unless a judge is scandalous or considered weak on crime. An attorney who loses a challenge to an incumbent judge will eventually be back in front of that judge on a case and will be afraid that the client will pay the price for having challenged the judge.

Depending on the local population, a judicial district may have one judge who handles all cases or 350 or more judges hearing various cases on any particular day. One judge becomes the presiding judge (PJ), either based on seniority, election by other judges or the public, or gubernatorial appointment. The PJ acts as an administrator in assigning other judges to departments such as criminal, civil, probate, family law and juvenile. The cases assigned depend on the judge's experience and training.

Education

Most states require judges to participate in some form of legal education. Some states provide their own training, while others send their judges to The National Judicial College in Reno, Nevada, which provides classes and training for new and established judges from all 50 states and 130 foreign countries. Courses include orientation for new judges, how to conduct trials, how to treat people fairly, judicial ethics, and classes on specific topics, such as family law, computers, domestic violence and sentencing.

Judge's Chambers

Duties

Judges issue warrants; set and revoke bail; manage the speed at which cases proceed through the court system; preside over hearings, trials and sentencing; determine what law applies in each case and what evidence is admissible at trial; and preserve order in the courtroom.

Appellate judges review briefs and trial court records, hear oral arguments and decide if a trial court has erred in any rulings or decisions. They are limited to the trial court record, which consists of the pleadings, exhibits and transcript that were developed by the trial attorneys. They only consider errors raised by attorneys in their appeals. They generally do not review the entire case.

Most judges now use computers to draft their decisions, though many still use dictation equipment for some matters. Most judges' chambers are lined with law books. However, these now are usually just for decoration and are not kept up to date because most legal research is done on computers. Of course, there are some judges who have not embraced the computer age, and they would rather pull a book off the shelf than boot up their desktop.

Teleconferencing is becoming more popular. Court appearances are made by telephone with the judge on a speakerphone in court and the attorneys in their offices connected with each other on a conference call. These are held in nonevidentiary hearings and for out-of-town attorneys.

To maintain respect for the law and the judicial process, judges manage activities in their courtrooms. If a defendant engages in disruptive conduct by blurting out comments, stomping feet, banging the table or refusing to remain seated, then the judge can order him shackled and gagged. If the defendant continues to disrupt the courtroom by, for example, moaning or rocking his chair, he can be removed from the courtroom. Some courts are set up so a defendant can be in an adjoining soundproof room and watch the court proceedings via closed-circuit television, thus satisfying the constitutional requirement that he be confronted by his accusers. If a judge believes a defendant or member of the public is dangerous, he can have additional uniformed law enforcement officers in the courtroom and have members of the public attending the trial pass through a metal detector and be photographed as they enter the courtroom. The judge also decides if the media will be able to use cameras in the courtroom or if only sketch artists are allowed to reproduce images of the proceedings.

Discipline and Removal

Judges are subject to ethical rules and a code of judicial conduct. For improper or unethical behavior, they can be disciplined by private or public reprimands or reprovals, censured or removed from the bench. If a judge has a personal bias or prejudice toward a party, or has an interest in the subject matter of the case, he must disclose it and disqualify himself. It's often said that even if there is an appearance of an interest in a matter or bias to a party, the judge should remove himself.

In federal courts, judicial discipline is accomplished through regional judicial councils, which investigate complaints of any conduct prejudicial to the effective and expeditious administration of the business of the courts. In serious cases the council can recommend impeachment of the federal judge to the U.S. Congress.

State judicial councils, usually made up of judges, attorneys and laypeople, investigate complaints about state judges' conduct. In serious offenses, a hearing is held, and the council can recommend appropriate discipline. The discipline is subject to approval by the state's highest court.

STORY IDEAS

A former judge who jumped from the bench and bit a defendant on the nose was acquitted of violating the man's civil rights. The judge was accused of confronting the defendant after the defendant repeatedly cursed at him while being led from the courtroom. The former judge had already pleaded no contest to state charges and served five days in jail for assaulting the defendant. He resigned from the bench rather than face a judicial disciplinary hearing.

Comments From Judges

Appointment: "It took perseverance for me to get appointed as a judge. I tried three times before I succeeded. It took a lot of letter writing and getting support from politicians and business people. I was involved with local politics, and eventually I got the governor's attention."

The Job: "Becoming a judge was better for me, because everything was laid out. There was a calendar and the cases were set. As a lawyer I used to procrastinate. I would put aside things I didn't want to deal with and the next thing I knew I was in big trouble. I had 'crash days' when I was trying to catch up or get ready for a trial."

"Being a judge seems to be less work, but more emotional. I have to put people in jail; I have to deal with the bad side of a lot of things, people's marriages, and the terrible things that happen to juveniles. I often go home with tears in my eyes after dealing with a day of tragedies. But that's my approach. Some judges get through the day and go out and play racquetball, no problem. It depends on your personality."

"I like to bring some humor into the case to put the jury at ease. When there is a lull in the proceedings after the first day or two, I will take the microphone and pull it close to me and say, 'You know it's times like these that are dangerous in the courtroom. I have a captive audience, a microphone and I'm getting this urge to sing *Moon River*.' But you know who doesn't like that. The district attorney in criminal cases and the insurance attorneys in personal-injury cases. They want it cold in there."

"I think the push for efficiency in the judicial system is occurring at the expense of judges taking the time to give a fair hearing to a case."

"I treat it as theater, sitting on the bench. The curtain goes up, and there is a cast of characters, and if you are one of the lawyers, you are one of the characters. I take in the entire audience. I can see the nuances of things, and sometimes you can get a feel for some injustice going on, and if you've got the patience and time, you can come to the right conclusion."

The Jury System: "I think the jury system works in almost all cases. It's an aberration when a jury comes back with a wrong verdict. If it's bad enough, the judge can correct it if one side is smart enough to make the right motions and back them up with sufficient points and authorities."

"I ask questions. If I have a question in my mind I assume the jury has a question too, so I ask it. I also let the jury ask questions. They have to submit them in writing to me, and I review them with the attorneys, and usually one of the attorneys will ask the question. If the attorney isn't brave enough to ask the question, I will ask it. Sometimes the question asked by the juror is embarrassing to one attorney or the other because it points out a hole in their case."

Lawyers: "The ideal lawyer is one who is prepared. The nightmare attorney is one not prepared. If the attorney is wasting the court's time, not advancing the case, then it's up to me to control the time the attorney takes in court. Sometimes I have to cut them off and tell them to sit down and be quiet."

"In small counties, almost all attorneys are good. They play ball the way they should, their word is good, when they say they are going to do something they do, when they say somebody agreed to something, that means they did agree to it. They don't have to put it down in writing. In big cities some attorneys engage in a backstabbing type of practice . . . no attorney will take the word of another attorney."

"Really good lawyers have a good demeanor. Even if I rule against them, they say 'Thank you, your honor.' When a witness gives an unexpected answer, they take it in stride. They make a good record and argue a little more strenuously, but they don't waste time. Some lawyers argue about everything and waste time. I love a lawyer who is prepared, has things organized on his table where he can find them. Most of the really good ones will give you a trial brief or a brief on a crucial point to help you along."

Typical Day: "As presiding judge I start work at 8:00 A.M. and coordinate the day's cases with the calendar clerk for fifteen to thirty minutes. At 8:30 I call the cases on the master calendar and assign them to whichever judges are available. Sometimes that takes quite a while. This morning we had fourteen cases for jury trial—twelve criminal, two civil. We have only seven judges. So, as happens every Monday morning, we try to make that last-minute settlement on the courthouse steps. We have already been through at least one mandatory settlement conference in civil cases and at least one pretrial conference in criminal cases to try to get a settlement. This morning we got either all cases settled or to a courtroom for trial. That was a joint effort of three judges working to settle the cases. The rest of my day is spent on administrative matters, except today I will hear two juvenile matters for disposition. There was an adult involved in the crime, and the DA is trying to get cooperation from at least one of the minors to put away the adult for a long time. Tomorrow I may have to take a court trial. I try not to take jury trials because I have too much administrative work to be tied up for two or three days in a jury trial."

"As a line trial judge I would be waiting at 8:30 to accept whichever trial the PJ sends out from the calendar. I may have a criminal trial one week and a civil trial the next. Once the trial ends, I notify the clerk, who sends me another one. Some judges have a specialty calendar on Friday, e.g., family law, law and motion, probate, mental health or domestic violence, and then settlement conferences on Friday afternoon. Trial days are usually Monday through Thursday."

Rewards: "The rewards are in resolving problems for people. That's what the courts are here for, to solve disputes. To the extent that you can get that done in ways that allow people to get on with their lives, that is very satisfying. It's a very interesting job because there is something different every week. It's never boring."

"The reward is walking through the community and having people say, 'Hi Judge, how are you? Do you remember me? Ten years ago you did the right thing on my case.' "

Frustrations: "The major frustration is seeing what people do to their children, or what they don't do. I am particularly aware of that from time spent in juvenile court and family law. The major issue in both cases is children. It's very, very frustrating. I think it's the cause of most of our societal problems. I see kids in juvenile court where things are done to them; they need protection from their family. Later they are delinquents doing things to others. Then I see them again in criminal court where they are doing worse things and they end up in jail and then prison. Then five or ten years later they are back and I have to send them off to do another prison term. It's discouraging. The reason a lot of the parents are not doing their job is because their parents didn't do the right job."

Court Personnel
Bailiff

The bailiff is responsible for the security of the courtroom and personnel, and for enforcing courtroom rules of etiquette and order. Usually the bailiff is a member of the county sheriff's department, has been trained through a police academy and been assigned to the jail and transportation of prisoners from jail to the court, prior to being selected, usually by the judge, to serve as the judge's bailiff. The bailiff has a desk next to the "bar," or railing that separates the audience from the court personnel. Where security is less a concern, some counties use a court attendant rather than a bailiff.

A bailiff has to be able to take the initiative in the courtroom in dealing with the public and the custodies (defendants in custody). The judge has to feel safe with the bailiff since part of his job is to protect the judge, as well as the public and the custodies.

Training is on the job. The bailiff will typically start work at 7:45 A.M., opening the courtroom, making sure the tables and chairs are in order, and inspecting the courtroom to make sure nothing's been left behind and that no one has put anything in the courtroom that does not belong there.

If the court has a grist calendar (criminal arraignments and sentencings) that morning, he may run a transportation check on the computer to make sure the custodies that are to appear have been transported from the jail. Transportation starts at 6:00 A.M., and they are supposed to be in a courthouse holding cell by 7:30 A.M. The bailiff then goes to the holding cells and escorts custodies to the courtroom. The custodies always have leg irons and at least one hand cuffed, and they may be all hooked together with a chain so they can be led as a group. They are seated in the jury box. The bailiff makes sure they don't slouch in their chairs and that they do not talk to each other or communicate in any way to the audience. They don't allow them to communicate with the audience because they can't know what the custodies are saying. They could be arranging for weapons or drugs to be tossed over to them from someone in the audience.

STORY IDEAS

A kidnapping defendant, hearing jurors declare him guilty, pulled out a homemade plastic knife and stabbed two deputies during a courtroom struggle that ended when a third bailiff shot him to death. The two deputies were hospitalized, but their wounds were described as not life threatening. Jurors convicted the fifty-one-year-old man of kidnapping for the purpose of rape and sexual battery. When the deputies tried to take him into custody, he stabbed them.

When the judge enters the courtroom the bailiff says: "All rise—the superior court of Local County is now in session, the honorable Jerry Judge presiding. Be seated," or something similar.

During court proceedings, the bailiff enforces the judge's courtroom rules and makes sure people in the audience do not talk, read newspapers, chew gum or eat. Baliffs also maintain quiet outside the courtroom and sometimes have to break up fistfights between overzealous attorneys.

When custody cases are called, the bailiff makes sure they don't walk through the well (the area between judge's bench and counsel table), instead making sure they come around behind the counsel table and stand with their attorneys. The bailiff makes sure they pay attention to what's going on and makes sure they sign any necessary papers. The custodies are usually led in groups of two or three back to the holding cells by other bailiffs so the judge's bailiff can always remain in the courtroom. After the morning calendar, jury trials usually commence and can last the rest of the day.

In a civil trial, the bailiff may escort the jury panel from the jury assembly room to the courtroom. In a criminal trial with a defendant who is in custody, the bailiff will remain in the courtroom to guard the defendant, and a clerk will bring the jury panel in. The bailiff will hand out a blank biographical sheet to each juror before they go into the box, to use in answering the judge's questions during voir dire (the process of selecting an unbiased jury). After the jury is picked, the bailiff makes sure the members are comfortable, that they have the supplies they need, e.g., notebooks, pens, sharp pencils, coffee and water. The bailiff may assist when evidence is presented. He may help witnesses to the witness stand, instruct them where to stand to take the oath and adjust the witness's microphone. If there are guns introduced as evidence, the bailiff will clear them before they are presented in court and keep the ammunition and weapons separate. If defendants are in custody, the bailiff always has to be aware of what they are doing. The bailiff may inform people entering the courtroom that, if they are witnesses, they cannot sit in the courtroom until they are called to testify.

When the jury is ready to deliberate, the bailiff is in charge of them, escorting members to and from the jury room or to meals and making sure no one disturbs them during deliberations. During deliberations, the bailiff makes sure the jury has all the evidence it is allowed to have. Each jury room has a buzzer members can push if they have a question. The bailiff responds to the buzzer, goes into the deliberation room and has the jury foreman write the question on a piece of paper. Then he brings it back to the judge. When the jury reaches a decision, the bailiff makes sure the verdict form is signed and dated and escorts the jury back to the courtroom. After the judge asks the jury if it has reached a verdict, the bailiff takes possession of the verdict and hands it to the judge. After the judge reads it, the bailiff gives it to the clerk for it to be read aloud.

Sometimes while court is in session, the bailiff will be talking quietly on the telephone. The call is probably with co-workers or the sergeant about how things are progressing in court. When court is not in session, the bailiff may run errands for the judge, such as delivering files, books or other items to other judges or court staff.

At the end of each day, the bailiff makes sure the courtroom is in order for the next day, searches it and makes sure nothing has been left, and gets his calendar ready for the following day.

Bailiffs have the full complement of devices used by sheriffs and police officers, including a gun, disabling spray and handcuffs. They may also have a restraint chair where an unruly or dangerous criminal defendant can be shackled without the shackles being visible to the jury. These chairs have a flap in the back that covers the restraints. They may also have a react-belt. This is a remotely controlled belt that has a voltage pack on the back. A react-belt is strapped onto potentially dangerous defendants. A remote button in the bailiff's possession can deliver a disabling shock to the defendant. These belts have been challenged as cruel and unusual, and some courts do not allow their use.

Courtroom Clerk

The courtroom clerk sits below the judge's bench, usually on the opposite side of the witness stand, when court is in session. The clerk also has an office next to the judge's chambers for when court is not in session. Most court clerks started as file clerks in the court clerk's office. They usually have experience in a number of other jobs, including microfilm clerk, domestic relation's filing clerk and criminal section clerk, prior to becoming a courtroom clerk, where they are assigned to one judge. They are the representative of the court clerk's office in the courtroom and are in charge of the files of cases that are assigned to their judge. Clerks let the judge know when the parties to a case are present. They hand files to the judge. They use worksheets to write down the names of the attorneys who are appearing, any requests the attorneys make and any orders the judge makes. After the court hearing they use the worksheets to prepare the minute order for each file. Attorneys often request copies of the minute order (clerk's summary of judge's decision) from clerks to see exactly what the judge ruled, since sometimes during heated courtroom exchanges details are missed.

Clerks also call names from the jury panel for jurors to walk up and sit in the jury box for voir dire questioning. They keep track of which jurors are selected and which are excused so jurors can get paid. They administer oaths to jurors and witnesses. They mark and keep control of exhibits offered by each attorney during trial by using a sheet with the number or letter of the exhibit along with a short description and whether the exhibit has been marked for identification only or has been admitted into evidence. (Only those that went into evidence can go into the jury room.) In some counties they read the jury's verdict and, if attorneys request, they poll the jury to see how each juror voted. They make sure all exhibits are accounted for in case there is an appeal. They make sure the exhibits are taken to the exhibit clerk where they are kept in a storage room for a period of time. When court is not in session, they are the contact people between the attorneys who want to talk to the judge, and the judge.

They give notices to attorneys or parties as requested by the judge and answer questions from attorneys about the judge's ground rules, such are whether attorneys should stand or remain seated when the judge enters the courtroom or ask permission before approaching a witness. They also record the jury's verdict and prepare bail papers.

In the late afternoon they usually pick up the files and calendar for the next day from the clerk's office. They also make sure the judge sees any necessary documents for the next day.

During jury trials the clerk, bailiff and reporter often discuss the case during breaks and reach their own opinion on the guilt or liability of a party. Sometimes they put money into a pool and bet each other to see who comes closest to the jury's decision.

Clerks use typewriters and computers to prepare minute orders and usually have an array of rubber stamps with dates, times, the clerk's name and the judge's name, for pleadings. Some courts track their cases on computers that are tied in with the DA, PD, probation department and sheriff's office. When the clerk enters a judge's ruling on the minute order on the computer, the information is available instantly to all departments.

Comments From Clerks

Nature of Work: "There are never enough hours at my desk in the courtroom or office next to the judge's chambers. I go early, work through lunch, stay late, sometimes work Saturdays. I never have time to take a vacation. Sometimes I work until 11 P.M. and I'm back the next day at 7 A.M. I've been there until 1:00 A.M. when a jury is in deliberations. It's actually the clerk's signature on the pink form that sends a person to prison, not the judge's signature."

"We see gruesome exhibits in murder cases, an ear in a jar, photos of victims. I can't believe what I hear goes on sometimes. For all these years, all I see is the seamy side of life. The only thing pleasant is the adoptions done in chambers: People were happy; life was being helped. We usually make jokes about the unpleasant stuff to keep our sanity."

"A lot of people assume that if the courtroom is dark (meaning the judge is not on the bench), he is not working. Not true. He is usually in chambers reviewing cases or talking with attorneys."

"One time a criminal defendant rushed toward the bench and the judge drew a gun. Not long after that a judge was shot in another county."

"One time when I was swearing in a witness, she raised her right hand and the elastic on her skirt broke, and it fell off. One time a female juror locked herself in the bathroom and refused to deliberate with the other jurors. The judge declared a mistrial. One time the jury came back after deliberating only one minute. The plaintiff had hired a high-priced attorney and the jury decided he didn't need any money awarded by them."

Insights on Lawyers: "It was good to see good lawyers and scary to see bad ones. One lawyer would twirl his eyebrow and another would click his ballpoint pen to distract the jury while the opposing attorney was talking or questioning his witness. Some lawyers are not taught proper appearance or courtesy. The judge would tell lawyers not to put their hands in their pockets and tell women lawyers not to wear slacks—they had to wear dresses, but that's changed now. We would try to guess who would be the foreperson and what the verdict would be."

"One lawyer carried an old tattered briefcase looking for sympathy from the jury. There is one attorney who bought all his clothes at the Salvation Army. He always looked wrinkled and the jury felt sorry for him and his client. Some lawyers didn't wear watches so they wouldn't unconsciously glance at it and appear to the jury like they had somewhere else to go. Others had to be at the bar at twelve noon sharp for a drink."

"I was impressed by attorneys who could remember every juror's name and address them without notes."

Court Reporter

Court reporters, who usually sit just below the judge's bench and face the witness stand, make a record of court proceedings. They are trained (sometimes requiring several years) to use a stenographic machine, a tiny typewriter-type device with keys that are struck in combination (like striking a chord on the piano) to record syllables onto a strip of paper. Before computers, when asked for a transcript the reporter had to type from notes. Now the keystrokes are recorded digitally on a disk that can be placed into a computer and converted into complete written form electronically. They still keep the paper notes as a backup. The job may involve recording highly technical terminology used in a number of fields. Transcripts of court proceedings are usually only made when an attorney requests one to have an exact copy of a witness's testimony, or for purposes of appeal.

Most reporters started reporting depositions for private attorneys prior to working for the court. Some reporters have a signal for the judge to let him know when the reporter is having a problem reporting, e.g., she cannot hear or understand the witness, two or more people are speaking at once, a speaker is talking too rapidly, she needs to change the paper in her machine or she is fatigued. During rapid questioning and answering the reporter has to intensely listen to each and every word to get an accurate record of the proceedings.

Some courts have replaced the stenographer with an audio or video tape recorder, which is monitored by a technician to ensure proper recording of court proceedings. Some are connected to computers for easier monitoring and editing. Court reporters are usually hired by the judge and work directly for him.

Comments From Reporters

"I prefer court reporting because there is a judge on the bench who controls what is going on. I've been in situations in depositions that have gotten totally out of control. I was much younger and didn't have the ability to exert the control that I would have liked. In a courtroom you've got a judge and a bailiff, and the bailiff has a gun to keep people from talking on top of each other."

"I start at 8:30 A.M. in the courtroom and report all proceedings. I work on transcripts if I'm not reporting in court. I have a laptop to work at home because I don't always have time to complete transcripts during the day."

"I get fatigued about three or four in the afternoon. I have a pain that runs up my arm. I think I will have it the rest of my life."

"I never try to second-guess a jury."

"I enjoy doing my job. A lot of it is very boring. Some of it's very distressing. When you get into child-custody cases, those are not fun. I enjoy doing criminal work the most. That's the most interesting."

"I can connect my stenograph machine to my laptop, so the transcript comes up on the screen as I am writing. I can have a second laptop on the bench so the judge can have a screen in front of him. If an attorney brought a laptop into court, I could connect to his laptop, and he could have testimony in real time on his screen."

Court Interpreter

Court interpreters translate for criminal defendants from their native language to English. They interpret court proceedings, hearings, interviews and court-related events and documents. Depending on the court's demands, they may be full time, part time or on an "as needed" basis, and the languages translated depend on the local population.

Law Clerk

Appellate judges almost always have law clerks, while trial judges vary on their use of clerks. Most law clerks who work for judges have graduated from law school and are either waiting to take the bar exam or have taken it and are waiting for their results. Some have already passed the bar but choose to spend their first year clerking rather than practicing law. Clerking for top appellate judges and Supreme Court justices is very prestigious and highly competitive. Usually graduation near the top of one's class from one of the best law schools along with excellent writing and analytical skills are required. Clerks perform legal research, prepare legal memoranda and draft proposed decisions. Most serve for one year.

Research Attorney

Research attorneys are usually full-time licensed attorneys who provide research at the request of judges. They often are assigned to a particular calendar, such as the civil law and motion calendar or probate calendar. They also provide additional research on such matters as ex parte motions and writs of habeas corpus from prisoners.

They typically review motions or pleadings submitted by attorneys, summarize the facts, highlight salient or contradicting points, review for accuracy and relevancy the law and cases cited by the attorneys, and provide the judge with memos of one-half to three pages in length with their findings and their recommended ruling. Usually the day prior to a hearing, the judge will review the motion or matter on calendar and review the research attorney's memo. Then the judge will either request further research by the research attorney or discuss the case with the research attorney to bounce off thoughts and to clarify his thinking and decide what questions he may have for the attorneys involved at the hearing. The research attorney often sits in court during the hearings to listen to the attorneys' arguments and to be able to discuss new points raised with the judge prior to his making a decision.

The research attorney may be liberal and the judge conservative, so they may differ in their conclusions how a case should be decided. But most judges know their own and their research attorney's biases and make their own decisions.

Comments From Research Attorneys

"I enjoy my work. It's like a puzzle. I try to figure out the solution. From the facts and the law, the correct answer usually becomes clear."

"I am kind of invisible since I am not up front in the courtroom, but I enjoy being involved."

"The most frustrating parts are the time limits and dealing with attorneys who are bad writers or don't focus on the relevant points, preferring to take a shotgun approach."

Clerk of the Court

The clerk of the court, or chief clerk, is elected in some states and appointed by the presiding judge in others. They are responsible for the administrative functions of the court. They coordinate the processing of cases, supervise the work of the individual court clerks, hire and evaluate personnel, usually perform some accounting and provide monthly and yearly reports of the court's operation. They usually have good interpersonal skills and work closely with and usually under the direction of the presiding judge.

Filing Clerk

The clerk with most public contact is the filing clerk, who receives pleadings and examines them to make sure they adhere to the basic requirements for filing (i.e., signed by the attorney or the party), stamps them with the date received (which can be critical if the statute of limitations becomes an issue), collects filing fees, gives each case a docket number, makes sure the papers are placed in the correct files and routes the files properly.

Family-Court Mediator

Most family-court mediators are trained counselors, usually holding a master's degree in psychology or social work, licensed by the state, and with at least several years' experience in family therapy. In contested custody-visitation cases, the family court usually requires the parents to meet with the family-court mediator before the judge will hear the case. The mediator, whose office is usually in the courthouse, helps the parents resolve custody and visitation differences by helping the parents focus on the present and future needs of their children, rather than on the past upsets from their failed marriage. They will often give input on what psychological and social studies indicate is best for children of divorce. The mediator and parents usually sit in chairs facing each other, with no table in between. If an agreement is reached, the mediator usually uses a form to record the terms of the agreement and the parties sign it, but have a certain number of days during which they can change their minds and cancel the agreement. Family-court mediators have about a 70 percent success rate. If the parents cannot agree, the mediator, in some cases, provides a recommendation to the court what would be the best custody-visitation arrangement. They may also recommend the parents receive psychological counseling. Most mediations last about two hours, and most mediators handle two to three mediations a day.

On occasion parents in mediation are potentially violent, and the mediator might request a court bailiff be outside the door, or present in the mediation room, to maintain security. Also, some mediator's offices are equipped with an emergency buzzer to summon police if violence erupts.

Comments From Mediators

"Sometimes the hardest mediations are between parents who are professionals, e.g., therapists, lawyers and doctors. They are people used to having their own way and they are articulate and assertive in stating their positions. They each think they know what is best for their children."

"It's nice to get people in the beginning and get them on the right track to constructive decisions regarding parenting, preventing them from going down a road that they don't know what they are getting into, financially and emotionally."

"I hate to see kids getting hurt as a result of their parents' divorce."

Jury Commissioner

The judges of the jurisdiction usually appoint the jury commissioner. The commissioner probably previously worked as a court clerk and in court administration. The job includes overseeing the compilation of jury lists, monitoring policies used in eliminating potential jurors, reviewing requests for postponement of service dates from potential juries, ensuring that an adequate number of qualified jurors are available and managing the daily operation of the jury assembly room. Staff often includes a deputy jury commissioner and assistants who send out juror summons, handle phone calls from prospective jurors who are usually trying to postpone or avoid service, and process return mail regarding juror qualifications and availability.

The commissioner annually creates a master list for the county, drawn from source lists, such as department of motor vehicles lists of licensed drivers and identification card holders, the registrar of voters list and sometimes utility cus-

Jury Assembly Room

tomer lists. The system of selection cannot intentionally exclude members of a racial, religious, ethnic, geographic or other identifiable group (Sixth Amendment requirement). From the master list a sufficient number of names are randomly selected and mailed summons to appear for jury service, usually on a Monday. Those that report for service become the jury pool. When a judge needs a jury panel, his clerk contacts the commissioner in the jury assembly room and sufficient names are called (typically forty, but sometimes several hundred in a high-profile case), and they become the jury panel.

Law Librarian

Many courthouses have law libraries, and depending on the size of the library and the court's budget, they may have no librarian (attorneys can check books out on the honor system), a part-time law librarian or one or more full-time professional law librarians. The librarian usually will assist a member of the public with legal research and the use of library computers. Law librarians are often asked by the general public, and particularly people representing themselves in court proceedings, for legal advice, which they cannot give. Some well-stocked law libraries are enormous, taking up two and three levels in large buildings. However, with the increased use of computers and availability of law books on CD-ROM, libraries are shrinking in size.

Probation Officer

Probation officers (POs) are usually trained in counseling, social work or criminal justice. They typically start in a juvenile intake unit interviewing juvenile offenders cited or arrested, investigating juvenile cases and recommending options for rehabilitation. After a year they may work with adult offenders, conducting presentencing investigations (PSIs) by conferring with the defendant, his attorney, his family, the victim and other concerned individuals. They will then prepare presentencing probation reports, which include statements from the prosecuting attorney, the police and correctional officers who observed the defendant during his presentence incarceration, along with relevant facts about the defendant's social history. The report usually includes a rehabilitation plan. The PO may testify in court and make recommendations regarding the "disposition" of the case, including conditions of probation or institutionalization of the offender. They also supervise individuals placed on probation (and in some states those on parole), and if they have cause, they can order probationers to submit to a search for weapons or a drug test. In some states probation officers are also peace officers and are authorized to carry weapons and arrest probation violators.

They usually speak in code (refering to offenses and procedures by the applicable state statute number, i.e., "a triple 7"), have a heavy workload, short deadlines and need to be able to work with upset, antagonistic or manipulative "clients" and their families.

Comments From Probation Officers

"When I first got into this field, I came in with a real altruistic feeling that I would be able to change everybody's behavior. I found really quickly that my success rate was not very high. My failure rate was much higher. So I changed my standards for what I consider success. Mine were completely unrealistic because I thought success meant that they would go to college, get a good job and get married and have a family. Success to me now is getting their high school degree or getting into school and actually attending school for several weeks at a time. The majority of kids able to do that are ones that have moved from their old environment."

"Once in a while I get a card or someone calls me or stops me and says, 'Do you remember who I was? You had quite an effect on my life.'"

"Sometimes I get involved with these kids cause it's hard to separate and be professional all the time because you really do like them and respect some of them. Then they end up dead because of the decisions they made. I've attended a lot of funerals. That's hard."

STORY IDEAS

A woman convicted of cutting off her boyfriend's penis was sentenced to seven years in prison after correctional authorities concluded she was exaggerating her stories of abuse at the hands of her victim. She must serve 85 percent of the sentence before she is eligible for parole because the crime was a serious and violent felony. The woman's attorney had asked that she be placed on felony probation, arguing that her actions were precipitated by long-term emotional, physical and sexual abuse by her boyfriend, abuse that had left her suffering from battered woman's syndrome. Those arguments were rejected by the judge, who concluded that she was not an accurate historian. He said if the gender tables were turned, probation would never have been proposed as an option. "If a man had intentionally damaged a woman's sex organs while she slept, there would be no doubt that man would go to prison," he said.

Expert Witnesses

Individuals with special knowledge, skill, experience, training or education can usually qualify and testify as expert witnesses. An expert can give his opinion as to how something occurred. He may be allowed to express his opinion on the ultimate issue being tried, i.e., the defendant's product was defective or the defendant committed the crime, essentially invading the territory of the jury in deciding how something happened or who is guilty.

To elicit an expert's opinion, attorneys usually ask a hypothetical question using the facts of the case and then ask the expert their opinion based on those facts:

"Doctor, assume that a patient came into a doctor's office complaining about left arm pain and the doctor sent him away with just pain pills. Based on your training and experience, do you have an opinion about whether or not that is appropriate treatment?"

"Yes."

"And what is that opinion?"

"That treatment falls below the reasonable standard of care of the medical community. In other words, Dr. Quack, the defendant, was negligent in his treatment of the plaintiff."

There are experts willing to testify in every imaginable field, from accident reconstruction to zoology. Experts vary in their integrity and reputations. Some will give an honest opinion, whether it helps or hurts the attorney hiring them. Others know who is buttering their bread and will testify accordingly. Experts usually have a Ph.D. in their field, or a master's degree with a great deal of experience. Some experts have only a bachelor's degree but their practical experience in their field, such as motorcycle racing, makes up for their lack of formal education. Experts charge attorneys for their time to review the facts of a case and to give an informal opinion, usually $500 to $2,500. If the attorney then decides to have the expert testify, the additional cost is billed at the expert's hourly rate, usually from $100 to $500 per hour.

STORY IDEAS

A court-appointed psychologist has concluded that an eighteen-year-old man accused of killing two women is faking or exaggerating symptoms of mental illness to avoid prosecution. "I cannot diagnose the defendant because it is impossible to sort out which of his reported symptoms, if any, are true," the doctor concluded in his written report to the court. The defendant is accused of shooting two women at point-blank range for no apparent reason.

Jury
Grand Jury

All grand-jury proceedings are usually secret. People called to testify before a grand jury usually cannot have an attorney with them while they testify, though they can consult with an attorney before and after testifying. If faced with a difficult or surprise question, they can ask for a brief recess to consult with their attorney, who can be waiting outside the grand-jury room. A person being investigated by a grand jury is not entitled to be present at the proceedings, but if they are subpoenaed to testify, they can take the Fifth and refuse to testify or seek immunity from prosecution before testifying. If they are granted immunity they can no longer take the Fifth and they can be ordered to answer. If they do not answer, they can be found in contempt and jailed until they answer or until the grand-jury term ends, whichever occurs first. The secrecy of grand-jury proceedings is justified to prevent outside pressure or influence on the prosecutor or grand jury members.

Qualifications for grand jurors are similar to trial jurors, i.e., citizens of the U.S., over eighteen, residents of the county for one year, in possession of their natural faculties, ordinary intelligence, sound judgment, fair character and possession of a sufficient knowledge of the English language. They usually elect a foreman, or the judge supervising the grand-jury proceedings appoints one.

A criminal grand jury consists of from twelve to twenty-three (depending on the state) local citizens selected from the jurisdiction's jury pool, who agree to meet usually once a month for a year. Their function is to listen to evidence presented by the prosecutor and determine if "probable cause" exists to "return an indictment" against the person being investigated so that he will be tried for the crime. If they return an indictment, unless the person indicted is already in custody or voluntarily surrenders, a judge usually issues a bench warrant for the arrest. His attorney usually is entitled to a transcript of the grand-jury proceedings ten days later, and ten days after that the transcript usually becomes a public record. However, it can be sealed by the court if making it public may prejudice the defendant's right to a fair and impartial trial.

A civil grand jury, sometimes called a blue-ribbon grand jury, usually consists of twelve to twenty-three prominent local citizens who volunteer and are appointed by the presiding judge. Their function is to investigate any alleged wrongdoing by government officials or agencies and bring indictments or make recommendations in their annual grand-jury report.

Petit Jury

A petit jury, known commonly just as a "jury," consists of twelve people in most state courts. Their decisions must be unanimous in criminal cases and at least nine of twelve in civil cases. Federal court juries are usually six, eight or twelve people, depending on the local court's rules. Verdicts usually must be unanimous in both civil and criminal cases, although some allow less than unanimous verdicts in misdemeanor cases. The parties can stipulate to fewer than twelve jurors and a less than a unanimous verdict.

Jurors

On the designated date and time of their summons, prospective jurors report to the jury assembly room where roll is taken and general instructions are given.

From this pool a jury panel is selected at random by the clerk or jury commissioner, and sent to a courtroom. The actual jury need not mirror the community makeup as long as it's drawn from a representative cross section of the community. Depending on the luck of the draw, a jury panel may have disproportionately more of one gender, economic or educational level, or racial or religious makeup, thus favoring one party over the other.

The only requirements for a juror are that they be a citizen, not a minor, a resident of the state and jurisdiction of the court, not an ex-felon, understand English and be legally competent. A person cannot automatically be disqualified because of loss of sight or hearing, inability to speak or lack of mobility. They can be challenged and excused, however, if one of these senses is required to decide the facts of the case. A juror can have one of these disabilities if the attorneys stipulate to the presence of a sign-language interpreter, reader or speech interpreter. The only group automatically exempt from jury service is peace officers.

A juror can be excused only for undue hardship, e.g., no transportation, excessive distance to court, extreme financial hardship (loss of income that would disrupt the person and his family), need to care for another or appearance for jury service within the last twelve months.

Jury Room

A juror who has been summoned and does not show up as required can be arrested, fined and ordered to immediate jury service; if they refuse, they can be jailed. Jurors receive fees and mileage for each day served.

The jury decides questions of fact, e.g., was the defendant intoxicated, did he intend to shoot his wife, was he legally insane. The judge decides questions of law.

Jurors evaluate the credibility of witnesses, e.g., is the alibi witness honest or lying, is the defendant telling the truth when he says he didn't do it or is he a habitual liar who can tell a lie as easily as the truth.

The jury renders a verdict after hearing all the evidence and being instructed by the judge on the law.

In some states, after a defendant is found guilty, the jury determines the sentence. In other states, juries recommend the sentence, while in others the judge decides the sentence.

Some jurors, from the time they arrive at the courthouse to be on jury panel until the time they are dismissed after reaching a decision, are hyperalert to the appearance and behavior of the attorneys and parties and witnesses and even the judge and bailiff and other court personnel. Most trial attorneys realize they are on stage while in the jury's presence and they make sure that their clothing, jewelry, walk, talk and entire demeanor convey the best impression for their client.

STORY IDEAS

A prospective juror who claimed to know nothing about a torture-murder case sat with her mouth agape as she heard the charges against the defendant, then stared at him and gasped, "Did you do that?" The defendant sat still, staring at the woman but showing no reaction. The unusually combative jury candidate repeatedly asked the lawyers for explanations, rather than giving answers. She was allowed to remain on the tentative jury panel despite her declaration that "I don't want to be on this case."

Criminals

From the issuance of search and arrest warrants to arraignments, pretrials, trials and sentencing, it's probably fair to say that at least half of a court's time is allocated to criminal matters.

Criminals come in all sizes and shapes, from the one-time offender who has no further dealings with the legal system to the career criminal who may know the law and procedure better than many lawyers. Some consider a journey though the criminal justice system and imprisonment a right of passage, while others feel lost and victimized by the system.

Victims of Crime

Many courts permit the victim or his family to make a victim's impact statement at the sentencing stage of criminal proceedings.

"Lock him so far down that when he dies he'll be closer to hell, where the devil belongs" and "He's diabolical, evil, cunning, a murderer" are examples of statements made by families of victims at sentencing.

Judges usually have decided ahead of time what the sentence will be, but the opportunity to express grief, pain and anger serves a therapeutic purpose and makes those most affected by the crime feel more a part of the justice system.

Some states provide for restitution to victims from state funds or by the convicted criminal. Many states have established victim service agencies that provide counseling and assist victims through the criminal justice process. Victims of crimes have the right to sue the perpetrator for the damages caused, such as wrongful death of a family member, or physical injury, medical expenses and pain and suffering. However, this move is usually impractical because most criminals have no money to pay a judgment.

Plaintiff

The plaintiff (in some cases called the petitioner) is the initiator of a civil court proceeding, e.g., a husband divorcing his wife, an accident victim suing the negligent driver or a landlord evicting a tenant. The plaintiff cannot be a minor, though a parent can be appointed guardian for their child for purposes of suing on the child's behalf. A conservator can sue on behalf of an incompetent person, and a person can assign his right to sue to another person, who can then become the plaintiff in the case. A corporation can sue in its own name. If the plaintiff has no or low income, he may qualify to have the court filing fees waived.

Defendant

The defendant (in some cases called the respondent) is the party being sued. Anyone or any entity can be sued, though in the case of minors or incompetents or businesses, an adult person is usually appointed or chosen to appear on behalf

The no-brainer approach of many criminals is to flatly deny they committed the crime. The intensity and persistence of their denial convinces some, but not those experienced in the criminal legal system. If you believed all the denials of those charged with crimes, you would wonder who was committing the crimes, since those apprehended say they aren't. A more sophisticated criminal, or a good defense attorney, will attempt to explain away the evidence linking the accused with the crime. Sometimes the explanations become rather extreme. Witness the following: A nineteen-year-old woman alleged that she was kidnapped, beaten and forced to orally copulate her captor before being left naked in a parking lot. On the stand, the woman testified that she was at a friend's house where several people had gathered for a barbecue. Shortly after arriving, she and the accused left in his car to get a CD from a nearby house. After getting the CD, the accused did not return to the party. He was smoking marijuana and parked at the end of a street and told her he wanted her to perform oral copulation. When she refused, the man began to choke her and told her he would "cut my head off and leave me in the park" if she tried to get away. Out of fear, she complied. Over the next couple of hours, the woman said, the man drove around town pulling her head down by her hair, forcing her into seven acts of oral copulation. At one point he made her take her pants off, then all of her clothes. He repeatedly hit her, threatened to kill her and her family and, more than once, made her lie on the rear floor of the car. He finally dropped her off in a parking lot, but before leaving her naked and alone, he told her to call the police and tell them she had been carjacked by two men who held her at gunpoint. The victim said she tried unsuccessfully to reach a friend and called 911 but was disconnected before she saw the man running up the street toward her again, having wrecked his car a few blocks away. Expecting that the police would be arriving, he ordered her to climb up a small hill and lie in the grass. After lying next to her for a while, he got up, kicked her in the eye and left.

The accused testified at his trial as follows: He and his wife and children went to a gathering at a friend's house. The woman arrived a short time later and began flirting with him, which surprised him since his wife was present. He asked the woman's friend if she had a CD she'd borrowed from him, and she told him he could take the victim and retrieve it from her house a few blocks away. He took the victim to the house and got the CD but on the way back she began talking about sex and asking him why he never tried to "hit" on her and offered to perform oral copulation on him. He told the woman he was married. The woman persisted so he stopped the car and she performed oral sex. "It was more than consensual. She started it. She seduced me," the man testified.

When the two were refastening their clothing, he heard footsteps and then heard the handles of the car's rear doors being lifted. The doors were locked, but the interior light was triggered and he saw two men standing outside the door. He quickly started the car and sped away, watching in the mirror as the two men ran for a vehicle. He had been in a barroom brawl several days earlier and he feared it was the same men coming for retaliation. He soon began to suspect his passenger was involved. He began to outrun his pursuers, when the woman told him he should just pull over because "all they want is your stereo . . . I'm sure they won't hurt you." After repeatedly telling him to pull over, he became sure the woman was involved. He said he slapped her four to five times during the ordeal and elbowed her in the back once. He drove around town in an effort to lose his pursuers, then finally stopped and told the woman to get out. The woman begged him to give her a ride home and removed her shirt, saying he wouldn't leave her stranded topless. He told her he would give her a ride if she told him what was happening. She confirmed her involvement and told him the men chasing them were the same who had attacked him several days before. He ordered her out of the car and told her to remove her pants to humiliate her. He then threw her clothes out of the car as he drove away.

A few blocks away he wrecked his car against a tree. Fearing that he was still being chased and that police would show up and find a naked woman, he decided to flee. At this point he stripped naked. "I guess my Army instincts came back. I thought I would be less visible without bright clothing."

You be the judge! Whose story is the most credible?

---

of the defendant. If the defendant countersues the plaintiff, for purposes of the cross-complaint, the defendant is called the cross-complainant and the plaintiff is called the cross-defendant.

Alternative Dispute Resolution (ADR)

The trend in recent years is toward resolution of disputes either outside the court system or short of a full court or jury trial. Courts are encouraging and often ordering alternative dispute methods, and many attorneys are encouraging their clients to choose this option as a time- and money-saving measure.

Mediation

In mediation the disputing parties agree to meet with a neutral third party, called a mediator. The mediator acts as a facilitator to help the parties stay focused on the issues involved in the dispute and to avoid or at least minimize the emotional component. The mediator helps the parties explore various options for resolution and reach their own agreement. The mediator does not decide the outcome.

Attorneys are usually not present at mediations. Mediations can last an hour or two, several days, or consist of multiple meetings over several months.

Arbitration

Unlike the mediator, an arbitrator decides the outcome of the dispute by acting as an informal judge. The arbitration usually is held in the arbitrator's office, library or conference room. The disputing parties or their attorneys each present their side of the case, and the arbitrator gives his decision. Arbitration can be binding, where the arbitrator's decision is final, or nonbinding, where the arbitrator's decision can be rejected if either party is displeased. The case then goes to a formal trial.

Rent-a-Judge

A number of retired judges act as mediators or arbitrators, often earning much more than they did on the bench. When the arbitrator is a former judge, the process is sometimes referred to as rent-a-judge, and the parties agree to pay the former judge for his time, often up to $400 to $800 per hour or more. Judges are often selected based on their background, with former supreme court and appellate court judges usually in the highest demand, followed by trial judges. Some work through mediation-arbitration firms. Regulars in litigation, like insurance companies, have judges they prefer based on their past decisions.

In Pro Pers

Increasingly people are representing themselves "in pro per," short for the Latin "In Propria Persona," meaning "in person." Criminal defendants sometimes choose to represent themselves at trial as a strategy to gain sympathy or to intimidate witnesses. The number of divorcing people representing themselves is increasing.

The old saying "A lawyer who represents himself has a fool for a client" is definitely true for nonlawyers in all but routine matters. It is contrary to human nature to be able to separate emotions from actions, so those that represent themselves often use the judicial system to ventilate their emotions rather than present facts that would support their best legal position.

A Typical Day in a Courthouse

The sheriff's bus arrives at 7:00 A.M. transporting the custodies—those who were in jail the night before—to the holding cells in the courthouse. Judges, staff and

Proper presentation of a case by a skilled attorney saves the court's time. Good attorneys sift through the relevant facts in advance, put them in logical order, offer their legal consequences and narrow the legal matters to the crucial points. There are some "in pro pers" who present their cases better than some attorneys, but others wander and expect special favors and treatment. Most judges tell them that in a court of law one is expected to know the law and procedure. It's not the judge's job to take public time to teach or educate or help. One judge said it this way:

> "You represent yourself at your own risk. It's like medicine. Some people can clean their own wounds and avoid infection. Others don't have the skill and need a doctor. But few of us would perform our own brain surgery or heart transplants. If you have a serious legal matter, you better get a qualified attorney, or you may just be committing legal suicide."

court personnel arrive at 8:00 A.M. Members of the public with morning court appearances start arriving at 8:00, milling around outside the courthouse or courtroom, talking nervously or looking glum, waiting for their attorneys or friends. If it's Monday, people called for jury duty may be waiting outside, usually with a paperback book in hand.

There is a line of people at the clerk's window, checking which courtroom they are supposed to be in or asking questions about paying fines or continuances.

Each courtroom has a printed calendar posted outside the door, with the date, courtroom number, judge's name, type of proceeding (criminal, probate, family law), docket number (same as case number), last name and first name of the party, and their attorney's name or just the initials "PD" if represented by the public defender.

Lawyers in coats and ties and carrying files or briefcases arrive, looking for their clients, who they then stand or sit with and flip through papers and explain what to expect in court.

At 8:15 a bailiff opens the courtroom doors from the inside, allowing the public to pass through a metal detector and sit down. The custodies will already be seated in the jury box, with their bright-colored jumpsuits and manacled hands and feet. Several bailiffs will make sure the custodies and the public sit properly, speak quietly and show respect for the court proceedings.

The court clerk is seated below the judge's bench, organizing files and preparing for the morning's business, and the court reporter, seated opposite the clerk, is checking her equipment in preparation for recording the proceedings.

The district attorney arrives caressing a pile of files and takes her seat at the counsel table, followed by the public defender, who usually has fewer files, and private attorneys, who sit between the bar (railing between the public and the court personnel) and the counsel table.

Waiver of Rights and Financial Statement forms sit in a box for defendants to read and complete prior to their cases being called.

At 8:30 the bailiff tells everyone to rise and the judge enters and takes the bench. She calls private attorneys' cases first so the attorneys can get back to their offices, then the custodies' cases so they can be returned to jail, then the cases of defendants who are not in custody.

The proceedings move fast as there is usually a "full calendar" and these matters are very routine for the court. A defendant's name is called, he stands, the charges are read and he is asked how he wants to plead. If he pleads not guilty his case is set for pretrial, usually about two weeks later. If the defendant pleads guilty in a minor case, he may be sentenced immediately. If the defendant is in custody and requests an attorney, the judge will assign the public defender, who will sit with the party to obtain initial information. As the judge finishes with a file she passes it down to her clerk, who has entered the defendant's appearance, plea and next court date onto a form. The form is placed in the file and she hands a copy to the bailiff, who passes it to the defendant or his attorney.

If the defendant's native language is not English, a court translator for that language will stand and call the defendant's name and translate the judge's words. If no translator is present, the case will be continued until the court can have one present.

Once the custodies are done, a bailiff will escort them out a rear door back to the holding cell and eventually back to jail. If the judge calls a defendant's name and he is not present, the judge will issue a bench warrant for his arrest.

At 9:00 the courtroom next door opens for business, with primarily older attorneys arriving to appear on probate matters. The judge calls each case along with a tentative ruling. These rulings were available to attorneys the night before by telephone. If the attorney agrees with the tentative ruling (which is usually approving the papers filed by the attorney), she need not make an appearance. If the court needed further information or the attorney does not agree with the tentative ruling, he can appear and discuss the matter with the judge.

At 9:30 the probate calendar is finished and the judge calls the law and motion calendar. These are technical legal issues raised by one attorney hoping to improve his client's position in the dispute with the opposing side. Some of the attorneys are new and nervous and uncertain of themselves, while others are calm and confident from years of experience. The judge makes rulings from the bench on some matters, and takes others under submission for further thought. After these matters, the judge calls the family law calendar, with disputing spouses appearing in various degrees of anxiety, anger and pain to argue over child custody, visitation and support. These tend to be the most emotional matters the court hears. Parties are often yelling or crying in the halls. Attorneys are trying to explain the reason for the judge's decision. The bailiff has to come out and tell everyone to keep it quiet.

In the third courtroom attorneys are dressed in dark blue or black suits and carry salesmen sample cases or cardboard storage boxes full of documents. They will be giving their final arguments to a jury in a civil case. Afterward, the judge will give the jury instructions on the law and how they should proceed with their deliberations.

Most courts take a morning recess at 10:30, a one-hour lunch at 12:00, an afternoon recess at 3:00 and finish court proceedings at 4:30 to 5:00. During the recesses attorneys usually check in with their offices by phone, reorganize papers or go for a walk to reduce their anxiety. Judges return to their chambers, review other cases and return phone calls.

Throughout the day in the courthouse there are attorneys sharing war stories, filing papers with clerks, requesting a judge sign temporary restraining or other emergency orders, or arriving in the afternoon for settlement conferences or one- to two-hour court trials.

Most filing clerk's offices close at 4:00 P.M. and most court personnel finish their workday at 5:00. Sometimes, if a jury is deliberating and is close to a decision or disputing parties are close to resolution during a settlement conference, the judge, his staff and the attorneys will stay past 5 P.M., but rarely past 6 P.M.

CHAPTER THREE

Crimes, Defenses and Punishments

"When Cobb reached the second step from the floor and Willard was three steps behind, and Looney was one step off the landing, the small, dirty, neglected, unnoticed door to the janitor's closet burst open and Mr. Carl Lee Hailey sprung from the darkness with an M-16. At point-blank range he opened fire. The loud, rapid, clapping, popping gunfire shook the courthouse and exploded the silence. The rapists froze, then screamed as they were hit—Cobb first, in the stomach and chest, then Willard in the face, neck, and throat. They twisted vainly up the stairs, handcuffed and helpless, stumbling over each other as their skin and blood splashed together.

Looney was hit in the leg but managed to scramble up the stairs into the holding room, where he crouched and listened as Cobb and Willard screamed and moaned and the crazy nigger laughed. Bullets ricocheted between the walls of the narrow stairway, and Looney could see, looking down toward the landing, blood and flesh splashing on the walls and dripping down.

In short, sudden bursts of seven or eight rounds each, the enormous booming sound of the M-16 echoed through the courthouse for an eternity. Through the gunfire and the sounds of the bullets rattling around the walls of the stairway, the high-pitched, shrill, laughing voice of Carl Lee could be plainly heard.

When he stopped, he threw the rifle at the two corpses and ran. Into the restroom, he jammed the door with a chair, crawled out a window into the bushes, then onto the sidewalk. Nonchalantly, he walked to his pickup and drove home."

—John Grisham, *A Time to Kill*

Categories of Crimes

Crimes are generally categorized as either felonies or misdemeanors. Felonies are more serious. In early common law there were originally only nine. Today, by statute, there are more. Punishment for felonies is usually death or over one year in state prison. Punishment for misdemeanors is usually less than one year in county jail.

Elements of a Crime

Two things must be present for a crime to be committed: an act, which is the physical element, such as the killing of a person, or the burning of a building,

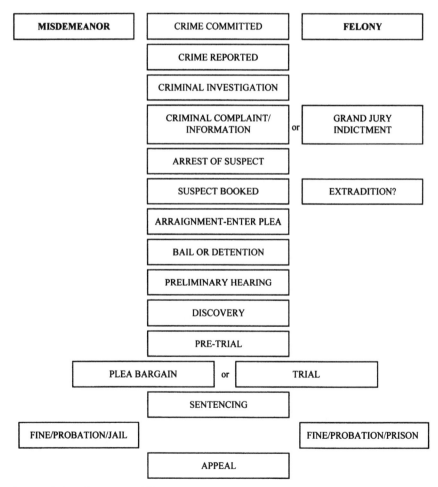

Criminal Case Sequence of Events

and a particular state of mind, which is the mental element. The mental element is the person's intent to do the illegal act. An act is not a crime if done without a guilty mind. Killing someone is not a crime if purely accidental or justified self-defense, because there is no wrongful intent. And intent needs an act to be a crime. Merely thinking about doing something illegal is not a crime, no matter how evil the thoughts. There is no physical act.

Corpus Delicti

In every prosecution for a crime, the corpus delicti, or elements of the crime, must be established. These include the fact of the injury, loss or harm, and the existence of a criminal agency as its cause. To prosecute for murder, merely having a dead body does not establish the corpus delicti. The prosecution must show that a criminal act was the cause of the dead body.

Preliminary Crimes

The crimes of solicitation, conspiracy and attempt are preliminary crimes, since they occur before the intended crime. They are punishable, however, because they go far beyond merely thinking about committing an illegal act—they are preparation for committing the anticipated crime.

Solicitation

Solicitation is asking someone to commit a crime for you or to help you commit a crime, or advising someone how to commit a crime. The crime solicited need not actually occur. The most common form of solicitation is associated with prostitution, offering a person money for sex. Since payment for sex is a crime, offering someone money to commit the crime is solicitation. The person need not agree to engage in sex, and the sexual act need not occur. The mere offering constitutes the crime.

Conspiracy

Conspiracy requires an agreement between two or more persons to commit a crime, and at least one of the conspirators must do an overt act that furthers the conspiracy. If Mack and Jerry agree to murder Fred, they have agreed to commit a crime, but at that point they have not committed a conspiracy, since neither has committed an overt act. However, if Mack purchases a gun intending to use it in the murder of Fred, he has committed the required overt act, and both he and Jerry are guilty of conspiracy to commit murder.

Attempt

Attempt is intending to commit a particular crime and coming dangerously close to completing it. Said another way: The person enters the zone of perpetration, where he is close enough that he could actually commit the crime. If Sally takes a hammer and chisel to an ATM machine but fails to gain access to the money, she has committed an attempted burglary. If she gained access to the money, the burglary was completed. Usually the attempt merges into the completion of the crime and she would be charged only with burglary, not attempted burglary *and* burglary. If she was arrested at home with a hammer and chisel and a map of the bank and location of the ATM machine, she has not come dangerously close to completing the burglary, so no attempt has occurred.

Crimes Against the Person

Assault

Assault is generally defined as attempted battery.

Battery

Battery is the deliberate harmful or offensive touching of someone else without their consent.

> **STORY IDEAS**
>
> *Three twelve-year-old girls who laced their teachers' coffee and soft drinks with laxatives pleaded guilty to charges of aggravated battery. The prank sent three teachers to the hospital, where they were treated and released. In exchange for their guilty plea, prosecutors dropped food-tampering charges against the three sixth-graders.*

> **STORY IDEAS**
>
> *A seventy-eight-year-old man allegedly shot at five people in a casino and was caught as he tried to shuffle away using his walker. None of those shot at were hit. The man may have been jealous that his girlfriend was at the casino with another man. The man was charged with assault with a deadly weapon.*

False Imprisonment

False imprisonment is the deliberate confinement of a person without consent or without legal justification. The confinement can be physical (locking a person in a room) or psychological (threatening to beat someone up if they try to leave).

> **STORY IDEAS**
>
> *Two photographers were found guilty of misdemeanor false imprisonment stemming from a run-in with actor Arnold Schwarzenegger and his wife. Photographers were accused of boxing in the couple's car with their car in an effort to videotape them outside their son's preschool.*

Kidnapping

Kidnapping is moving a person from one place to another against his will. It can be accomplished through force against the person or threats of force against the person or a family member.

STORY IDEAS

A millionaire businessman was sentenced to life in prison for luring his New Jersey bus company rival to Florida, kidnapping him, then killing him by shooting him in the head, wrapping his body in plastic and dumping it into the Atlantic.

Rape

Rape is sexual intercourse with a woman without her consent. In most states a man cannot be raped, but he can be sodomized. Force or threat of force is sufficient, and a woman does not have to resist if resistance would be futile and subject her to more danger. Statutory rape is sexual intercourse with a female under a certain age, usually fourteen to eighteen years old depending on the state. Girls under that age are legally incapable of giving consent to sexual intercourse. In some states it doesn't matter if the man thought the girl was over the legal age or the girl led him to believe she was over the legal age.

STORY IDEAS

A woman who admitted on a TV talk show to having a relationship with a sixteen-year-old boy has pleaded guilty to rape. The woman, twenty-four years old, admitted that she had sex with the teen, who is the son of a neighbor. Police began their investigation after the woman discussed the relationship during the talk show.

Mayhem

Mayhem is a deliberate act of maiming a person or causing permanent disfigurement. If Larry chops his girlfriend's arms off because he is jealous of the attention other men are showing her, he is guilty of mayhem.

Homicide

Homicide is the killing of one human being by another human being. By itself it is not a crime, because some killings are accidental or are committed in self-defense. Homicides that are crimes are murder, voluntary manslaughter and involuntary manslaughter.

Murder

Murder is the unlawful killing of one human being by another with malice afore-thought. Malice aforethought means having a particularly evil or heinous state of mind, and includes:

1. Intentionally killing the victim—a deliberate act without legal justification. Scorpio, a hired assassin, walks up behind his intended victim, points a .22 caliber pistol at his head, fires and kills him. This is the classic premeditated murder, often called murder in cold blood.

2. Intending to seriously harm the victim. Steve, angry with Jerry for coming on to his girlfriend, beats him with a baseball bat, intending only to teach him a lesson. Jerry dies. Steve is guilty of murder because there is likelihood that death can result from beating someone with a baseball bat.

3. Killing someone during the course of a dangerous felony, such as burglary, robbery, rape or arson. This is known as the felony-murder rule. Harry robs a bank and escapes in a getaway car. While speeding away from the bank, Harry's car collides with another car and kills the driver. Harry is guilty of murder since bank robbery is a dangerous felony and the other driver was killed during the course of the felony.

4. Doing something that has a high risk of death or serious injury, in disre-gard of the consequences. Carlos drives past a house where a rival gang member lives. He doesn't know if anyone is home but he fires three shots through the front window as a calling card. One of the bullets hits a baby in a crib in a back bedroom and kills her. Carlos is guilty of murder. This class of murder is sometimes called a depraved heart killing.

STORY IDEAS

A son who had been embarrassed since age thirteen about his father's homosexuality was convicted of shooting his dad's lover to death and blinding his father. The man, now thirty-six, shot and wounded his sixty-year-old father and killed his father's forty-five-year-old companion as the two men sat in a parked car outside a restaurant.

Degrees of Murder Most states classify murder into first degree and second degree. The difference is based on the suspect's intent in committing the crime or the manner in which he carries it out. Punishment, which can include the death penalty, is more severe for first-degree murder.

FIRST DEGREE

First-degree murder includes a murder that was willful, deliberate and pre-meditated (murder in cold blood); murder caused by the use of poison, torture, explosives or ambush (lying in wait); and killings committed in the course of certain felonies, usually arson, burglary, robbery, rape and mayhem.

SECOND DEGREE

Second-degree murder includes murder in which the suspect intended to kill the victim but the killing was not premeditated (a spur-of-the-moment killing); murder in which the suspect intended to seriously harm, but not kill, the victim (a depraved heart killing); and killings committed in the course of a felony, other than those listed under first-degree murder.

Manslaughter

Manslaughter is the unlawful killing of a human being by another human being, but without malice aforethought. There are two types, voluntary and involuntary. Voluntary is more serious and receives a stiffer punishment.

Voluntary manslaughter is an intentional killing without malice aforethought, usually in the heat of passion. William comes home and finds his wife in bed with Fred. William grabs a gun from the dresser drawer and kills them both. There has been no premeditation, just a reaction to a situation. He is guilty of voluntary manslaughter. He must, however, have killed them before an ordinary person would cool off. If he left and made plans how he was going to kill them, then killed each of them two days later, his "heat of passion" had time to cool off, and he would be guilty of premeditated murder.

Involuntary manslaughter is an unintentional killing caused by a person's criminal negligence. Justin is trying out his new Camaro and drives it at 65 mph down a residential street. He loses control and the car hits and kills a woman sitting in her front yard. Justin is guilty of involuntary manslaughter. He did not mean to kill anyone, he was just criminally negligent by speeding.

The misdemeanor-manslaughter rule applies where a person accidentally kills another during the course of a misdemeanor. Henry calls Joe a jerk. Joe pushes Henry, and Henry falls and hits his head on the curb and dies. The pushing was an assault and battery, a misdemeanor, but since Henry died, Joe is guilty of misdemeanor-manslaughter.

Torture

Torture is the intentional infliction of great bodily injury on another. Frank wants to know if Jack squealed to the police about a murder Frank committed.

Frank uses a blowtorch and pliers to burn and peel the skin off Jack's face. Frank is guilty of torture.

Robbery

Robbery is the use of force or threat of immediately using force to take money or property from a person. It's a crime against a person rather than his property.

STORY IDEAS

A man strolled into a bank and held up the teller with a hamburger. The man handed a teller a note demanding money and indicating he had a bomb in a fast-food restaurant bag, which he placed on the counter. The teller handed the man $500 and he ran away. The bank employees and customers were evacuated, but police quickly determined that the bomb squad wasn't needed because they could smell the hamburger in the bag.

Carjacking

Carjacking is the forcible taking of a motor vehicle from another person. A rash of incidents where people were forced off the highway and pulled from their cars so their cars could be stolen resulted in this specific crime being defined. Though other crimes were being committed, such as assault, battery and robbery, the specific act of taking someone's car from them while they are in it was made an additional crime by many states.

STORY IDEAS

A woman made a daring escape after a carjacker stabbed her three times, puncturing her lung and breaking a rib. The woman had stopped for coffee at a doughnut shop when the assailant jumped in the passenger seat through the unlocked door. The suspect fled but was later caught and arrested for attempted murder, carjacking and evading arrest.

Stalking

With a rash of people, usually movie stars, being followed and some being attacked and killed, many states created the crime of stalking. It is the willful, malicious and repeated following or harassing of another person and making threats with the intent to place that person in fear for his safety or the safety of his immediate family.

Sex Offenses

Sodomy is one person using threat or force to have his penis penetrate another person's anus.

Oral copulation is one person using threat or force to have contact between one person's mouth and the sexual organ of another person.

Penetration by a foreign object is where one person causes the penetration of the genital or anal openings of another person by any foreign object by force or threat.

STORY IDEAS

A male chiropractor accused of giving at least nine teenage boys drugs, money and pornography and then forcing them to have sex with him was arrested on a $1.5 million warrant. He was captured while trying to make a withdrawal from his bank account. He was charged with multiple counts of sodomy and oral copulation, furnishing marijuana and possession of obscene material.

Crimes Against Property

Theft

There are three common-law crimes that most states combine under the statutory crime of theft.

Larceny is the unlawful taking and carrying away of another person's personal property with the intent to permanently deprive the owner of the property. Jimmy is walking past a neighbor's open garage. He sees a bicycle inside, runs up and takes it, intending to sell it to a friend at school. Jimmy is guilty of larceny.

Taking under false pretenses is inducing someone to part with both possession and title to property by making a false statement or creating a false impression.

Embezzlement is wrongfully taking something that someone else has entrusted to you.

> ### STORY IDEAS
>
> *An ex-con posing as a banker tricked a Roman Catholic priest over the telephone into handing over $1.4 million in church funds, saying he was going to invest the money. The man had been convicted eight years before of swindling fifty priests out of $130,000 by pretending to be a needy parishioner. He got two years in prison for taking money under false pretenses.*

> ### STORY IDEAS
>
> *A former bank teller who used a trusting friendship with two elderly sisters to embezzle $100,000 from their accounts was sentenced to twenty-eight months in prison. Because of their advanced age, the sisters had difficulty filling out their deposit and withdrawal slips, so the teller would help them, sometimes delivering cash to their home. The man, who had no prior record, said he initially began embezzling the funds to pay off credit card debt run up when he was "young and stupid." He would fill out a withdrawal slip for the amount the sisters requested and have them sign it. Then he'd add a number to it and keep the extra money.*

Grand Theft

Taking property that exceeds a certain monetary amount, usually $200 to $400, depending on the state, is grand theft, a felony and usually punishable with at least one year in state prison and a fine.

> ### STORY IDEAS
>
> *An appeals court upheld the conviction of a former sheriff's deputy for stealing money while serving in an elite drug enforcement squad. Prosecutors said he stole money that was seized by deputies during drug investigations. He was sentenced to six years in prison for grand theft.*

Petty Theft

Petty theft is taking property under a value of $200 to $400, depending on the state, and is a misdemeanor and usually punishable with less than one year in county jail and a fine.

Extortion

Extortion is obtaining property from someone by threatening to hurt them or a member of their family or threatening to destroy their reputation. Marcia tells Bill that if he doesn't give her $100,000, she will tell Bill's wife that they had an affair. Marcia is guilty of extortion, sometimes called blackmail.

Forgery

Forgery is making or altering a writing that has some legal significance.

STORY IDEAS

A fourteen-year-old boy used a color computer scanner to make at least a dozen counterfeit $1 bills. He tried to use one of them to buy a soda, but the machine spit the fake dollar out. He then crumpled the bills and dropped them around the school to watch other students find them. Unsuspecting students used the fake money to buy Twinkies at the snack bar. Suspicious snack-bar attendants called police. Police allowed the boy to return to class, but later he got a visit from the Secret Service.

Receiving Stolen Property

Receiving stolen property is taking possession of property you know to be stolen. Paying for it doesn't relieve you of the crime if you know or should have known it was stolen.

STORY IDEAS

A former criminal defense attorney was sentenced to three to six years in prison for possessing stolen art, books and computers from schools, museums and libraries that he apparently received from clients he had defended. He admitted to sixty-five counts of receiving stolen property worth thousands of dollars.

Burglary

Burglary is entering a structure at any time with the intent to commit larceny or any felony. Unlike the common-law definition of burglary, modern burglary doesn't require stealing something. If the criminal breaks into a house to commit any felony, i.e., murder, rape or arson, he is guilty of burglary. The crime of burglary has been committed when the criminal enters the structure, whether or not the intended felony is accomplished. Rocky sees a house that is dark and decides to steal a television. He sneaks around to the backyard, finds an unlocked sliding door, opens it and enters. A silent alarm is triggered and Rocky is caught before he gets out of the house with the television. He is guilty of burglary.

Arson

Arson is the deliberate burning of any structure owned by another person. Burning a structure that you own is not arson, but it might be insurance fraud.

STORY IDEAS

A landlord who wanted a family out of her property gave an arsonist a dog in return for having a fire set that killed four children. When the fire was set the children were trapped in the house, which had security bars over most of its windows.

Crimes Against Public Health, Safety and Morals

Illegal Weapons

Most states have laws against possession of certain weapons, such as assault rifles, silencers and nunchakus. Also, most states have laws against carrying concealed or loaded weapons without a license or permit.

STORY IDEAS

A federal law adding five years to the prison sentence of anyone who carries a gun while selling or buying illegal drugs can apply to those who keep a gun locked in a car's glove compartment or trunk, the Supreme Court has ruled. Drug traffickers arrested while in or near their cars can be convicted of carrying a gun even if it is not immediately accessible.

Prostitution, Pimping and Pandering

Prostitution is engaging in sexual activity in exchange for money or property. It is a crime for both the prostitute and the customer. Pimping is soliciting on behalf of a prostitute or deriving support from prostitute's earnings. Pandering is procuring a person to become a prostitute.

STORY IDEAS

Three women face prostitution charges after filing a complaint with the police that a man who had sex with them gave them a bad check for $1,500. Police also arrested the man who gave the women the bad check and charged him with three counts of patronizing a prostitute.

Obscenity

Obscene material is material that, when taken as a whole, under contemporary statewide standards, appeals to the prurient interests of an average person by depicting or describing sexual conduct in a patently offensive way that lacks serious literary, artistic, political or scientific value. Enforcement of laws against obscenity usually bumps up against First-Amendment rights to freedom of expression.

STORY IDEAS

The Barnes & Noble bookstore chain was indicted on obscenity charges for selling three books that feature photographs of nude children. The books had received some critical praise but a state grand jury claimed they might violate state obscenity laws. However, the district attorney agreed to drop obscenity charges against Barnes & Noble after it promised to keep the books out of the reach of kids.

Loitering and Vagrancy

Loitering and vagrancy is sitting or standing around a public place with apparently no place to go. Laws against such activity are often ruled unconstitutional for being too vague or for prohibiting lawful conduct.

Unlawful Assembly, Rout, Riot

Unlawful assembly is an assembly of two or more persons to do unlawful acts or to do lawful acts in a violent, boisterous or tumultuous manner. A rout is an assembly making a concerted attempt to riot. A riot is the use or threat of force or violence that disturbs the public peace.

Disturbing the Peace

Fighting or challenging someone to fight in public, disturbing others with loud or unreasonable noise, or the use of offensive words in a public place that are likely to cause an immediate violent reaction all constitute disturbing the peace, usually a misdemeanor.

Malicious Mischief

Malicious mischief is defacement of property. Raymond uses a can of spray paint to write his name on the side of city hall. He is guilty of malicious mischief.

Bigamy

A person who has a spouse living and who marries another person is guilty of bigamy. Some states allow a defense of good faith belief that you were divorced.

STORY IDEAS

A police detective who was married to three women at the same time has pleaded guilty to bigamy. The officer, who recently divorced all his wives and remarried one, pleaded guilty to the misdemeanor and was fined $750.

Incest

The law prohibits sexual relationships between persons who are within certain degrees of relationship, e.g., brothers and sisters, parents and children, or half-brothers and sisters.

Gambling

State and local laws extensively regulate gambling. Games such as cards, slot machines, dice, roulette and bookmaking are allowed in some areas and outlawed in others.

Brandishing a Weapon

Drawing or exhibiting a deadly weapon in a rude, angry or threatening manner is illegal. Jim pulls out his new .44 magnum and shakes it at Ted, saying: "This will take care of you." Jim is guilty of brandishing a weapon.

Driving Under the Influence

Driving a motor vehicle while under the influence of alcohol or any drug is illegal. A person with a blood-alcohol level of 0.08 percent or higher is presumed to be under the influence in most states.

Controlled Substance Offenses

It is illegal for any person to possess any controlled substance unless he has a legal prescription or is in the legal chain of distribution to people with prescriptions. Controlled substances include legal drugs, e.g., stimulants and depressants, and illegal drugs, e.g., marijuana, narcotics and hallucinogens.

Forfeiture of Property

Any money or property used in or gained from the sale of specified amounts of controlled substances is subject to forfeiture. The forfeited property becomes the property of the state and sometimes the agency that made the arrest.

Crimes Involving Minors

It is a crime to contribute to the delinquency of a minor, such as getting a minor to shoplift, drink, engage in sexual activity or commit other crimes.

School Crimes

To protect children and school activities, most states have laws relating to activities on or near schools, such as restrictions on unauthorized people being on school property or loitering near a school.

Criminal Street-Gang Activity

Most states have specific laws against criminal gang activity, such as participating in gang activity, committing crimes for the benefit of the gang, and using a building for gang purposes.

Miscellaneous Crimes

Bribery

Bribery is the giving or taking of a bribe for certain governmental action. Mike tells the highway patrol officer who is writing Mike a speeding ticket that he will buy the officer's pen for $100, then the officer won't have anything to write the ticket with. If the officer accepts, both he and Mike are guilty of bribery.

Perjury

Perjury is knowingly giving false testimony regarding a material matter while under oath. Vicki testifies in court that her boyfriend was with her at the time of the murder. She made this up to give him an alibi. Vicki is guilty of perjury.

Subornation of Perjury

Subornation of perjury is procuring someone to commit perjury for you. If Vicki's boyfriend talked her into giving false testimony, he is guilty of subornation of perjury.

> TIP: State legislatures and the federal government, in response to evolving criminal activity, pass legislation creating new crimes by statute. Carjacking, stalking, computer crimes and crimes on the Internet are examples. Watch for pending legislation creating these new crimes to include them in your book or screenplay.

Federal Crimes

Some crimes, by their nature, are only federal crimes.: counterfeiting U.S. currency; violations of customs regulations; embezzlement and theft of federal property; crimes committed through the mails; espionage and treason; piracy; assault, kidnapping or assassination of the President. These crimes are usually investigated by the Federal Bureau of Investigation and prosecuted by U.S. Attorneys in the U.S. Justice Department.

Accomplices and Accessories

Accomplice

Anyone who participates in any way in a crime is an accomplice and is generally as guilty as if he actually committed the crime. Fred drives Terry to a bank that

---

Terry is going to rob. Fred waits outside while Terry robs the bank. Although Fred did not go inside the bank, he is still guilty of bank robbery.

Accessory

An accessory before the fact (called an aider and abettor in some states) instigates, advises, incites, aids or abets someone in the commission of a crime. Sam lends his car to Jerry to drive to a bank that Sam knows Jerry is going to rob. Sam is an accessory before the fact, or an aider and abettor. Generally the accessory before the fact is as guilty as the person who actually commits the crime.

An accessory after the fact is someone who knowingly conceals a criminal, helps a criminal escape or otherwise deliberately acts to prevent a criminal's capture. The accessory is not guilty of the main crime but is criminally responsible for harboring or concealing the fugitive.

If a person deliberately conceals another person's felony, he is guilty of misprision of felony. If a person accepts money or property and agrees to not report or prosecute another's crime, he is guilty of compounding.

Multiple Offenses

Most criminal actions involve the commission of multiple crimes. Robbing a bank can include solicitation, conspiracy, assault, battery, false imprisonment, burglary, robbery and possession of a deadly weapon. Typically the prosecuting attorney will charge every possible crime, knowing that some will be easier to prove than others, and also knowing that, in plea bargaining, he can offer to dismiss some of the charges in exchange for guilty pleas to others.

Multiple Prosecutions

Some offenses violate both state and federal laws. For example, blowing up a federal office building is a state crime and a federal crime. Possession of firearms can be both a state and a federal crime. Since the offense violates both state and federal law, a defendant can be prosecuted for violating both laws. It is not double jeopardy, since it is not the same jurisdiction prosecuting the defendant twice for the same crime. It just happens that the crimes arise from the same actions by the defendant. Usually the federal and state prosecutors agree on where the prosecution will be and do not each prosecute, due to limited resources. However, some high-profile crimes are prosecuted both by the state and the federal government.

Defenses

If a person commits a crime but has a valid legal excuse or justification (defense) for his actions, he may be acquitted.

76

Consent of Victim

Some activities are not crimes if the parties involved consent. For example, if a woman of legal age agrees to have sexual intercourse, it is not rape. But consent is never a defense to more serious crimes such as murder or mayhem, or to crimes against the general public such as prostitution or selling drugs.

Self-Defense

A person is entitled to use reasonable force to protect themselves when it reasonably appears that they are in danger of immediate harm from someone else. Rudy approaches Jerry and starts pushing him. Jerry can grab Rudy and restrain him. If Rudy claims that Jerry committed assault and battery, Jerry can claim self-defense since he used reasonable force to protect himself from Rudy harming him.

A person can use deadly force (force that is likely to result in the death or serious injury to a person) when they are in immediate danger of death or serious injury and deadly force is reasonably necessary to protect themselves. Before Jerry could grab Rudy to restrain him, Rudy pulled out a knife and lunged at Jerry. Jerry could shoot Rudy and claim self-defense since Jerry was in immediate danger of death or serious injury from Rudy and his knife attack. In some states a person is required to retreat before using deadly force, except if they are in their own home or they cannot retreat safely.

STORY IDEAS

The daughter of one of the world's biggest arms dealers was convicted of voluntary manslaughter instead of murder after claiming self-defense in the shooting death of her boyfriend. The woman testified that she shot her lover after he slashed her arms with a knife and threatened to kill her. She was sentenced to sixty days in jail and fined $2,500.

Defense of Others

This defense used to apply only if the person was defending a member of his own family. Today, a person can defend anyone if they are in immediate danger of serious harm. They can use only that force that the person in danger could use if they were defending themselves. If Tommy saw Rudy attack Jerry with the knife, Tommy could shoot Rudy and claim defense of others, since Jerry could have shot Rudy.

The "battered woman's syndrome" defense to murder developed when a woman who had been raped later received a threatening telephone call from one of the perpetrators. She grabbed a rifle, hunted down and shot one of the men who had restrained her and stood by laughing as she was raped. Prior to that case the treatment of the woman by the man she killed was not admissible as a defense.

Defense of Property
A person can use force to protect property in certain situations, e.g., a person can use reasonable force to prevent someone from breaking into their car. However, a person is usually required to warn the criminal to stop and leave before using any kind of force, unless doing so would put the person in danger. If Ed sees Joe breaking into Ed's car, Ed can grab Joe and keep him from breaking into the car, but in most states he would have to tell Joe to stop first before he could grab him.

Usually a person cannot use deadly force to protect property, with the main exception being protecting your home when you are inside and a criminal is breaking in.

Prevention of Crime
The police can use reasonable force, including deadly force if necessary, to prevent a crime or to apprehend or prevent the escape of the person who has committed a felony or a misdemeanor involving a breach of the peace. A private citizen can use reasonable force to prevent a felony attempted in their presence.

Insanity
Insanity in legal proceedings has a legal definition, not a psychiatric one. The psychiatric equivalent of legal insanity is psychosis or loss of touch with reality. Most states use one of two tests of legal insanity.

The first, developed by the American Law Institute as part of the Model Penal Code, provides that: "A person is not responsible for criminal conduct if at the time of such conduct, as a result of mental disease or defect, he lacks substantial capacity either to appreciate the criminality (wrongfulness) of his conduct or to conform his conduct to the requirements of law."

The second test, called the M'Naghten Rule, defines legal insanity as: "At the time of committing the act the party accused was laboring under such a defect of reason, from disease of the mind, as not to know the nature and quality of the act he was doing, or as not to know that what he was doing was wrong."

Diminished Capacity
Diminished capacity is not a complete defense to a crime. It is just a means of reducing an offense to a less serious charge by showing the person did not have the ability to form the required mental state necessary to commit the crime charged.

Intoxication
Voluntary intoxication generally is not a defense to a crime, but it may reduce the charge in a few cases where a specific intent was required, e.g., the defendant

> ### STORY IDEAS
> *A World War II veteran who claimed flashbacks to his days as a prisoner of war caused him to kill his son-in-law was sentenced to thirty-five years to life in prison. The jury rejected the former Marine's contention that he thought he was shooting a Japanese guard when he shot his son-in-law, then chased him down and fired four more times.*

was unable to premeditate the killing because he was so drunk.

Involuntary intoxication (someone spiked the punch or slipped drugs in your drink) can be a defense if the defendant wasn't sober enough to realize what he was doing and could not control his actions.

> ### STORY IDEAS
> *A teenager who killed two people while driving drunk was sentenced to carry pictures of the victims in his wallet for the next ten years. The judge, known for his creative punishments, gave the teen ten years probation with strict conditions that included carrying pictures of the victims and watching an autopsy.*

Acting Under Threats or Coercion

A person is not normally liable for crimes committed while acting under physical duress or coercion. If Barry steals a car because Nick said he would kill Barry's son if he didn't steal the car, Barry has the defense of acting under a threat when he committed the car theft. However, this cannot be used as a defense to murder or manslaughter.

Entrapment

Entrapment is a defense to certain crimes, e.g., solicitation for prostitution and selling drugs. But it is not a defense to crimes involving physical injury or injury to property, e.g., murder, rape, arson or robbery. Entrapment occurs when the police talk a person into committing a crime that person would not otherwise be predisposed to commit. The police put the thought into the defendant's head and the police help plan and instigate the crime.

Domestic Authority

Parents—and, in some states, schoolteachers—are entitled to use reasonable force to discipline their children or pupils without being criminally liable for assault or battery. However, if the punishment is excessive and the child is injured, this privilege is lost and the person is liable for assault and battery.

Children

Under common-law rules that some states still apply, a child under the age of seven is legally incapable of committing a crime. Children between ages seven and fourteen are presumed incapable of committing a crime. However, a child can be convicted of a crime if the evidence shows that the child was sufficiently mature to understand what he was doing.

Double Jeopardy

If a defendant has already been tried and convicted or acquitted, he cannot be tried a second time by the same jurisdiction for the same crime.

Statute of Limitations

Most crimes have a time limitation on how long after the crime charges can be filed. However, there is no statute of limitation for murder.

STORY IDEAS

A judge dismissed charges against a man accused of molesting his niece more than two decades ago in a case that challenges the constitutionality of a state law extending the statute of limitations. The woman claimed that she never told anyone about the alleged molestation until twenty years later when she discovered other family members came forward with tales of abuse and she learned that her uncle had a new seven-year-old stepdaughter living with him.

Discriminatory Enforcement of Statute

This defense is available if the defendant establishes that the prosecution was pursued and the defendant was singled out because of intentional and purposeful discrimination, e.g., because of the defendant's race, religion or gender.

Proving Defense
The defendant generally has the burden of proving any defense to a criminal offense.

Punishments
Punishment for crimes usually consists of fine, incarceration in a county jail, imprisonment in a state prison or death.

Determinate Sentencing
Some states provide for determinate sentencing, providing by statute for an upper term for aggravated crimes, a middle term for routine crimes and a lower term where mitigating circumstances exist.

Aggravating Circumstances
Factors that make a crime aggravated include use of great violence, causing great bodily harm, acts of great cruelty, use of a weapon or crimes against a victim who was particularly vulnerable. Other factors include multiple victims, a defendant who induced others to join in the crime or acted as a leader, and a defendant who threatened witnesses.

Mitigating Circumstances
Factors that constitute mitigating circumstances include a defendant who was a passive participant or played a minor role in the crime, a victim who provoked the crime and a defendant who had no predisposition to commit the crime but was induced by others to participate in the crime. Other factors include a defendant who tried to avoid harm to person while committing the crime, a defendant who was motivated by a desire to provide necessities for himself or his family, a defendant with no prior record, a defendant who voluntarily acknowledged his wrongdoing prior to arrest or at an early stage of the criminal proceedings, and a defendant who made restitution to the victim.

Sentence Enhancement
A sentence enhancement is an additional term of imprisonment added to the base term. For example, if the crime involved intentional infliction of great bodily harm, an enhancement of three years is added in some states, and if the crime involved a loss of over $100,000 in property, an enhancement of two years might be added.

Consecutive vs. Concurrent Sentences

Sometimes the sentencing judge has the discretion to impose consecutive or concurrent sentences for multiple offenses. A consecutive sentence is the linking of sentences for two or more offenses end to end, to extend the overall sentence. A concurrent sentence is the joining of sentences for two or more offenses together so the defendant serves two or more sentences at the same time, making his overall time in prison shorter.

Misdemeanor vs. Felony

Misdemeanors are generally punishable by a fine of up to $1,000 and confinement in county jail for up to one year. Felonies are generally punishable by a fine of up to $10,000 and imprisonment in state prison for over one year, or if the crime was a capital offense, by death.

Credit Against Sentence

Often a defendant has spent anywhere from a few days to several months in custody prior to conviction. The sentencing judge must give the defendant credit for this time served.

Credit for Good Time

Some states provide that prisoners will receive good-time credits for each day the prisoner either works or participates in educational programs. Typically one day is taken off the time the defendant must serve for each one day of good time. These credits can be lost for violating prison rules.

Death Penalty

Certain crimes, such as first-degree murder, train wrecking, treason or the killing of a police officer or public official, are punishable by death. These factors, sometimes called "special circumstances," if found to exist, require a separate trial, called the "penalty phase," where the possibility of the death sentence is considered by a jury.

Additional Penalties

In addition to fine and incarceration, a defendant may lose the right to hold certain licenses, such as a license to practice law or drive a motor vehicle. He

STORY IDEAS

A woman will join her husband on death row for submerging their four-year-old niece in a bathtub of water so hot it peeled the skin from her body. The same jury that convicted the twenty-eight-year-old woman of murder recommended that she be executed for the death of the little girl. The woman's husband is already on death row for the child's murder.

may lose the right to vote, to hold office and, after release, he may have to register his presence in the county where he lives.

Shock Incarceration

Some states and counties have programs where young first offenders are sentenced to boot camp correctional facilities where they are confined for short periods under rigid standards and strict military discipline.

CHAPTER FOUR

Search and Seizure, Arrest and Confession

"The poorest man may, in his cottage, bid defiance to all the force of the Crown. It may be frail; its roof may shake; the wind may blow through it; the storm may enter; the rain may enter; but the King of England may not enter; all his force dares not cross the threshold of the ruined tenement."

—William Pitt, Earl of Chatham, speaking in 1763 in the English House of Commons against allowing general search warrants

Nazi "SS" troops storm people's apartments in the dead of the night, searching randomly for anything incriminating and dragging the occupants away to interrogations, torture, concentration camps and death. Millions of ordinary citizens disappear for unknown offenses into Stalin's Gulag, with no charges, no trials and no one defending their interests or challenging the evidence against them. A SWAT team in Chicago armed with a no-knock warrant enters the wrong house in the middle of the night, terrorizing an innocent family erroneously believed to be drug traffickers. All these frightening incidents occurred in the absence or abuse of search-and-seizure rules.

What can be searched and when can a search be conducted? What can be seized? What information must the authorities possess before they are entitled to a search warrant? When are citizens entitled to privacy? Under what circumstances do they have to allow police to enter their homes, search their vehicles and examine their bodies? The rules of search and seizure developed over the centuries, providing objective standards for measuring the proper and improper use of police power in invading the privacy of people's homes, possessions and bodies. The boundaries of those rights are tested daily by the police, prosecutors, the courts and criminal defense attorneys in their never-ending battle between the need for a safe society and the rights of individuals. This constant struggle can provide gripping fare for your readers and viewers.

Search and Seizure
History
Virtually unlimited search powers were used for years in England to seek out books and other publications as a means of restricting freedom of press. Under general warrants authorities essentially looked for anything, anywhere—entering people's homes and searching until they found something incriminating. Therefore, to formally protect individual privacy and security against arbitrary invasions by government officials, the founding fathers adopted the Fourth Amendment to the U.S. Constitution:

> "The right of the people to be secure in their persons, houses, papers and effects, against unreasonable searches and seizures, shall not be violated, and no warrants shall issue, but upon probable cause, supported by oath or affirmation, and particularly describing the place to be searched, and the persons or things to be seized."

Definition
The courts consider a search to be an exploratory investigation, looking for or seeking out that which is concealed. A search takes place whenever the government (police, FBI agents, marshals, sheriffs, etc.) intrudes into a person's privacy to discover and gather incriminating evidence. A policeman in someone's residence, sliding a stereo forward just a fraction of an inch to look at the serial number, is conducting a search.

A seizure occurs when there is some meaningful interference with an individual's possession of property. Seizure takes place as soon as the police exercise control over the property, whether they have actual physical possession of it or not. Eavesdropping on or recording a telephone conversation is a seizure of the conversation.

Expectation of Privacy

The Constitutional search-and-seizure provisions protect our reasonable expectations of privacy, our "right to be left alone." The most protected areas are our persons, our homes (including temporary homes, such as a hotel rooms or mobile homes), our offices (areas not open to the public), our papers and our effects. There is less expectation of privacy in our vehicles and for children attending school. We have no expectation of privacy on public property or in open fields. If we have papers inside a closed briefcase, we reasonably expect they will remain private since others do not have access to them. But if we leave papers scattered on a public library table we reasonably don't expect them to be private since we are exposing them to public view and anyone who happens by.

We have an expectation of privacy in most things in our home, except for things hanging in the window that can be seen by a passerby, since we have voluntarily placed them where others, including the police, can see them. The test is did the individual have a reasonable expectation of privacy in the area searched? The courts decided that a homeless person living in an open-ended cardboard box located on a public sidewalk in violation of a local ordinance had no reasonable expectation of privacy in the box as his home, and thus the police could make a warrantless search of the box.

Who Is Protected?

The Fourth Amendment protects all persons within the boundaries of the United States, whether adults, minors, citizens, aliens (legal or illegal), parolees, probationers or corporations.

Whom Are We Protected From?

The Fourth Amendment only protects us against searches and seizures by the police and government, or at their direction or by their agents. It does not protect us against searches and seizures by private parties. So if a victim of theft, without the knowledge, consent or direction of law enforcement personnel, carries out a search of the suspect's residence and while there sees his stolen property, what he discovers can provide probable cause for the police to obtain a search warrant to enter themselves. But if the theft victim tells the police he is going to break into the suspect's house to see if his stolen property is there, and the police do nothing to protect the suspect's right to privacy against the intrusion, the entry by the theft victim is done with government involvement and evidence cannot be used against the suspect.

Search Warrants

A search warrant is an order in writing in the name of the People, signed by a magistrate (judges of state and federal courts are magistrates), directing a peace officer in the court's jurisdiction to search for a person or thing.

Requirement

In general a search is not valid unless it is conducted pursuant to a warrant. The warrant requirement is intended to protect our privacy from unrestrained police efforts to locate evidence. The law requires a neutral and detached magistrate with a "cool, objective mind" to review the police request for a warrant. The magistrate cannot act as a "rubber stamp," approving all requests for warrants without even reading the application and supporting affidavits. The magistrate must make an independent judgment from the information set forth in the sworn affidavit submitted to him that the requested warrant is supported by probable cause.

Probable Cause

To obtain a warrant, a law enforcement officer (or any government official) needs to submit information to a magistrate to establish probable cause, which means it is "substantially probable" that there is specific evidence of criminal activity at a particular place. The evidence can be contraband, such as stolen property, illegal drugs or firearms, or evidence of a crime, such as a murder weapon or blood stains. (See Search Warrant on page 89.)

Probable cause is more than a mere hunch or suspicion but less than evidence beyond a reasonable doubt. Probable cause must be based on credible and reliable information.

Source of Information

Informant: If the source of the information that contraband or evidence of a crime exists at a specified location is an informant, the magistrate must consider how the informant obtained the information and what the credibility or "track record" of reliable information from this informant is. If the informant is a criminal with a record, the magistrate has to take into account that criminals

STATE OF CALIFORNIA - COUNTY OF MONTEREY

SEARCH WARRANT AND AFFIDAVIT

(AFFIDAVIT)

⌐etective Mike _____ swears under oath that the facts expressed by him in the attached and incorporated statement of probable cause are true and that based thereon, he has probable cause to believe and does believe that the property described below is lawfully seizable pursuant to Penal Code Section 1524, as indicated below, and is now located at the locations set forth below. Wherefore, affiant requests that this Search Warrant be issued.

_____,   NIGHT SEARCH REQUESTED: YES [X]   NO [ ]
Signature of Affiant

(SEARCH WARRANT)

THE PEOPLE OF THE STATE OF CALIFORNIA TO ANY SHERIFF, POLICEMAN OR PEACE OFFICER IN THE COUNTY OF MONTEREY: Proof by affidavit having been made before me by **Detective Mike** _____ that there is probable cause to believe that the property described herein may be found at the locations set forth herein and that it is lawfully seizable pursuant to Penal Code Section 1524 as indicated below by " X " (s) in that it:

___   was stolen or embezzled;
--X--   was used as the means of committing a felony;
--X--   is possessed by a person with the intent to use it as a means of committing a public offense or is possessed by another whom he or she may have delivered it for the purpose of concealing it or preventing its discovery,
--X--   tends to show that a felony has been committed or that a particular person has committed a felony;
___   tends to show that the sexual exploitation of a child, in violation of Penal Code Section 311.3, has occurred or is occurring.

YOU ARE THEREFORE COMMANDED TO SEARCH:

3245   Circle in the City of   This is a dark tan over stucco single story residence with the numbers
'3245' on curb in front of house.   Police Detectives are currently securing the house at this time.

⌐.reas to be searched to include all rooms, attics, safes, parking areas, garages, hidden compartments, the surrounding grounds, outbuildings of any kind, storage areas, trash containers, mailboxes, and any other area designated for the specific use of 3245   Circle in the City of

FOR THE FOLLOWING PROPERTY:

A handgun, possibly a .38 caliber or .357 magnum, or similar type weapon. Additionally, experience teaches that those who use firearms also possess ammunition, cleaning equipment and containers for such firearms, along with associated documents such as receipts related to transfer and repair, within their residence and/or vehicle.

The personal belongings of Christopher _____ , including letters, memos, writtings, pictures and any other items belonging to Christopher around the time he was 16 years old.

AND TO SEIZE IT IF FOUND and bring it forthwith before me, or this court, at the courthouse of this court. This Search Warrant and incorporated Affidavit was sworn to as true and subscribed before me this _28th_ day of _Jun_ , 19_78_ ,at _11:00_ a.m. / p.m. Wherefore, I find probable cause for the issuance of this Search Warrant and do issue it.

_____   NIGHT SEARCH APPROVED: YES [X]   NO [ ]
Signature of Magistrate

⌐.udge of the Superior/Municipal Court, ___ _Satum_ Judicial District

03000.

Search Warrant

STATEMENT OF PROBABLE CAUSE

Your affiant, Mike   , has been a   Police Officer since 8-24-88. I attended the Santa Rosa Basic
Police Academy and I currently posses an Advanced POST Certificate. I have received an Associates of Arts
Degree in Administration of Justice from Hartnell College. I am working towards a Bachelors Degree in
Management. I am currently a Detective with the   Police Department, working in the Investigation
Division. I have investigated and assisted with the investigation of crimes involving murder, attempted murder,
assault with deadly weapons, robbery and kidnapping. I have attended several POST schools, receiving
specialized training in many of these areas. I have also received informal training from other experienced
investigators, both from my agency as well as outside agencies. I have interviewed multiple persons charged
with and convicted of these types of crimes and have questioned them regarding the manner in which they
commit these crimes. I am thoroughly familiar with the manner in which many of these crimes are committed
within the City of

On 1-27-98, Officer Bud   and Corporal John   of the   Police Department received a
call to go to 248   Drive for a report of a possible body under the kitchen area of a house. The owners of
this house are Diana and Eric   . Approximately two weeks ago Eric and his father-in-law Robert
crawled under the house to install vents for the bedrooms. While under the house they noticed what
they thought were a pair of tennis shoes sticking up out of the dirt under the kitchen area. Initially they thought
this was a prank and did not give it any more thought. They never went near the shoes. On 1-24-98 Diana
received a letter from the   Police Department that said there was a missing person report generated at the
residence in 1984. The Salinas Police Department letter said the case was still open and they wanted to know if
that person had returned. Diana then remembered that Eric had told her about the shoes in the dirt.

On 1-27-98, Diana was talking to a friend and challenged the friend to go under the house to check on the shoes.
The friend, Noemy   , put on some overalls and went under the house and up to the shoes. She tugged on
the shoes and they did not move. Noemy crawled out from the house and Diana called the police.

Corporal   crawled under the house and checked on the shoes and believed there was a good chance that
this was a buried body. He notified Detectives   and   and a crime scene was established and the
kitchen floor was cut open. Crime scene technicians and two anthropologists from University of Santa Cruz
responded to process the scene.

There were skeletal remains buried in a shallow grave. The skeleton appeared intact and appeared to be a male
approx. 5'8" long. This fits the description of the missing person from 1984. This person was then 16 years old.
In 1984 the mother reported to Officer Rick   of the   Police Department that she had not seen her
son for 3 months. She said he left without his clothes, or any other personal belongings. She could not give any
reason for him leaving. She said Christopher was last seen wearing a rock-type shirt, levis pants and white
tennis shoes. Dale said her son was wearing an earring in his left ear.

On 1-27-98, Detectives   and   contacted Christopher's girlfriend at the time, Carlota
Carlota said she clearly remembers Christopher and said she was very surprised when he just disappeared. She
said she asked Christopher's mom what had happened to Christopher and she told Carlota that Christopher
packed up all his clothes and left and she does not know where he went.

2

02000

Search Warrant (continued)

While processing the crime scene, Detectice   found two spent and deformed bullets in the chest area of the skeleton. The skull of the skeleton was broken along the front and there was a hole on both the right and left side of the head. Investigators also found an earring near the skull.

On 1-27-98, I went to the autopsy of the skeleton male. This was conducted by Dr. John   of the Montery County Sheriff's Department and he found the following; there was a bullet hole in the skull which entered from right and exited through the left. There was also two bullet holes going through the right shoulder blade and entering from the back. The male was wearing pants, which were mostly gone, but there was a Levi tag attached to the threads. The pockets were intact and inside one of them was a set of keys. One of the keys appeared to go to a honda motorcycle. Detective   said that when he spoke with Christopher's girlfriend, Carlota, she told him that Christopher did have a motorcycle. This all fits the description of Christopher   A dental record check on the skeleton is forthcoming.

On 1-28-98, Detectives   and   contacted Christopher's step-father, Jackson   at his work at 216   St. in Salinas. Jackson was married to Dale at the time of Christopher's disappearance. Jackson voluntarily came with Detectives   and   to the   Police Department. He told them that he did live there when his step-son disappeared and stayed there for four to five years after. He said that after Christopher disappeared his mother packed up all his belongings and boxed them in their garage. Jackson said that they have since moved to 3245   Circle in the City of   and they still have all of Christopher's belongings still in the boxes. Jackson said that he owns three weapons and all are at his current house in He described the guns as a Remmington .22cal., a Browning (not specific as to what type of weapon) and a Colt Python. A Colt Python is capable of shooting a .38cal. and a .357cal. bullet. This is similar to the type of bullets found in the rib cage of the body. Jackson said he has owned the python since 1978.

Detective's   ... and   asked Jackson if he had anything to do with the body under the house and he aid he did not. At this point it appears that the skeleton is Christopher   It was established through the autopsy that Christopher died as a result of multiple gunshot wounds to his head and back. Detective also found two bullets in the body. Christopher lived with his mother and step-father at the time of his disappearance and his step-father told detectives that he owns, and still has, a weapon that could have fired the bullets into Christopher.

At this time Dale   is at the   Police Department voluntarily and being questioned by Detective   Officers of the   Police Department are at 3245   Circle in the City of   freezing the residence in anticipation of this warrant being signed. At this time it is 2130 hours and it is unlikely we will be able to have the warrant signed before 2200 hours. Based on this fact, I am requesting night service endorsement.

Based on this information I believe that there is sufficient evidence to establish that a Christopher   was a victim of a homicide in 1984. I also believe that his parents would have to have participated, or known about the homicide and the disposal of the body.

I swear under the threat of perjury that the statements made in this statement of probable cause in support of the issuance of the warrant to search is true and correct to the best of my knowledge.

          Mike   , Detective
          Police Department

3

Search Warrant (continued)

often expect to personally gain from informing on each other and thus their information may be less reliable.

Victim: If information comes from a victim of the crime, from an eyewitness or from an ordinary citizen, the magistrate will usually treat the information as more reliable, since their motive is usually to see the law enforced.

Anonymous tip: By itself, an anonymous tip is not sufficient to establish probable cause. The tip must include sufficient information for the magistrate to conclude the informant is honest or his information is reliable, and must give a basis for the informer's knowledge. However, since the informer might be an undercover law enforcement officer, a criminal who is providing continuing useful information or an ordinary citizen who is concerned for his safety, the magistrate can allow the police and prosecution to keep the informer's identity confidential to protect him from retaliation.

The information in the affidavit can be based on hearsay, or even double hearsay, e.g., Bill tells informant that Bill and Joe have drugs for sale. Informant tells police. Police tells magistrate. If the magistrate considers the informant reliable then the informant's statements are sufficient to establish probable cause.

Describing the Place to Be Searched

The description of the place to be searched must be sufficiently specific for a police officer with the warrant to identify the place and not confuse it with some other place. Sufficient descriptions include a street address, an apartment number, a building style and color, and a vehicle by license number.

Describing the Things to Be Seized

To prevent general, exploratory rummaging in a person's belongings, the thing to be seized must be described to distinguish it from other things. Sufficient descriptions include "controlled substances," "gambling equipment" and "fibers and hairs and other trace evidence for comparison." But descriptions such as "stolen property," "jewelry" and "any papers, things or property of any kind relating to criminal activity" are not specific enough.

Application Procedures

Any law enforcement or prosecuting officer may apply for a warrant. He must give an oath or affirmation that the statements in his request are true. Some jurisdictions allow oral statements (usually later reduced to writing), but most jurisdictions require a written affidavit. If the magistrate believes the affidavit has established probable cause, he will sign the warrant.

Most search warrants are issued in person by the magistrate, but some jurisdictions allow magistrates to issue search warrants over the phone. If the magistrate approves the request for a search warrant over the phone, he directs the police officer to sign the magistrate's name to the duplicate original warrant and the magistrate signs the other duplicate original in his possession. On return of the officer's duplicate, the magistrate signs it too and files both with the court clerk. Some jurisdictions allow this procedure only in emergency situations where time is critical.

Stale Information

The information that is the basis for probable cause cannot be stale. The police must get a warrant when the information is still fresh so that it is probable that the things to be seized are still in the place to be searched when the warrant is issued.

The nature of the criminal activity determines whether the information is stale or fresh. If ongoing criminal activity where it is reasonable to expect evidence is still present, e.g., a crime spree, growing marijuana, manufacture of drugs or bombs, then a lapse of time (ten to thirty days) between the police believing that evidence is in a particular place and their obtaining a search warrant is OK. If the criminal activity is a one-time event that occurred too long ago to expect evidence is still present, then an unreasonable lapse of time may make the information stale. A three-month delay between learning that stolen auto parts might exist in a building and requesting a warrant to search for them is not reasonable—the probable-cause information is stale.

It's OK if probable-cause information is anticipatory, i.e. that contraband is to be delivered to a specified location. A search warrant can be issued to search at a future date, as long as probable cause exists.

Timeliness of Execution

Most jurisdictions allow ten days for execution of a search warrant, although the magistrate can require the warrant be executed in a shorter time period. After the statutory time limit or the time limit imposed by the magistrate has passed, the warrant is treated as dead and any evidence seized as a result of the dead warrant can be suppressed.

Execution of Warrant

A warrant is executed by giving notice that the police have a warrant, entering the location where the things to be seized are located, serving a copy of the warrant on the person in control of the premises or leaving it there if no one is present, seizure of the items listed in the warrant, and return of the executed warrant to the issuing magistrate.

Some courts allow a search once the police are notified (usually over the police radio) that a warrant has been issued but before they physically have it. Other courts require the police to physically have the warrant before they search.

Knock-and-Announce Requirement

Most jurisdictions require officers executing a search warrant to expressly announce their presence and purpose prior to entering the premises to be searched.

"This is the police, we have a search warrant, open the door."

This obviously is meant to safeguard the privacy of citizens in their homes and to preclude violent confrontations between householders and police whose entry is unannounced and unexplained. Plain-clothes or disguised officers (dressed as a mailman or pizza deliveryman) must identify themselves as police. Officers in uniform are considered identified by their uniforms.

A police SWAT team with a search warrant yelled "Police, search warrant" as they kicked in the door while the defendant was in bed. This was found to be an inadequate notice, and the drugs they found were suppressed since no conditions justified destruction of the front door and need for immediate entry.

However, officers can be excused from the knock-and-announce requirement if by doing so they create peril to themselves or other persons or create risk that the suspect will escape or possibly destroy evidence. For example, if the suspect is known to habitually answer the door carrying a gun, the knock-and-announce requirement is excused.

Entry

Usually after knocking and announcing the officer must wait a reasonable period of time (usually considered to be thirty seconds) to allow the occupants to respond.

If, after the officer has announced his identity and purpose, the occupants refuse to admit the officer, or if while waiting the officer hears sounds in response to his knock indicating a denial of entrance, flight or destruction of evidence (flushing illegal drugs down the toilet), the officer may forcibly enter the premises. An express refusal is not required. Unreasonable delay (one minute) in responding to the officer's demand is considered a refusal.

If forced entry is justified, the officer may break open any outer or inner door or window of a house or any part of the house or anything in the house, to execute the search warrant.

Entry by Trick

Officers can use trick, ruse or subterfuge without using force, to gain entry and avoid the need to knock and announce. Usually these methods of entry are used if the officers anticipate some danger in gaining entry by knocking and announcing. Entry by an officer pretending to be a narcotics customer is legal.

No-Knock Entries

Some jurisdictions allow issuance of no-knock warrants where the object of the search is narcotics that can be easily disposed of or where weapons are known to exist inside. However, most jurisdictions require the police executing the warrant to make an independent determination, based on the circumstances existing at the time the search is about to be conducted, whether knocking and announcing can be done safely or should be dispensed with in favor of a no-knock entry.

Entry When No One Is Home

After knock and announce, officers may enter (forcibly if necessary) if it appears no one is at home. They need not try to locate owners or occupants.

Covert Entry: "Sneak and Peek" Warrants

To further the investigation of ongoing crime, a warrant can authorize entry into the premises to observe or take photographs of suspected illegal activity. It's necessary to show the magistrate the reasonable necessity of delaying notice of the search, and the appropriate persons must be notified of the search within a reasonable time after the entry.

Nighttime Searches

Most jurisdictions require search warrants be executed during daytime hours unless a special showing of a need for a nighttime search is made to the issuing magistrate and noted on the warrant. Most jurisdictions have defined nighttime as beginning between 7 to 10 P.M. and ending at 6 to 7 A.M. However, a warrant

authorizing a search at nighttime can be issued if the officer shows special circumstances that reasonably necessitate a nighttime search, i.e., his belief that
narcotics are sold only during the night at the suspected residence.

Extent and Intensity of Search

A warrant authorizing the search of premises includes the right to search auto-
mobiles owned or controlled by the owner of the premises that are found on
the premises. Also police cannot search a neighboring area, i.e., a warrant authorizing search of a garage for a stolen lawnmower did not authorize search of an
upstairs bedroom. A search that is excessive in scope is unreasonable. Officers
who discover evidence of casual marijuana use in the passenger area of a car
cannot search the trunk, and officers who entered an apartment with consent to
search for contraband acted improperly in intercepting incoming telephone calls.

If a place may be searched pursuant to a search warrant, the fact that it is
locked or inside a closed area does not prevent the police from entering to search.
A search warrant to locate a gun justifies breaking the padlock on a metal box
that could contain the gun, but search of envelopes, a notebook or medicine
vials is not justified since they are too small to contain a gun.

Length of Search

In executing a search warrant for a dwelling, the police may remain on the
premises only as long as it is reasonably necessary to conduct the search, usually
several hours. However, search of a residence for two days may be reasonable
where chemical tests are needed to analyze bloodstains found on the first day.

What Evidence May Be Seized?

Evidence of the crime described in the search warrant may be seized. Also, other
evidence can be seized if the searching officers have probable cause to believe it
is evidence of a crime or criminal activity and the officers come across it in
"plain view." For example, when searching pursuant to a warrant for a sawed-
off shotgun, officers could lawfully seize bags filled with a brown, powdery substance that, based on the officers' experience, appeared to be heroin.

Search After Objects Found

Once officers seize the objects called for in the warrant, the warrant is considered
fully executed and the authority of the police to search pursuant to the warrant
has expired. Any further searching or intrusion into the searched premises must

cease. So once officers discovered a stolen stereo, they could not continue to look in closets for other possible stolen objects not specified in the warrant.

Damage or Destruction of Property

Can officers tear apart the interior of a house or apartment in their search and then leave it that way after they are finished? Courts have held that if damage is reasonably necessary to make a search, it is within the scope of the warrant. So a warrant for drugs justified an extensive search including minimal destruction of property and leaving the house searched in substantial disarray, and a warrant for evidence of narcotics justified jackhammering a newly poured concrete slab in the yard. But police cannot use a warrant as an excuse to unreasonably destroy property, so if the search or destruction was unnecessary to find the objects called for in the warrant, the police have exceeded their search and may be liable for civil damages for the destruction caused.

Exceptions to Warrant Requirement

Obtaining a search warrant is unnecessary under certain circumstances. However, the police still must have probable cause to believe it is substantially probable they will find evidence. A warrantless search is considered unreasonable unless the prosecution can show, by a preponderance of the evidence, that it was made pursuant to an exception to the warrant requirement. Exceptions are:

Plain View

If evidence is in plain view and observed by an officer who has the right to be in the location used to observe the evidence, it can be seized without a warrant. An officer can enter a second-story apartment with the permission of the owner to look down at a suspect's enclosed backyard to see marijuana plants growing there.

An officer can also use senses other than sight to detect the items in plain view. For example, an officer may use a drug-sniffing dog to smell objects in public areas. If the dog indicates he has smelled drugs, probable cause exists for the officer to search further. An officer can use his unaided hearing from a public place to detect or learn of evidence. So an officer can use a conversation overheard while he was in a public restaurant as a basis for probable cause.

Officers can use mechanical aids, within reason, to detect what is in plain view. If an officer could observe an object by the light of day, then he can use a flashlight to detect it at night. And most courts allow the use of binoculars or sound amplifiers to view or hear into homes to see or hear better what an officer could see or hear with his unaided eye or unaided ear.

Consent

If a competent individual who owns or possesses authority over the premises to be searched or items to be inspected gives his voluntary consent to a search, then no warrant is necessary. So a person can consent to the police searching the person's car or house, but a landlord or hotel clerk cannot consent to a search of a tenant's or hotel guest's room. A roommate can consent to a search of the apartment area that he has rightful access to, such as the kitchen, bathroom, hall closet and common living areas, but not his roommate's exclusive areas or private stuff.

Parents can give consent to search areas in the family home in which all members of the family have equal access. But some courts don't allow parental consent to search their child's private stuff, like a locked metal box in the child's personal desk in his personal room. Generally a minor cannot give consent for the police to enter and search the family home. However, the minor's consent might be allowed if the search is for evidence of a crime committed against the consenting child.

Generally an employer cannot give consent to search areas that an employee has a reasonable expectation of privacy over, such as his desk.

Usually a high school principal can give consent for the police to search student lockers, since students know that school authorities maintain combinations of lockers and thus have access. But a college dean could not give consent to search a student's dormitory room, since students have a reasonable expectation of privacy in their own rooms.

How about if the police point at the suspect's neck and order him to spit out the drugs he is trying to swallow or they will blow his head off? The courts held the consent was not freely given and the evidence the suspect spit out was inadmissible.

Where an officer said: "If you have nothing to hide, you would let me search," the courts decided the consent was coerced and not voluntary and the evidence discovered was inadmissible.

Officers can only search within the boundaries of the consent, e.g., "You can search everywhere except in my briefcase." Officers must respect any limitations of the consent, and if the consent is withdrawn they must stop their search, unless they have already found something incriminating that would give them probable cause to make an arrest.

Exigent Circumstances

If circumstances exist requiring immediate action without the delay required to obtain a search warrant, the police may search without a warrant. For example, when officers saw through an open door a man placing white powder into baggies and the man saw the officers, they could enter without a search warrant because there was a strong possibility the man would destroy the evidence before the officers could return with a warrant. And the police may make a warrantless entry into a residence in response to a 911 call that originated from that residence.

Hot Pursuit: If the police are in immediate pursuit of a fleeing suspect, they can enter private property without a warrant and search for the suspect. The concern for the safety of the public who may encounter a fleeing felon and the need to prevent the escape of the suspect override the need for a warrant. However, most courts look to the seriousness of the offense committed by the fleeing suspect in deciding if the police had the right to enter a private residence without a warrant. Most courts hold that the offense must be a felony. However, some courts have held that where a police officer tried to issue a citation for a traffic violation to a person who ran from the scene into the family home, entry into the home without a warrant was justified.

Searches Incident to Arrest

Since a person arrested may be carrying a weapon that could threaten the officer's safety, or could be concealing evidence that could be destroyed, the officer can conduct a warrantless search as part of the arrest. However, the search must be limited to the person and areas within his immediate control. If the suspect is in an automobile at the time of the arrest, the officer can search the passenger compartment, including the glove compartment. If the officers have entered a residence to make the arrest, they may make a "protective sweep" of closets and other spaces immediately adjoining the place of the arrest from which another person could attack the police. They may also "sweep" the entire residence if they believe there is someone in the residence dangerous to the officers.

Warrantless Search Not Justified by Results

Courts have consistently held that the reasonableness of a search and seizure is judged at the time of the search. A warrantless search is never justified by its results. So even though the search finds evidence of multiple homicides, if the search was not legal at the time it was conducted, it is not justified merely because what was discovered is significant.

Searches of People

Students

Generally minors have the same Fourth-Amendment rights as anyone else. But while in school, if a teacher or a school official has reasonable grounds to suspect that a search of a student or the student's personal property will produce evidence that the student has violated or is violating the law or is violating the rules of the school, then the teacher or school official can make a reasonable search. They must consider the age and gender of the student and the nature of the suspected infraction. For example, after several shootings at school, the principal ordered the search of students' lockers for guns. The school security guard randomly searched lockers and found a gun and cocaine in the jacket of one student. The court held the search was proper, and the evidence was admitted in the prosecution of the student.

Persons in Custody

During the booking process, officers can require the suspect to remove from his body all his personal belongings to both safeguard the belongings and to prevent contraband or weapons from entering the jail facility. Courts have held that during this process, officers can search the suspect's wallet and read papers on his person, and push the suspect's pager button to obtain the number of the person who called the suspect.

The less intrusive the search, the less Fourth-Amendment protection there is and therefore the less is the need for a warrant. So courts have allowed the police to do the following without the need for a warrant: fingerprint and photograph the person arrested, require him to give voice, handwriting, hair and fingernail samples, and require him to stand in a lineup for identification purposes. However, probable cause and necessity must exist before a blood sample may be withdrawn without a warrant to determine if the suspect is under the influence of alcohol or drugs or to compare to blood found at a crime scene. And some courts require a warrant to obtain a sample of the arrested person's pubic hair since it is more intrusive into a private area of the body where the arrested person has a greater expectation of privacy.

Full-Body Searches

Most courts have held that when a suspect is taken into custody the police can conduct a full-body search, including a strip search, if it's possible the person is hiding a weapon or contraband on his body. The person conducting the search cannot touch the breasts, buttocks or genitalia of the person being searched. Also, cross-gender body searches of women has been considered cruel and unusual punishment.

A physical body-cavity search usually requires a search warrant and must be conducted by medical professionals under sanitary conditions. If these guidelines are violated, the suspect may sue those who violated the rules.

Some courts allow the police to use reasonable force to prevent a person from destroying evidence by swallowing it. However, most courts do not allow the police to choke or threaten the suspect. They do allow an officer to put his hand on the back of the suspect's head and force his chin to his chest, making swallowing more difficult but not cutting off air. Other courts allow officers to place a chokehold on a suspect to prevent swallowing.

Probable cause must exist for further intrusions into the body, and some intrusions may be considered cruel and unusual punishment and not allowed under any conditions. For example, in one case the police forcibly entered the suspect's room and, after observing the suspect place two capsules in his mouth, tried unsuccessfully to extract them by force. They then took the suspect to the hospital where a doctor forced an emetic solution through a tube into the suspect's stomach, resulting in vomiting and retrieval of the two capsules. The search and seizure was ruled illegal as an offensive intrusion.

The courts are split on whether to allow minor surgery on a suspect to remove a bullet that is evidence in a crime. Most courts consider a warrant not sufficient, and require a hearing and determination that the value of the evidence and probable cause that the surgery will produce the bullet justify the surgery. The surgery must be minor, and reasonable medical precautions must be observed. Where the bullet is lodged next to the suspect's spinal cord and there is risk of death, no surgery is allowed.

Prisoners

By the very nature of prison, inmates have little expectation of privacy and may be searched, including anal and genital inspections (sometimes called "strip-and-probe searches") as required for reasonable security of the prison and protection of guards and other prisoners. Such searches can be made on a routine basis even in the absence of any suspicion that contraband will be found. Searches can be required before and after the prisoner receives visitors in prison, whether physical contact visits or not, and before all court appearances. Prisoners can be required to submit to urine tests to determine if they are using drugs and sometimes blood tests to determine if they are infected with HIV.

Prisoners have little expectation of privacy of their prison cells so searches of their cells, called cell "shakedowns," unannounced and at irregular intervals, aimed at discovery of contraband, drugs or weapons, do not violate Fourth-Amendment rights.

Incoming privileged mail, also called "legal mail," which is correspondence from attorneys, courts, governmental officials and sometimes the media, may be opened or inspected only in the presence of the inmate it is addressed to, and the inspection has to be limited to locating contraband. The letter itself cannot be read or censored. Outgoing privileged mail may not be opened or inspected, unless the authorities have probable cause to believe wrongdoing is occurring, such as threats by letter to witnesses or judges.

Nonprivileged incoming or outgoing mail may be inspected only to further a substantial government interest and only to the degree necessary to accomplish the government interest.

Probationer and Parolee

A person released on probation or parole usually waives his Fourth-Amendment protections of search and seizure as a condition of release. Officers can search him without probable cause and without a warrant. However, officers cannot use this waiver to undertake searches for harassment or arbitrary reasons. Any search must be for legitimate law-enforcement purposes.

Searches of Places

Dwelling

Entering and searching a house usually always requires a warrant. As described above, the police usually must knock first, announce who they are and why they are there, wait a reasonable time and, if no one lets them in, they can then use force to enter. The police need not knock and announce if people inside would likely destroy evidence or if doing so would put police in danger of being shot or seriously hurt by the people inside. The most common exceptions to the warrant requirements are hot pursuit of a dangerous suspect who police believe is in the dwelling, and when the police have reason to believe that a crime victim is inside the house and needs assistance.

A magistrate issuing a warrant and the police executing the warrant must balance the means of entry with the potential risks and results. Consider this case. The police had inside information that a residence was a "rock house," a home being used to manufacture and sell crystallized "rock" cocaine. The residence was fortified. It had iron bars and wire mesh over the windows, multiple steel doors, multiple deadbolts, an electronically controlled locked cage at the front entrance and cameras monitoring outside activity. The police concluded it was impossible to enter by conventional methods before evidence would be destroyed so they wanted to use a motorized battering ram to break in. They obtained a search warrant and prior authorization from the magistrate to use the ram but they were still required at the time of entry to determine that there were exigent circumstances amounting to an immediate threat of injury to officers executing the warrant or reasonable grounds to suspect that evidence would be destroyed. In authorizing the use of the battering ram, the magistrate had to determine if the use was appropriate, considering the reliability of the ram as a rapid and safe means of entry, the seriousness of the underlying criminal offense and society's interest in obtaining a conviction, the strength of law-enforcement suspicions that evidence of the crime will be destroyed, the importance of the evidence sought and the possibility that the evidence could be recovered by alternate means less violative of Fourth-Amendment protection. This had to be balanced against the likelihood of injury to innocent third parties as well as occupants and police officers, and the extreme property damage that would occur to the target house and neighboring structures.

Unoccupied Premises

If officers have previously determined that the premises they are preparing to search pursuant to a warrant are unoccupied, they need not state their authority and purpose before forcibly entering.

Businesses

The courts have held there is a lesser privacy interest in business premises. However, generally a search warrant is still required. Because of First-Amendment freedom-of-expression issues, though, courts usually look closely at any searches of newspaper offices or television stations. If probable cause exists to believe that contraband or evidence of a crime exists in a newsroom or television station, even though the business and its personnel are not suspected of any crime, some courts allow searches pursuant to a warrant. However, other courts state that less intrusive methods should be used first, such as requesting the business to turn over the evidence, or a summons or subpoena.

The same guidelines apply to the search of a nonsuspect's attorney's office because of the attorney-client privilege that applies to client's files. Most courts allow a search if the warrant clearly describes the items sought and narrowly specifies the area to be searched. For example, the search of a law office for evidence of commodity trading violations was OK, but the search of a law office for financial records of a former client was held unconstitutional where the executing officers seized the entire client file. Some states require a special master appointed by the issuing magistrate be present during the search of a law office. However the police cannot search a suspect's lawyer's office. It would be a clear violation of the attorney-client privilege.

Courthouse

To prevent violence in courtrooms, magnetometers are often used to detect metal on people entering. Their briefcases and parcels may also be searched. No warrant is required. And to preserve order in their courtrooms, judges have the authority to order the search of a person in the courtroom.

Border

To protect the national interest, our borders are closed to the unauthorized entry of people and things. Therefore, routine inspections at the border are constitutional when made to prevent the illegal entry of people and goods. Customs officials may stop all entrants for routine investigation including questioning and limited searching of effects, vehicles and clothing. There is no need for probable cause or a search warrant. The questioning and search can be made at the border when entry is made by land from the neighboring countries of Mexico and Canada, at the place where a ship docks in this country after having been to a foreign port, and at any airport in the country where international flights land. Routine inspections can include requiring a person to submit to a pat down, remove a coat, roll up a sleeve, remove boots and socks, and lift an ankle-length skirt to just above the knees.

Full-Body Searches at Border

Abnormally intrusive searches must be justified by "real suspicion," which is some objective evidence that the person attempting to cross the border is concealing something illegal on his body in an attempt to transport it into the U.S. Real suspicion can be based on such things as the person's excessive nervousness or unusual conduct, evasive or contradictory answers, or unusual traveling habits such as carrying little luggage, traveling alone, returning from a short vacation or having no purchases to declare. Many of these characteristics are contained in a smuggling profile used by customs agents to identify potential smugglers. For example, in the case of a person flying into Miami from Bogota alone after an alleged vacation carrying only one small suitcase, appearing very nervous and pale, saying he was an unemployed truck driver with a wife and children, a strip search was justified.

When a pat down or other routine inspection of a person crossing a border uncovers contraband, a full search of the person, including body-cavity inspection, can be conducted without any further level of suspicion. A traveler suspected of being a swallower (a person who ingests cocaine placed in small balloons or cut-off fingers of surgical gloves) could be strip searched and detained for eighteen hours to monitor her bowel movements. The agents could have forced her to submit to a X ray, but the detention in a "dry cell" was less intrusive.

Customs agents may search mail and packages crossing the international border. Envelopes can be opened and examined without a warrant if the agents have a reasonable belief they contain contraband, e.g., drugs. However, the First Amendment prevents customs agents from reading the mail.

The Coast Guard can stop and board vessels in the territorial waters of the United States to conduct a document and safety inspection. If during the inspection they observe any obvious customs or narcotics violations, they may search further to investigate them.

Roadblocks

If police officers believe that stopping all vehicles moving in a particular direction is reasonably necessary to permit a search for the perpetrators or victims of a felony, they can order drivers of vehicles to stop and may search vehicles to the extent necessary to accomplish their purpose. For example, where three felons escaped from jail, a roadblock on the only highway leading away from the jail and the search of any spaces in vehicles where a person could hide was proper.

Airport Searches—Hijacker-Detection System

The inconvenience accompanying air travel of walking through a magnetometer that detects metal and inspection of carry-on luggage by X ray and possibly by hand is considered a valid administrative search conducted under Federal Aviation Administration guidelines. But these preboarding inspections must be confined to minimally intrusive techniques designed solely to disclose the presence of weapons. A person can avoid the search by deciding not to board the airplane. However, some courts have held that if a person fails a magnetometer test, he cannot then decide not to fly and avoid a search.

Regulatory Searches

If someone engages in a licensed or extensively regulated business or activity, they may be required to consent to warrantless periodic inspections. Such businesses include the alcohol beverage industry, auto repair and dismantling, massage parlors, pawnshops, nursing homes and fire-alarm dealers. The courts have said that one who accepts the benefits of the license must also accept the burdens. However, the searches must be for legitimate regulatory purposes conducted at reasonable times and must be reasonable in scope.

Searches of Things

Mail

Police agencies occasionally request postal authorities to make a record of information on the "cover," or outside of a person's mail. The postmark showing where the letter was mailed from and the return address are recorded before the mail is delivered. This technique is usually used on a person suspected of committing a crime to determine who his associates are, or to discover the whereabouts of a fugitive by recording information on the cover of letters received by his family or friends. For example, a "cover" was done on a person suspected of dealing in narcotics. The information taken from the cover of a letter from his bank led to the discovery of an account with a large amount of money that no tax had been paid on. The suspect was prosecuted for income-tax evasion. The "cover" technique is not considered a search since the information on letters' covers is available to postal employees. There is no reasonable expectation of privacy. Opening mail, however, would require probable cause and a search warrant.

Telephone

A "pen register" is a device attached to a telephone line at the central telephone office. It records the number called by that telephone. It is not a search or seizure since the contents of the call are not obtained and a person has no expectation of privacy of the numbers called on his phone. Other devices used for the same purpose are digital pagers and clone beepers, which enable the user to see the numbers displayed on another beeper without disclosing any conversations. These techniques are like the "cover": They allow the police to see whom the targeted person is associating with either through the mails or over the telephone.

Computers

To search the contents of a computer, probable cause and a warrant are generally required. A computer may be an instrument of crime, i.e., where a counterfeiter uses a computer and scanner to scan currency and a color printer to print the money. A computer may contain evidence of a crime, i.e., a drug dealer stores records of drug transactions, customers or money made in a computer.

If the police track, through the Internet, which Web sites you visit, do they need a warrant, or is it like a cover or pen register? This question hasn't reached the Supreme Court yet.

Vehicles

A car cannot be searched when a driver is stopped for a minor traffic violation. The officer may, in his discretion, require a driver who commits a traffic violation to exit the vehicle, but he cannot search either the person or the vehicle unless he has probable cause. However, when an officer stops a vehicle, he usually runs a radio check on the person and vehicle to see if there are any outstanding warrants on the person and if the vehicle is reported stolen or wanted in the commission of a crime. The check may be of local records, but increasingly these checks go through The National Crime Information Center, which is a national database.

If from this check or for other reasons the officer has probable cause, he may search the vehicle without obtaining a warrant. The courts have held that, because vehicles are mobile, they may be long gone before a search warrant can be obtained, and the time required to obtain a warrant could give the occupants time to dispose of contraband or evidence. Also, courts consider that people have less expectation of privacy in their vehicles than in their dwellings. This applies even for motor homes used as a dwelling. So if the police have probable cause to believe that a vehicle contains items subject to seizure, they may immediately search the vehicle and any container in it, including pockets of clothing, the glove compartment and the trunk. They may search the vehicle at the scene or remove it to the police station for a later search. For example, the police stopped a vehicle in an area of gang activity. The driver reached under the seat and the officers heard the sound of metal on metal. They had probable cause to search the vehicle. Also, observation of a knife or other weapon in plain view in the vehicle provides probable cause to search the entire vehicle. The smell of alcohol in the vehicle gives an officer probable cause to search the passenger compartment of the vehicle for containers of alcohol. But if an officer smells burnt marijuana only on the driver, he cannot automatically search the passengers. He must suspect the passengers of illegal activity to have probable cause to search them.

When an officer has made a lawful custodial arrest of the occupant of an automobile, he may search the passenger compartment of that automobile, and if a vehicle is impounded because it is improperly parked, or it cannot be secured at the scene when the driver is arrested, an inventory search may be conducted to make a list of what is being taken into custody. Any contraband or evidence of criminal activity discovered is admissible.

Obscene Material

The ordinary rules of search and seizure do not apply to the search for and seizure of obscene material. To protect the violation of First-Amendment rights to freedom of expression during the search and seizure for obscene material, a search warrant is usually always required. Obscene material cannot be seized under the plain-view doctrine or incident to an arrest. Before a magistrate can issue a warrant he must determine that there is probable cause to believe that the items to be seized are obscene. The affidavit supporting the application for the search warrant must describe with "scrupulous exactitude" the facts that make the material obscene. An affidavit describing a single drawing or only one frame of a motion picture with a general description of the obscene acts depicted is generally insufficient. Detailed descriptions of the material plus the opinions of qualified experts that the material is obscene are usually required.

Warrants for "obscene, lewd, lascivious and filthy material" are too general, as are ones for "materials depicting or describing natural or unnatural sex acts." These give too broad discretion to the officers executing the warrant. It becomes their judgment what is obscene rather than society's judgment as determined by statute and previous cases.

STORY IDEAS

A federal judge has ruled that police unconstitutionally seized copies of the Academy Award-winning movie The Tin Drum. *Police officers had seized copies of the film after a judge said it violated a state law that bans any depiction of minors having sex. The judge ruled that police illegally removed the film from public access. He reserved a decision on whether the film is child pornography and set a trial on that matter.*

Garbage

Once items are left on the public street where they are accessible to animals, children, scavengers, the homeless and garbage men, a person no longer has any reasonable expectation of privacy in the items. This includes shredded documents placed in a plastic garbage bag. No search warrant is required for the police to search and seize these items.

Business Records

A person has no reasonable expectation of privacy of records submitted to a bank, since he has voluntarily disclosed their contents to bank personnel. No search warrant is required for the police to look at these items.

Evidence of Another Crime

If during a valid and legal search evidence is discovered of another crime, e.g., during a valid search for drugs a murder weapon is discovered, that evidence is admissible in the prosecution of the crime.

Search Methods

Wiretaps

Bugging a phone and listening and recording the conversation is clearly a search and seizure under the Fourth Amendment, especially where both parties had a reasonable expectation that their conversation would be private. In some states, one party to a telephone conversation can record, or give permission to the police to record, their conversation without the other party being notified. In other states, a telephone conversation cannot be recorded without the permission of both parties, or unless a search warrant is issued. Because the intrusion into a private telephone conversation is such a violation of privacy, phone tap warrants are generally issued only in serious cases, such as murder, kidnapping, bombing and significant sale of drugs. They are usually issued for a limited period of time, like a week or two, and they are closely monitored to avoid abuse.

Electronic Tracking Devices

Sometimes called a "bug," these devices broadcast only a signal, not a conversation. They are usually placed in prepacked money given to bank robbers, packages of drugs and vehicles. They transmit a low-frequency signal that is received by a directional finder that tracks the location of the beeper. Generally the courts do not consider the use of these devices to be a search or seizure under the Fourth Amendment, and therefore no search warrant is required.

Infrared Thermal Surveillance

These sensors, when pointed at a building, measure the heat being emitted by a structure and also heat differences within the structure. They are usually used to scan the heat pattern of residences to determine if heat lamps are being used to grow marijuana. Some courts hold that a person has an expectation of privacy of the "heat signature" of his home activities, and thus a warrant is required. Other courts say this is just a measuring device of heat being emitted from the structure and no search warrant is required.

Wired Informant

You have just had what you think was a confidential conversation with a friend, and the next day you discover they were wearing a "wire," or tape recorder, and what you told them is on the front page of the newspaper or, worse yet, it is used as evidence against you. The courts have held that no warrant is required for use of a wire, saying that the Fourth Amendment provides no protection for wrongdoers' misplaced confidences.

Video Surveillance

Using video cameras to record a suspect's activities is not a search or seizure if the police are where they have a right to be, generally in a public place, when they videotape the suspect. Also, placing closed-circuit television cameras on utility poles in high-crime areas and monitoring the television screens from the police station is not a search or seizure since the cameras are just observing what the public can observe anyway.

Interception of Cordless or Cellular Telephone Conversations

The signal from a cordless telephone is transmitted over public airways. Therefore some courts have held that the public has no expectation of privacy and the police can listen to public airways without a warrant. Other courts hold that the public has a reasonable expectation of privacy in these conversations and require a warrant. Cellular phones also transmit over public airways, though the airway is not one commonly received on generally available scanners. Therefore, there is a greater expectation of privacy in cellular conversations.

Dogs

The use of dogs trained to sniff drugs or explosives or to follow a person's scent generally does not require a search warrant, since they are not intruding into any private space. If the dogs enter onto private property, however, a warrant would be required.

Aerial Searches

The police can fly over property and observe it from above without a warrant as long as they are flying in public airspace and following FAA regulations. Since the general public can fly in those same places and observe what is below, the person in the property observed has no reasonable expectation of privacy. The limit is that what the police observe must be observable by the unaided eye. They could not use high-powered cameras or spy satellites to observe what the unaided eye could not see, unless they had a warrant.

Searches by Private Parties

The constitutional protections against unreasonable searches and seizures apply only to the police and other government agents. Any evidence seized by them without observing constitutional procedures is not admissible against the person whose rights have been violated. However, evidence gathered in searches by private citizens not acting as police agents is not subject to exclusion under constitutional provisions and is admissible.

A private citizen can search for his missing property, an airline employee can search bags, a vehicle repossessor can search a repossessed vehicle and, in most jurisdictions, a merchant can stop a customer they reasonably suspect of shoplifting and search their bags and a library employee can stop a patron reasonably suspected of removing books unlawfully. Any contraband, instrumentalities of a crime or other evidence of a crime (such as weapons, drugs or stolen property) discovered during the search, can be turned over to the police and is admissible in court.

Receipt, Return and Inventory of Items Seized

Most jurisdictions require officers executing a search warrant to leave a copy of the warrant and a receipt for all of the items seized with the owner of the items or at the place searched. The officers are then to promptly file a "return" with the issuing or designated court, reciting when the search warrant was executed and giving a detailed inventory of all the items seized pursuant to the warrant.

Custody

The items seized usually are tagged and referenced with the name of the defendant, the officer who seized the items and the date and location of seizure. The items are usually retained by the police in evidence lockers or rooms until needed for trial.

The Exclusionary Rule

Evidence found in a search that violates the Fourth Amendment cannot be used against the defendant in court. It is excluded to deter law-enforcement authorities from conducting unlawful searches and seizures. Also, any other evidence found as a result of the illegally found evidence cannot be used. This evidence is called "fruit of the poisonous tree." Since the original evidence was unlawfully obtained, other evidence obtained as a result of that unlawfully obtained evidence is tainted by illegality. For example, if the police illegally seize business records containing a list of names and they search the homes of those named and find additional incriminating evidence, they cannot use the list because it was illegally seized, and they cannot use any evidence found at the homes of those named in the list, since it is the "fruit" from the illegally seized list.

But if the police would have discovered the people on that list and searched their homes from an independent, legally obtained source other than illegally seized business records, the exclusionary rule would not apply and the evidence seized in the homes would be admissible.

The exclusionary rule has been criticized because sometimes application of the rule suppresses criminal evidence that allows a clearly guilty defendant to go free. In response to this criticism, the U.S. Supreme Court has said that the "Constitution sometimes insulates the criminality of a few in order to protect the privacy of us all."

Standing

It must be the defendant's own Fourth-Amendment rights that have been violated for him to assert the exclusionary rule. The defendant cannot assert the

Fourth-Amendment rights of someone else if the evidence was seized at that other person's residence. For example, if the police illegally enter Joe's residence and find evidence that Bill murdered Jane, only Joe can raise the illegal search and attempt to suppress the evidence. Bill cannot raise the objection; he does not have "standing" since it was not his rights that were violated by the search.

Timely Motion

To have the illegally seized evidence and any fruits from it excluded, the defendant must make a timely motion to have the exclusionary rule applied to suppress the evidence. The defendant has the burden of proving that the warrant or its execution was unconstitutional. If the search was made without a warrant, the prosecution has the burden of proving that a warrantless search was justified. The standard of proof in each case is by a "preponderance of the evidence." The motion to suppress the evidence is usually heard before trial, at a special evidentiary hearing, before the magistrate who issued the warrant. Testimony is usually obtained from the police officers who conducted the search and seizure, people present or nearby when the search was made and sometimes the defendant. Inconsistencies between the notes, reports and testimony of police officers can undermine their believability and raise doubt about how the search was conducted. Testimony from independent witnesses, such as passersby or people present but not involved in any criminal activity, can often be the most believable. If the properness of the search comes down to the credibility of the police versus the defendant, most judges find police officers more believable than accused defendants, and the motion to suppress will probably be denied.

If the motion is granted, the evidence is not admissible against the defendant at trial, unless the defendant testifies and the evidence can be used on cross-examination by the prosecution to impeach the defendant's testimony. For example, if the defendant testifies he never possessed a gun, and one was illegally seized at his residence, the prosecution can use the fact of the seizure of the gun, though illegal, to impeach the defendant's credibility.

Stop, Search and Arrest

Street Encounter

A police officer can, in a noncoercive manner, approach, question and request identification of a person on the street without having reasonable suspicion of criminal activity as long as the officer does not detain the person. There is no detention if the person voluntarily cooperates and feels free to leave at any time.

Investigative Detention

If an officer has a reasonable suspicion that a person is engaged in criminal activity, he can temporarily detain the person to make an investigation into what aroused the officer's suspicions. "Reasonable suspicion" is less than the probable cause required to arrest, but more than a whim or hunch. There must be specific and articulable facts that cause the officer to suspect that some criminal activity has taken place, is taking place or is about to take place. Reasonable suspicion can be based on the time and place of the detention, what the officer sees, hears or smells, how the suspect is dressed, looks, acts and behaves, or on a tip from a reliable informer. Suspicious conduct could include walking back and forth in front of a store and peering into the window, nervous or excited behavior or furtive gestures like appearing to hide a weapon or contraband as the officer approaches, attempts to avoid or flee a uniformed officer, wearing a bulky heavy coat on a hot day and matching a drug courier profile. For example, an investigative detention was found to be reasonable when the officers encountered four men at 2 A.M. standing on a corner in a residential high-drug-traffic area.

The officer can only detain the person for as long as it is necessary to deal with the reason for the detention. A person stopped for a suspected vehicle equipment violation cannot be detained after the officer determines there was no such violation.

The officer may use reasonable force to make an investigative detention, and most courts find that reasonable force includes use of a drawn weapon, handcuffs or a roadblock. If the officer has a reasonable belief that the person stopped is carrying a weapon and may threaten the officer's safety, he can make a frisk for the weapon. If during the search the officer feels a hard object the size and shape of a weapon, he may remove it and seize it. If he doesn't feel an object that reasonably could be a weapon, he cannot search further. If the search turns up an object that is not a weapon but that is contraband, e.g., a jar full of drugs, the search is still legal and the object can be used as evidence for prosecution of a crime.

Detention Following Routine Traffic Stop

If a police officer has a reasonable suspicion based on specific facts that a vehicle code or other laws have been, are or are about to be violated, he can stop the motorist to conduct a brief investigation. He can examine the driver's license and vehicle registration and make a routine warrant check. He can order the

MUNICIPAL COURT FOR THE SALINAS
JUDICIAL DISTRICT, COUNTY OF MONTEREY

WARRANT OF ARREST UPON PROBABLE CAUSE

COUNTY OF MONTEREY   WARRANT #
STATE OF CALIFORNIA

THE PEOPLE OF THE STATE OF CALIFORNIA   FELONY [X]
TO ANY PEACE OFFICER IN THE COUNTY OF MONTEREY   MISDEMEANOR [   ]

Proof, by affidavit, having been made this date before me, by **Detective Mike**   of the
        Police Department, this court finds that there is probable cause to believe that the
offense(s) of, **187 PC** has been committed on or about **Jan, 1984** as outlined in   Police
Department report # **98-011**   by **Jackson**   , dob **11-13-54**.

Wherefore, you are commanded forthwith to arrest **Jackson**   and to bring said person
before the Municipal Court for the Salinas Judicial, County of Monterey, State of California.

Defendant may be admitted bail in the amount of $ _1,000,000 . 00_ (One million)

[   ] For good cause shown. I direct that this warrant be served at any hour of the day or night.

If the above [   ] is not checked the hours of service are limited to 7:00 A.M. to 10:00 P. M.

_____   _2/5/98_
Judge of the Municipal Court   Date
County of Monterey

_____

RETURN TO ANY PEACE OFFICER

I certify that I have executed this warrant by arresting and taking into custody the within named
Jackson   on _____ as provided by law.

_____   _____
Name and Title of Peace Officer   Signature

                                                                02000

Warrant of Arrest

APPEARANCE DATE ON ADMISSION TO
BAIL OR RELEASE ON OWN RECOGNIZANCE

[ ] Bail in the form of (cash, bond, other) _____ of $ _____ was

deposited with me by (name and address) _____

_____ .

[ ] Released on own recognizance with the Promise to Appear.

I am directing _____ to appear in Department number _____,

Municipal Court for the SALINAS JUDICIAL DISTRICT on _____, 19___ at
_____ A.M./P.M.

_____
Signature, Date

_____

That based on the aforesaid information, your affiant believes that there exists probable cause to arrest Jackson   , **dob 11-13-54** for the crime(s) of **187 PC**.

Wherefore, your affiant prays that a warrant of arrest be issued for the arrest and seizure of the person of Jackson   , **dob 11-13-54**.

_____, DETECTIVE   2-5-98
Signature and Title of Affiant   Date

Sworn to, before me under penalty of perjury and subscribed in my presence on FEBRUARY 5, 1998, at 1536 A.M./P.M. in Salinas, California, County of Monterey.

_____
Judge of the Municipal Court

2

02000.1

Warrant of Arrest (continued)

COUNTY OF MONTEREY, STATE OF CALIFORNIA

AFFIDAVIT IN SUPPORT OF ARREST WARRANT

Your Affiant, Mike   personally appearing and being duly sworn, deposes and says:

I am a regularly employed Police Detective with the   Police Department.

On 1-27-98, Officer Bud   and Corporal John   of the   Police Department received a call to go to 248   Drive for a report of a possible body under the kitchen area of a house. The owners of this house are Diana and Eric   . Approximately two weeks ago Eric and his father-in-law Robert   crawled under the house to install vents for the bedrooms. While under the house they noticed what they thought were a pair of tennis shoes sticking up out of the dirt under the kitchen area. Initially they thought this was a prank and did not give it any more thought. They never went near the shoes.

On 1-24-98 Diana received a letter from the   Police Department that said there was a missing person report generated at the residence in 1984. The   Police Department letter said the case was still open and they wanted to know if that person had returned. Diana then remembered that Eric had told her about the shoes in the dirt.

On 1-27-97, Diana was talking to a friend and challenged the friend to go under the house to check on the shoes. The friend, Noemy   , put on some overalls and went under the house and up to the shoes. She tugged on the shoes and they did not move. Noemy crawled out from the house and Diana called the police.

The access to get under the house can only be made through the kitchen pantry. There is no outside entry to get under the house. There is an approx. 2' x 2' opening on the floor. Corporal   crawled under the house and checked on the shoes and believed there was a good chance that this was a buried body. He notified Detectives   and   and a crime scene was established and the kitchen floor was cut open. Crime scene technicians and two anthropologists from University of Santa Cruz responded to process the scene.

There were skeletal remains buried in a shallow grave. The skeleton appeared intact and appeared to be a male approx. 5'8" long. This fits the description of the missing person from 1984. This person was then 16 years old. In 1984 the mother reported to Officer Rick   of the   Police Department that she had not seen her son for 3 months. She said he left without his clothes, or any other personal belongings. She could not give any reason for him leaving. She said Christopher was last seen wearing a rock-type shirt, levis pants and white tennis shoes. Dale said her son was wearing an earring in his left ear.

3

02000ü

Warrant of Arrest (continued)

On 1-27-98, Detectives   and   contacted Christopher's girlfriend at the time, Carlota   Carlota said she clearly remembers Christopher and said she was very surprised when he just disappeared. She said she asked Christopher's mom what had happened to Christopher and she told Carlota that Christopher packed up all his clothes and left and she does not know where he went.

While processing the crime scene, Detective   found two spent and deformed bullets in the chest area of the skeleton. The skull of the skeleton was broken along the front and there was a hole on both the right and left side of the head. Investigators also found an earring near the skull.

On 1-27-98, I went to the autopsy of the skeleton male. Dr. John   of the Montery County Sheriff's Department conducted this and he found the following; there was a bullet hole in the skull which entered from right and exited through the left. There was also two bullet holes going through the right shoulder blade and entering from the back. The male was wearing pants, which were mostly gone, but there was a Levi tag attached to the threads. The pockets were intact and inside one of them was a set of keys. A dental record check on the skeleton confirmed that the remains belong to Christopher

On 1-28-98, I went under the house and between the opening under the house and the grave I found a short handled hoe. This hoe was dirty and appeared to have been there for years. It could have been used to dig the grave. I photographed and collected the hoe.

On 1-28-98, Detectives   and   contacted Christopher's stepfather, Jackson   at his work at 216   St. in Salinas. Jackson was married to Dale at the time of Christopher's disappearance. Jackson voluntarily came with Detectives   and   to the   Police Department. He told them that he did live there when his stepson disappeared and stayed there for four to five years after. He said that after Christopher disappeared his mother packed up all his belongings and boxed them in their garage. Jackson said that they have since moved to 3245   Circle in the City of   and they still have all of Christopher's belongings still in the boxes. Jackson said that he owns three weapons and all are at his current house in   He described the guns as a Remmington .22cal., a Browning (not specific as to what type of weapon) and a Colt Python. A Colt Python is capable of shooting a .38cal. and a .357cal. bullet. This is similar to the type of bullets found in the rib cage of the body. Jackson said he has owned the python since 1978 and that he keeps it locked up. He said that he was the only one with a key to the gun.

Detective's   and   asked Jackson if he had anything to do with the body under the house and he said he did not.

On 1-28-98,   Detectives obtained a search warrant and served it at Jackson's residence in   We found a Colt Python in one of the bedrooms that Jackson said was his. The gun was in a briefcase and was locked with a trigger lock. We also found several bullets in a box in the closet of the same room. These items were collected.

4

020007

Warrant of Arrest (continued)

During the search warrant Detective _____ found a Monterey County Probation report dated August 14, 1983 written by probation officer Yvonne _____ Christopher had been arrested for stealing some of his mom's checks and cashing them. In the report Christopher told Yvonne that he is not able to get along with his stepfather "who does not talk to him and does not like him" Chris went on to say that he stays out late at night in an attempt to avoid being at home.

P.O. _____ then wrote in her evaluation that "it does appear that this entire situation revolves around a very poor relationship between this minor and his stepfather to the degree that the minor avoids having contact with the stepfather".

On 1-29-98, Detective _____ took the Colt Python to IBIS, Integrated Ballistic Identification System, which is a branch of Alcohol, Tobacco, and Firearms. Lab. Tech. Chris _____ examined the spent bullets found in the grave and determined that they were fired from one of three types of weapons. One of the weapons capable of firing the rounds was a Colt Python. _____ said that it would be difficult to match ballistics back to Jackson's gun. Coleman did say that the spent bullets might be able to be matched, but we should contact Department of Justice for further results. We are in the process of taking the bullets to DOJ.

On 1-30-98, Detective _____ and I flew to _____, Ohio to talk to Christopher's sister, Scherie _____. She has since changed her name to Maia _____. She was 12 years old at the time of Chris's disappearance. She told us that she does remember this time frame. Maia said that Jackson did not like either her or her brother. She said she thought it was because they were not his natural children. She said that she saw and heard Jackson and Chris get into constant arguments, but never hit each other. Maia said she remembers that Jackson was happy after Chris was gone.

Maia said she clearly remembers a very bad smell in the house around the time Chris disappeared. She thinks the smell started sometime in February of 1984. She thinks it lasted for several weeks. Maia said the smell was so bad that she and her mom checked the house every few days. She said they even cut a hole in the bottom of the couch, thinking Chris's gartner snake may have crawled into it and died. Maia said she associated the smell with rotting fish.

I asked Maia about the hoe and she said that she does remember that they had a short handled hoe. She said they used to keep it in the garage and she used it occasionally to garden. She does not know what happened to it, or when it disappeared. Maia said that the day after Chris disappeared, they received a telegram saying something to the effect of 'I will contact you when I get into the NFL'. Maia said that her mom showed her the telegram and asked her what she thought about it. Maia said she felt certain at the time that Chris did not send this telegram. She said that Chris never would have done that. She said she felt at the time that Jackson sent the telegram.

Maia said that Christopher did not have any enemies that she knew of. She said the only person in the house capable of dragging Chris's body under the house was Jackson.

5

020003

Warrant of Arrest (continued)

occupants out of the vehicle for the officer's safety. He may seize any weapons or contraband in plain view in the vehicle.

If the officer has a reasonable belief that the driver or passengers are dangerous and may have access to a weapon, he can make a limited protective search of the passenger compartment and glove compartment. He can conduct a patdown search of the driver and passengers if he reasonably believes the person searched is armed and dangerous. If the driver or passenger throws an object out of the car, it is considered abandoned property and can be recovered by the officer without a warrant, and is admissible as evidence.

Occupants of Search Premises

Police officers can detain the occupants of the search premises while the search is conducted. They need no additional warrant and no reasonable suspicion or probable cause that the occupants have committed any crime. When the magistrate issues the search warrant, he has determined the police have probable cause to believe that someone in the home has or is committing a crime. The connection between the home and the occupants at the time of the search gives the officer the right to detain them. But the police cannot search the occupants who are detained unless they are specifically identified in the search warrant. For example, the police had a warrant to search a bar for stolen property. While executing the warrant, the police searched all the customers present. The court found the search of the customers was illegal because the police had no reason to suspect the customers were involved with the stolen property or were armed or possessed any contraband.

Arrest

An arrest occurs when the police take a suspect into custody, either by the suspect submitting himself to the officer's custody or by the use of reasonable physical force or restraints by the police. An arrest occurs not necessarily when the police announce that the suspect is under arrest, but rather when the suspect reasonably believes he will be restrained and formally arrested if he tries to leave. Some courts hold that an arrest occurs once the police have probable cause to arrest a suspect, whether or not the police inform the suspect he is under arrest at that moment. "Probable cause" is when enough facts exist to lead a reasonable person to conclude that a crime is being committed or has been committed. Said another way, it is reasonably apparent that it is more likely than not that the suspect committed the crime. If the suspect is arrested pursuant to an arrest warrant, the issuing magistrate has already found probable cause. The police can arrest without a warrant if the crime is committed in their presence or they have probable cause to believe the person committed a felony.

Determining the moment of arrest is important is because it triggers the requirement for Miranda warnings before any further questioning can occur.

Use of Force

An officer who has probable cause to make an arrest can use reasonable force to make the arrest. He cannot use deadly force unless the suspect has committed a violent felony and is attempting to escape or poses a significant threat of death or serious physical injury to the officer or others. An officer can legally request the assistance of all people necessary to aid in the arrest, including ordinary citizens and passersby.

The person being arrested has a duty to not resist arrest. However, some courts hold that if the officer uses excessive force, the person can use reasonable force to defend his life and limb.

Extradition

Most suspects are arrested in the same community or at least the same state where the crime occurred. However, if the suspect has fled across the state line, he must be arrested in the jurisdiction where he is located (called the asylum state or country) and returned (extradited) to the state and county where the crime occurred (called the demanding state).

The procedure starts when a judge issues an arrest warrant. A limit can be placed on where an arrest warrant is served since the county bears the expense of bringing the person back from the asylum state or country. The crime has to merit the expense. So for minor offenses, the warrant will only be served if the person is in the state. For more serious offenses, the warrant may be served in adjoining states. For the most serious offenses, the warrant may be served nationwide or even internationally. When the person is taken into custody on the warrant, the local state court allows the person a hearing, but the hearing is only to establish whether or not this is the person named in the warrant. It is strictly an identification hearing, usually based on fingerprints and mug shots. The issue of guilt or innocence is not addressed.

If the accused fled to another country his extradition depends on the country and the crime. Some countries have no extradition agreement with the United

From police academy through street training, police are taught the following guidelines in increasing force when confronting an armed suspect.

1. *Presence:* An officer in uniform is often enough to convince a suspect to surrender quietly.
2. *Voice:* Ranging from quietly telling a suspect he's under arrest to yelling at him to put down his weapon.
3. *Hands-on:* An officer sometimes needs to make physical contact with a suspect before the suspect understands he is under arrest, whether that contact is simply pressure on the arm or a hold.
4. *Chemical or electrical deterrents:* Pepper spray or a stun gun will temporarily incapacitate a resisting suspect.
5. *Impact:* Police batons or similar devices will also temporarily incapacitate a suspect, though the risk of permanent injury is greater.
6. *Deadly force:* If a suspect is coming toward an officer with a weapon, the officer can defend himself with deadly force, but the officer must be able to justify the amount of force used.

States, so these countries will not cooperate officially in returning a person accused of committing crimes in the United States. Other countries have signed international extradition treaties with the United States. However, many will not return someone accused of crimes that are not considered crimes in the asylum country, and many countries that do not have the death penalty will not return an accused to the United States if the crime carries the possibility of the death penalty. Sometimes the United States avoids this problem by agreeing not to seek the death penalty if the asylum country will return the accused.

Extradition treaties usually say that a country does not have to extradite its own citizens who committed crimes in another country. Informally though, if the crime is serious enough, the country's state departments will cooperate in returning people to the jurisdiction of the crime.

If extradition is approved, law-enforcement officers from the state where the crime occurred travel to the asylum location where the defendant is held and escort him back for trial. Most people waive extradition.

Booking

After arrest the suspect is usually booked, which is the identification, fingerprinting and photographing of the suspect and recording of the arrest in police records. Personal belongings are taken for safe keeping and a receipt is given. If

---

STORY IDEAS

An acclaimed fertility specialist who fled to Mexico amid allegations that he stole patients' eggs won't be extradited on federal fraud charges. Since none of the crimes with which he's charged in the U.S. are crimes in Mexico and therefore do not fit within the framework of the extradition treaty, he is not extraditable.

---

an arrested person fails to cooperate or refuses to identify himself, he may be charged with resisting an officer. Also, it is a crime to provide false identification to an officer or to impersonate someone else.

The arrested person has the right to make a completed phone call (some jurisdictions allow up to three local calls free of charge). The police cannot listen in on calls to the person's attorney. An arrested person who is denied the right to make phone calls can bring a civil rights action against the officers who denied him access to a telephone.

We often see police officers from one city or town driving in another city or town, and we wonder: Can that policeman arrest me if he sees me committing a crime here, or does he have arrest power only in his town? Clearly a peace officer can arrest within the town that employs him. And generally he can make an arrest any place in his state if he is arresting for a crime committed or reasonably believed to have been committed in the jurisdiction that employs him. If the officer is in another jurisdiction within his state, he usually has to have the prior consent of the local police department to make an arrest in their jurisdiction. However, he can arrest if a crime is committed or he reasonably believes a crime has been committed in his presence and there is an immediate danger to persons or property or a threat the suspect will escape. This includes traffic violations. Also, an officer can arrest a person he believes is charged with or has been convicted of a felony in another state, and an officer who is in hot pursuit of a person who has committed a felony in his state can enter an adjoining state during the pursuit to make the arrest.

Who Can't Be Arrested?

Generally any person can be arrested. However, federal law grants immunity from arrest to foreign diplomats, ambassadors and ministers and members of their official household, including family members, attachés, secretaries and servants, while they are within the United States. Also, some states have limitations on arresting a person for prior crimes while in or passing through the state pursuant to a subpoena to attend and testify in the state or another state. And some states have immunities from arrest for nonfelonies for voters going to, while at, or returning from a polling place on election day.

Bench Warrant

If a defendant has previously appeared in court and then failed to return as ordered, the judge will usually issue a warrant from the bench to arrest the person and bring him before the judge for failing to appear.

Searches Following Arrest

Police can search the defendant after his arrest, and the search can include fingerprinting, placing the defendant's hands under an ultraviolet lamp, examining his arms for burns, swabbing his hands with a chemical substance, taking scrapings from under his fingernails, taking a small sample of hair from his head, obtaining a urine sample, giving a breathalyzer examination, swabbing his penis and taking pubic hair combings. Searches of the surface of the body are distinguished from intrusions into the body. If time allows, a warrant may be necessary for searches into areas where the defendant has a greater expectation of privacy.

The search of vaginal or anal cavities must be made by skilled medical technicians to ensure sanitary conditions and to avoid nonmedical people from conducting the search. Routine strip searches must be justified. They are not allowed for minor offenses. For example, a woman was arrested for speeding and because she could not post $50 bail, she was detained in the county jail. She was strip-searched for weapons and contraband pursuant to routine procedure before being placed in jail. The court found the search improper because she was not in a category of offenders who might possess weapons or contraband.

Remedies of Defendant

Besides a motion to suppress evidence obtained during an illegal arrest, a person improperly held after an arrest may seek release by petitioning the court for a writ of habeas corpus, which is an order to the police to bring the person into court and determine if he is being held improperly. A person illegally arrested (no probable cause or use of excessive force) may have a civil action for false imprisonment, monetary damages and violation of civil rights against the arresting officials. The mere fact that the person is found not guilty is not sufficient grounds for a civil action against the arresting officials. The officials must have acted illegally. The arresting officers may also be subject to criminal liability for an illegal arrest or use of excessive force.

Arrests by Private Citizens

A private person may make an arrest when a felony, misdemeanor or infraction has been attempted or committed in his presence. If a felony has been committed, whether or not in a private person's presence, he may arrest the person he reasonably believes has committed the felony. A citizen's arrest must be made at the time of the offense, in fresh pursuit of the offender or within a reasonable time (thirty minutes) after the offense was committed. The citizen making the arrest must take the arrested person to the police without unnecessary delay. Citizens who make illegal arrests or use excessive force are subject to civil liability.

Citation Procedure

A person who is arrested on an infraction, such as a vehicle code violation or a misdemeanor, may be issued a citation on his written promise to appear at a later date. This avoids the need of taking the person into custody and booking him.

Protective Hold

Some states have laws allowing a person to be taken into custody if as a result of mental disorder or inebriation, the person is a danger to himself or others or is gravely disabled. The person is usually taken to a medical facility for evaluation and can be held, usually for seventy-two hours, for the purpose of the evaluation.

Confessions

A confession is a complete and express acknowledgment of guilt of the offense charged.

"All right, I confess, I stole the money."

Short of a confession is an admission, which is a statement of specific facts that when considered with other evidence in the case may permit the drawing of an inference of guilt.

"All right, I was there."

Neither can be used as evidence if involuntarily made or coerced. For example, a black suspect who was beaten by white deputies and subjected to a mock lynching to obtain a murder confession did not give the statement voluntarily. And other types of less-obvious physical abuse may make the confession or admission inadmissible. Examples are: A defendant placed in a cell with a plank as a bed, awakened early in the morning and subjected to intense questioning, and denied food or medication until he confessed; police holding a gun to a wounded defendant's head to force him to confess; police stripped the defendant and left him naked for an hour before giving him shoes, socks and a blanket to cover himself; and police questioned a defendant for four hours while he was sedated and incapacitated in an intensive-care unit.

Threats can make a confession involuntary. Examples are: The police threatening to take the suspect's wife into custody if he didn't cooperate; the police told the suspect that unless he admitted that he had beaten his wife the officers would write the word *liar* on their report to the judge; the police told the suspect that unless she cooperated she would lose her welfare benefits and custody of her children; the police called a sixteen-year-old defendant a liar, threatened her with the death penalty and indicated that if she would change her story, she might be charged only as an accessory after the fact.

Psychological coercion can make a confession involuntary. Examples are: The police placing an informant in the defendant's cell, and the informant told the defendant that other inmates would attack him, but if he confessed to the informant, he would protect him; the police had a state-employed psychiatrist get the suspect to confess to killing his parents by using the guise of providing medical treatment, a sympathetic bedside manner, and appealing to the youth's feelings of guilt and fear.

Promises of leniency can make a confession involuntary. Examples are: The police promising the defendant that if he confessed, he would be released; the police promised the defendant that his confession would not be used against him; and the police told the defendant that the only way to avoid the maximum penalty was to confess.

The length of questioning can make a confession involuntary and inadmissible, i.e., the police questioned an ill and physically deprived suspect for six hours.

Trickery or deception does not make a confession inadmissible as long as the means used are not calculated to produce an untrue statement. Examples are: The police told a murder suspect that the victim was still alive, even though he was really dead; the police told the suspect they had found highly incriminating evidence that made his denials futile; that the suspect's fingerprints were found at the crime scene; that the suspect had been identified by the victim.

Being under the influence of drugs administered by the police makes the confession inadmissible, e.g., the police injected the suspect with a hallucinogenic drug that acts like a truth serum and the suspect confessed. However, being under the influence of self-administered drugs does not prevent a confession from being voluntary and admissible.

Miranda Warnings

A voluntary statement during casual conversation by a person who is not in custody is admissible. The Miranda rights need not be given during a routine traffic stop or during general on-the-scene questioning by police during an investigative detention. A suspect must be given the Miranda warnings, however, before the police conduct a custodial interrogation.

Custody occurs when the police deprive a person of his freedom of action in any significant way or if the person is reasonably led to believe he is deprived of his freedom in any way. The test is, would a reasonable, innocent person in the same circumstances conclude that he is not free to leave. If so, then custody has occurred.

Interrogation is questioning by the police reasonably likely to elicit an incriminating response from the suspect. Routine questions and booking are not interrogation and no Miranda rights need be given.

In the landmark case of *Miranda v. Arizona* in 1966, the U.S. Supreme Court ruled that an incriminating statement obtained during a custodial interrogation (one in which the defendant is not free to leave anytime) is not admissible in court unless, before police question the defendant, the defendant is advised of certain fundamental rights, which are:

The right to remain silent;

Anything said can and will be used against him in court;

The right to an attorney during questioning;

If he cannot afford an attorney, one will be provided without cost.

After advising of these rights, typically the police will ask the defendant if he understands the rights, and they may have him sign a statement that he has read or had read to him his rights, that he understands them and that he chooses to waive them.

After being told of his Miranda rights, a suspect can waive the rights if done voluntarily, knowingly and intelligently. In determining if a suspect properly waived his rights the courts consider the suspect's age, education, physical condition, any language barriers and sophistication with the criminal-justice system.

If a custodial interrogation of a suspect takes place without Miranda warnings and the knowing and voluntary waiver of the rights, the suspect's confession and admissions must be suppressed, evidence obtained through the use of information obtained in the confession or admission must be suppressed and the fruits of the questioning cannot be used to supply probable cause for a subsequent arrest or search.

CHAPTER FIVE

Outline of a Criminal Trial

"Now that she walks rapidly," the witness said excitedly, "I know that it was this woman. There's a peculiar way she has when she walks; that hurrying walk, that was just the way she walked when we saw her."

Mason smiled and said to Hamilton Burger, "That, Mr. District Attorney, concludes my cross-examination. Do you have any redirect examination?"

Hamilton Burger slowly got to his feet. "If the Court please," he said wearily, "I suggest that this matter should be adjourned until tomorrow morning at ten o'clock. There are some things which I feel should be investigated."

"I think so, too," Judge Kent said dryly. "The case is adjourned until tomorrow morning at ten o'clock, and in the meantime this defendant is released on her own recognizance."

—Erle Stanley Gardner, *The Case of the Deadly Toy*

With the instincts of a panther, the mind of a chess master and cross-examination skills that could penetrate a witness's toughest veneer, Perry Mason not only gained acquittal for his clients, but he usually solved the crime in the process, much to the chagrin of the district attorney.

In real life, criminal defense attorneys spend most of their time plea bargaining to reduce the number or severity of the charges against their clients, and to minimize the sentence. Ninety percent of all criminal cases are disposed of by plea bargaining, and of the 10 percent that go to trial, 80 percent result in convictions. Naturally the exceptions may make the most exciting grist for the writer's mill, but those are usually won, not on the witness stand, but only after completion of an extensive trial with the presentation of complex evidence, testimony of expert witnesses and extended jury deliberations.

To gain and retain credibility with your readers, thorough familiarity with the courtroom and courtroom procedures is crucial to an accurate portrayal of a criminal trial.

TIP: Call your local court and ask for the calendar clerk for criminal cases. Find out when the next case of the type you are interested in (murder, robbery, drunk driving) is scheduled for trial. Plan to attend, pencil and paper in hand. Take notes about the interactions of the attorneys and judge. Sketch the courtroom layout. During a recess, talk to the bailiff. To interview other court personnel you may have to send a letter to the court administrator. Some judges are flattered by requests for interviews and will arrange time to talk with you. Others may not. Just keep asking and eventually you will obtain the information you seek. Plan to interview one or more people who were on the jury after they are discharged by the trial judge. You can learn their impressions of the prosecutor and defense attorneys, the defendant and what swayed their thinking and led to their decision.

People vs. Ramon Valdez

Probably the easiest way to understand how a criminal case progresses through the court system is to follow a typical case. The following names and facts are fictional. They are used to demonstrate the law and procedures used in a criminal case.

On Friday night, June 21, three gunshots broke the silence in front of Joe Joe Torres's family home. Joe Joe's parents ran from the house to the garage where their nineteen-year-old son had been working on his car. His mother screamed in horror as she saw Joe Joe lying in the driveway, a stream of blood draining from his chest. Joe Joe was dead. His father called 911 and joined his wife in grief.

Over the next four days the police investigating the murder determined that Joe Joe was a member of a youth gang and had been secretly dating the sister of the leader of Los Diablos, an opposing gang. In the gang culture it was taboo for gang members or their families to have any friendly interaction with opposing gang members. An informant in Joe Joe's gang told police that Joe Joe knew that if his girlfriend's brother found out they were dating, he risked being shot.

The police obtained a search warrant and went to the house of Ramon Valdez, the leader of Los Diablos and brother of Maria Valdez, the girl Joe Joe had been dating. No one was home, so the police broke down the front door, entered the residence and discovered a .22 caliber gun hidden in a shoe in the closet. This was the same caliber as the murder weapon. Ballistic tests on the gun and murder bullet, which had been removed from Joe Joe's heart during an autopsy, proved this was the murder weapon. The police reviewed their case with the district attorney's office, which took the evidence before the county grand jury the next day. The grand jury found there was "probable cause" to believe that Ramon had committed the murder, they returned an indictment against Ramon for first-degree murder and a warrant was issued for his arrest. That night the police, with the warrant in hand, arrested Ramon Valdez, age twenty-four, on suspicion of the murder of Joe Joe Torres.

Here Comes the Attorney

Within an hour of his arrest, Ramon's family contacted Sheldon Rosen, a local well-respected criminal-defense attorney. Sheldon took immediate steps to protect Ramon's constitutional rights. He went to the jail and had a private meeting with him. Sheldon impressed on Ramon how important it was that Ramon not speak about anything to do with the charges against him, with the police or any other inmate in jail. When Ramon started to tell Sheldon his story, Sheldon stopped him and said:

"Don't tell me what you did, I don't want to hear that right now, tell me what they say you did."

Sheldon wanted to get a basic picture of what Ramon was charged with. From this information Sheldon and his investigator would start their work.

Bail

Each court has a judge, magistrate or bail officer on duty twenty-four-hours a day. The amount of bail (usually written out on a bail schedule) is based on the charges and the likelihood the defendant will flee the jurisdiction. An experienced criminal attorney can usually get his client released within hours of arrest. Sheldon's efforts to have Ramon released on bail were unsuccessful. Because of the seriousness of the crime charged and because Ramon was considered a threat to commit further violence and to possibly flee the court's jurisdiction to avoid prosecution, the arrest warrant was issued stating "no bail."

COUNTY FELONY BAIL SCHEDULE

FELONIES NOT LISTED BELOW ARE SET AT $5,000

PENAL CODE		STANDARD BAIL
187	MURDER	$500,000
207	KIDNAPPING	25,000
209a&b	KIDNAPPING FOR RANSOM	50,000
211	ROBBERY	10,000
215	CARJACKING	25,000
220	ASSAULT WITH INTENT	7,500
245a(1)	ADW	7,500
245a(2)	ADW	10,000
261	FORCIBLE RAPE	15,000
262	SPOUSAL RAPE	15,000
264.1	RAPE IN CONCERT/FORCE/VIOLENCE	20,000
266j	PROVIDING/TRANSPORTING CHILD UNDER 16 FOR PURPOSE OF LEWD OR LASCIVIOUS ACT	25,000
269	AGGRAVATED SEXUAL ASSAULT OF A CHILD (OPERATIVE 11/30/94 - 15 YRS TO LIFE SENTENCE)	100,000
273ab	ASSAULT ON CHILD W/FORCE LIKELY TO PRODUCE GBI RESULTING IN DEATH (OPERATIVE 11/30/94 - 15 YRS TO LIFE SENTENCE)	100,000
273.5	CORPORAL INJURY ON SPOUSE WITH PRIOR OFFENSES	7,500 20,000
286(c)	SODOMY VICTIM UNDER 14 OR FORCE	15,000
286(d)	SODOMY IN CONCERT BY FORCE	15,000
288(a)	LEWD ACT/CHILD UNDER 14	15,000
288(b)	LEWD ACT/CHILD UNDER 14/FORCE	25,000
288a(c)	ORAL COPULATION (14) OR FORCE	15,000
288a(d)	FORCIBLE ORAL COPULATION IN CONCERT	15,000

Count Felony Bail Schedule

PENAL CODE		STANDARD BAIL
288.5	CONTINUOUS SEXUAL ABUSE OF CHILD	25,000
289	RAPE BY FOREIGN OBJECT	15,000
422	THREAT TO COMMIT CRIME RESULTING IN DEATH OR GBI	7,500
451A	ARSON WITH GBI	25,000
451B	ARSON OF HOUSE	20,000
459	BURGLARY, FIRST DEGREE (RESIDENTIAL BURGLARY)	7,500
653f(b)	SOLICITING MURDER	50,000
664/187	ATTEMPTED MURDER	250,000
666/???	ATTEMPTED (ANY CRIME EXCEPT MURDER) HAS SAME BAIL AS UNDERLYING OFFENSE	*
1551	FUGITIVE FROM JUSTICE (SAME BAIL AS OUT-OF-STATE WARRANT)	*
4530	ESCAPE FROM PRISON	25,000
4532	ESCAPE FROM JAIL	25,000
	HEALTH AND SAFETY CODE	
11351	POSSESSION FOR SALE, OVER ½ OZ.	7,500
11352	SALE TRANSPORTATION, OVER ½ OZ.	15,000
11352	SALE TRANSPORTATION, UNDER ½ OZ.	7,500
11353	USE OF MINOR FOR DRUG TRANSACTIONS	7,500
11360	SALE OF MARIJUANA, OVER ½ LB.	7,500
11378.5	POSS FOR SALE PCP	7,500
11379	SALE/MFG/DIST CONTROLLED SUB	7,500
11379.5	SALE/MFG/DIST PCP	10,000
11383	POSSESSION FOR MANUFACTURING	10,000

*****IF A FIREARM IS USED - ADD $5,000 TO THE STANDARD BAIL*****
***** ALL OTHER FELONIES ARE $5,000 *****

(9/10/96)   2

Count Felony Bail Schedule (continued)

Postarrest Appearance

A defendant must usually be brought before the court within forty-eight hours of arrest. This short time period is to prevent unwarranted police interrogation, to ensure the defendant is informed of his rights, and to allow him to apply for bail. This appearance is usually combined with the arraignment.

Arraignment

The arraignment is the procedure where the accused is informed of the charges against him, advised of his rights and the consequences of a plea, and is asked to plead. Most courts hold the criminal arraignments first on the court calendar, usually at 8:30 A.M.

If he was not bailed out, the defendant has probably been held in the city or county jail since arrest, as Ramon was. He will be brought, along with others, by bus or van, to the courthouse an hour before court convenes. He will wait in a holding cell, probably in the courthouse basement. He will probably be dressed in an orange or red jumpsuit, and shackled hand and foot and to another prisoner.

At the scheduled time, he will be brought from the holding cell, probably up an elevator, down a back hall that passes the jury rooms and judge's chambers, through a door next to the judge's bench and into the courtroom to the jury box. If he does not have an attorney (either private or a public defender), when his case is called he will stand before the judge, who will inform him of the charges and his rights, as follows:

1. You have the right to an attorney. If you cannot afford one, one will be appointed.
2. You have the right to confront and cross-examine witnesses against you.
3. You have the right to a jury trial.
4. You have the right to not incriminate yourself.
5. You have the right to a speedy trial.
6. If you plead guilty (if this is a capital case), you could be sentenced to death or life in prison without possibility of parole. Do you understand these rights?

If he cannot afford an attorney (based on a financial statement he will have to complete), and about 70 percent of all defendants can't, a public defender, who probably is already in court on other cases, will be assigned to his case. They will talk before the defendant enters a plea. Many defendants and their families consider public defenders to be not very good attorneys or, since they are part of the government system, the defendants don't trust them.

If the public defender's office is too busy to represent a defendant or has a conflict in the case (already representing another defendant in the same criminal event), the court may appoint a private attorney from a list of qualified practitioners. In most cases appointed attorneys receive a set fee from the county for representing a defendant, regardless of how much time the attorney spends on the case and whether or not the trial is in front of a judge or a jury. So, as with the public defender's office, the quality of representation often is determined by economic factors. However, in a capital case, more money is available since the defendant faces the possibility of a sentence of death, and the U.S. Supreme Court will probably review the case prior to execution to determine if the defendant had adequate representation.

If a defendant or his family has money to hire a private attorney, they usually obtain the name of an attorney from a friend or acquaintance, as occurred in Ramon's case. If they have no source for a referral, they may look in the yellow pages and be drawn to an ad by an attorney specializing in criminal defense.

If the defendant was out on bail, he will arrive at court dressed in a coat and tie (if he has taken his attorney's advice), and when his case is called, he will stand with his attorney and enter a plea. Almost without exception, the plea is:

"Not guilty."

Alternate pleas are:

"Not guilty by reason of insanity," which is an admission of guilt, or

"Not guilty" and "not guilty by reason of insanity," which will cause a two-stage trial, considering the issues of guilt and sanity separately.

After entering the plea, the judge will set the case for a preliminary hearing and set a cutoff date for any motions. Arraignments usually move fast and can often be confusing or overwhelming to the defendant and to those unfamiliar with the criminal court system. One arraignment judge commented:

"I have, on a typical morning calendar, between twenty and thirty-five defendants to be arraigned within a sixty-minute period. I am thinking about two things: Advise them of their constitutional rights so they can plead, and get it done efficiently so I can get on with the rest of the court calendar. If I take too much time on arraignments, I am behind the rest of the day. I expect the district attorney, public defender and especially private attorneys to be prepared. I don't tolerate delays or inefficiency. We have to keep things moving."

Ramon was brought into court on Wednesday morning for arraignment. Sheldon was given the police report and the indictment returned against Ramon.

Sheldon would use this information to structure his investigation. Sheldon had previously represented a member of Ramon's gang and had his charges reduced and sentence set at eighteen months in state prison. Ramon knew Sheldon was an aggressive attorney, and his family came up with the initial retainer fee of $25,000 by giving Sheldon a lien on their home.

On the advice of his attorney, Ramon entered a plea of "not guilty." The judge scheduled a preliminary hearing for one week later, any pretrial motions for four weeks later, a pretrial conference for six weeks later and trial for seven weeks later. Sheldon could extend these dates later by waiving the mandatory time periods required for a speedy trial. He made arrangements to meet with Ramon in jail later that day to review in detail the police report and other evidence. He then arranged to visit the murder scene with his investigator, talk to some of his acquaintances in the Latino community familiar with gang activity, and look at the alleged murder weapon in police custody.

Some criminal defense attorneys use the "old wine defense," which says that the case gets better for the defense with age. Because witnesses forget, move or die and evidence gets lost or deteriorates, it's not uncommon for the defense to take the approach that the longer they can put the case off the better. Other attorneys take the opposite approach. They don't waive time and are always ready for trial on the scheduled trial date. Knowing that the prosecution is expecting the defense to seek delay, oftentimes they catch the prosecution by surprise and the prosecution has to scramble to be ready for trial, sometimes being poorly prepared and hurting their case.

Grand Jury Indictment vs. Criminal Complaint

In state courts prosecutors usually use grand juries in felony cases involving complicated issues, organized criminals or to protect the identity of a victim or a witness. All federal felonies must be brought by grand jury indictment unless the defendant waives this right.

Preliminary Hearing

If evidence is not presented to a grand jury to establish "probable cause" to indict the defendant, then the prosecution files a criminal complaint against the accused and a preliminary hearing is held in open court, usually within ten days of arrest. At the preliminary hearing, the prosecution presents its witnesses and evidence to determine if probable cause exists to prosecute the defendant for the crime. The defendant's attorney can cross-examine the witnesses, challenge the sufficiency of the evidence and present exculpatory evidence (evidence that indicates the defendant did not commit the crime charged). Judges at preliminary hearings invariably find that probable cause exists and hold the defendant over for trial. For this reason, many defense attorneys waive the preliminary hearing.

Gathering Evidence

Usually most of the prosecution's investigation has been completed before charges are brought against a defendant, as occurred in Ramon's case. The police and district attorney investigators take statements from witnesses, gather physical evidence in support of their case and have forensic scientists run tests on blood, clothing, vehicles and weapons. As the evidence comes together, they determine the most likely suspect and develop a theory for what occurred and why the suspect committed the crime, the all-important "motive."

"I have to resist jumping to the logical conclusion too fast," says Mary Gerard, who has prosecuted over twenty murder cases. "I want a complete investigation of all the evidence before we put it together and develop theories, motives or suspects. I know if I am not thorough I probably will come up against a highly paid defense attorney and his investigators and they will shoot holes in my investigation and case. I don't like to lose, so I want everyone on my team to gather and evaluate every shred of evidence before we proceed with prosecution."

The defendant's investigation will not start until he is charged and hires an attorney. A criminal defense attorney has a practical and legal obligation to promptly and adequately investigate the facts of his client's case. By delay, physical evidence can be lost, destroyed or deteriorated and witnesses can forget details, leave the area or otherwise become unavailable to provide information.

If a defendant doesn't have the money, the court will provide funds for payment of investigators and experts as a matter of the defendant's constitutional right to present an effective defense, particularly in a murder case.

Experts

Solving crimes, or freeing defendants, often comes down to the findings of forensic scientists. Experts in medicine, pathology, ballistics or psychology may provide valuable assistance to both the prosecution and the defense. But like everything in life, experts differ in their evaluations and opinions. The prosecution and defense will each have the best-educated, most experienced and most credible expert witness they can afford. The prosecution usually uses the state or federal criminal labs to assist in the preparation of their cases. Defense attorneys hire experts from private forensic labs. Check under "forensic" in the yellow pages to locate a resource for an interview.

Sheldon visited the crime scene with Mark Fisher, a private investigator fluent in Spanish who had helped Sheldon on many cases. Mark made a detailed diagram of the crime scene and photographed and videotaped it from all angles. While Sheldon left to meet his ballistics expert to look at the weapon in police custody and then meet with his client, Mark remained, knocking on doors to inquire what local residents saw or heard the night of the murder. Sheldon had already arranged for his medical expert to inspect and photograph the deceased's body at the coroner's office.

Pretrial Discovery

The days of surprise are supposed to be gone in criminal cases. After the prosecution and defense complete their initial investigations, they are each entitled to "discover" what evidence the other side has. In discovery, each side is generally required to provide the other with:

1. Names and addresses of persons to be called as witnesses at trial, along with any written or recorded statements made by those persons.

2. A list of all relevant real evidence, including fingerprints, bullets, weapons, clothing, photographs of the crime scene, and samples and specimens taken from the body or clothing of the victim.

3. All statements in the prosecution's possession made by the defendant, whether written, recorded or oral.

4. Reports of experts including results of physical or mental examinations, scientific tests or comparisons, which the parties intend to introduce at trial.

5. The above has to include all evidence in the prosecution's possession favorable to the accused, so-called "exculpatory evidence."

The sharing of evidence and evaluation of the strengths and weaknesses of one's own case and the opposition's case are intended to force each side to look objectively at their evidence and increase the chances of avoiding a trial and resolving the case by plea bargaining.

Through pretrial discovery, Sheldon learned that the police had a witness to the shooting, an elderly woman who was driving home when she heard gunshots and saw a car the same make, model and color as Ramon's speed away from in front of Joe Joe's house.

Sheldon had to reveal to the prosecution that he had a witness who would testify that Ramon was with her the entire evening of the murder, and that his ballistics expert would testify that the gun found by the police was not the murder weapon.

Theory of the Case

Before plea bargaining, each side must put the evidence together in a logical, believable manner (something a jury would accept) most favorable to their client. The prosecution, representing the people, wants to show that this defendant is a bad, dangerous, antisocial person who not only committed the crime charged, but who should be punished for it. The defense, representing the accused, wants to poke holes in the prosecution's case to prevent the judge or jury from finding, beyond a reasonable doubt, that the defendant is guilty.

The prosecution needs a motive for the crime (e.g., revenge, heat of passion, monetary gain), and the defense needs a defense (e.g., misidentification, self-defense, frame-up, accident). In Ramon's case the prosecution's theory was revenge. Sheldon's theory of the case was mistaken identity and frame-up.

Mental Competence and Mental Defenses

If the evidence against the defendant is overwhelming, his only chance may be to raise a mental defense. If the defendant is unable to understand the nature of the proceeding or to aid in his defense, he may be incompetent to stand trial. The criminal proceedings will be adjourned and the court must make orders geared toward returning the defendant to competency through treatment, usually in a state hospital. If the defendant regains competency he is returned to court and criminal proceedings are resumed where they left off.

The defendant has a number of mental defenses that he can raise during the trial, including:

1. Failure to form intent: If a person reasonably believes he has properly rented a car and therefore drives it away, he has not formed the necessary intent to steal the car even though he is charged with auto theft.

2. Unconsciousness: If a person is a somnambulist (sleepwalker) and one night, while sleepwalking, he takes his roommate's diamond ring, the defense of unconsciousness would apply since the taking did not occur as a result of a conscious act.

3. Voluntary intoxication: If a person voluntarily consumed a large amount of alcohol and while intoxicated received stolen property, his defense could be that he was so intoxicated that he did not realize the watch was stolen, so he did not form the intent to receive stolen property.

4. Involuntary intoxication: While at a party a person drinks what he thought was fruit punch. In fact, it contained LSD. While hallucinating, he punched someone else. Because of the involuntary intoxication he did not form the conscious intent to hit someone, so he has a defense.

5. Idiocy: A person who is an idiot is not of sound mind and cannot form the necessary intent to commit a crime.

If the defendant enters pleas of not guilty and not guilty by reason of insanity, his trial is bifurcated (divided into two phases). First the question of his guilt or innocence is tried (the guilt phase of the trial), and if he is found guilty, then the sanity stage is tried. Unlike the guilt phase, where the burden of proving the defendant's guilt beyond a reasonable doubt is on the prosecution, in the sanity phase of the trial the burden of proving insanity is on the defendant. The amount of proof required is not proof beyond a reasonable doubt; it is the lower standard of proof by a preponderance of the evidence. The jury must be unanimous in its verdict on the sanity issue. If the defendant is found insane and has not recovered at the time of the trial, he is usually committed to a hospital for treatment, or he could be treated as an outpatient, if appropriate.

Though Sheldon discussed with Ramon a possible defense of reduced mental capacity to form intent based on "heat of passion" when Ramon learned that Joe Joe was dating his sister, Ramon refused to allow it, not wanting to appear weak to the members of his gang. Ramon insisted he was innocent, that the witness was mistaken and that the gun was planted in his closet.

Defendant Acting as His Own Attorney
In a criminal prosecution, a defendant can act as his own attorney if the court determines that he understands the nature of charges against him and is able to act in his own defense. Ramon was smart enough to know that he stood no chance of being found "not guilty" if he represented himself.

Pretrial Motions to Suppress Evidence
Ramon could not be found guilty if there was not sufficient evidence against him. The first way to limit the evidence is to show that it was obtained illegally.

At the "suppression hearing," the circumstances surrounding the issuance and execution of the warrant and the search are presented to the judge. If he believes the warrant was invalid or the search was unconstitutional, he will grant the defense attorney's request to "exclude" the evidence. If the evidence excluded was crucial to the prosecution's case, the prosecutor may have no choice but to drop the charges against the defendant.

Sheldon filed a motion to suppress the .22 caliber pistol found in Ramon's house during the search by the police. He based it on the police breaking into the house when no one was home. He argued that there was no chance that any evidence would be lost or destroyed since there was no one in the house, and the police should have waited until Ramon or a member of his family returned before the police entered. This argument was creative, but the prosecution argued that if this principle were applied, then Ramon and his family could just stay away from the residence indefinitely and the police could never enter to make their search. The judge decided the prosecution's argument made the most sense and was consistent with the law, and ruled that the police did not have to wait until someone was in the residence before they could enter.

Sheldon's second argument was that the gun was not in "plain view" when the police entered and that the warrant did not allow the officers to open closet doors, therefore the gun should not have been seized. The judge held that the warrant specifically allowed a search for a gun and anyplace where the weapon might be hidden, and that included a closed closet and containers in the closet that might hold a gun, including inside a shoe. The gun would come into evidence.

Change of Venue

The term "venue" means the proper location for trial of a case. It is usually the county where the crime occurred, but in the interests of justice it can be elsewhere. Proper venue is balanced against the defendant's right to an impartial jury and a fair trial. Often pretrial publicity and media coverage in the community where the crime occurred cause so many potential jurors to form opinions about the guilt of the defendant that it is not "reasonably likely" that the defendant will obtain a fair and impartial trial. The solution often is to move the trial to a community that has not heard about the crime or that is much less affected by the crime. Sometimes the case is even moved to another state.

Ramon's case was not covered widely in the media. There was little concern that a jury of twelve impartial people could be obtained, so his trial was held in the local courthouse, about five miles from where the killing had occurred.

Let's Make a Deal—Plea Bargaining

Once each side evaluates the evidence and develops a theory of the case, they are ready to negotiate to see what's the best deal they can obtain. Just like card players slapping each card onto the table to see who has the better hand, the attorneys show what evidence they have and what weaknesses the other side has in their case. If the prosecution thinks they have a sure winner they are going to insist on a plea of guilty as charged (plead the sheet). If the defense believes they have a good chance at acquittal they will argue that the charges should be dropped, or they may plead to a lesser offense.

Some prosecutors "overcharge" a defendant; that is, they file more charges or stiffer charges than they expect to be able to prove. This gives them more bargaining room in the plea-bargaining process, so they can agree to reduce the charges (to what probably should have originally been charged and could be proved) in exchange for the defendant's plea of guilty. Experienced defense attorneys know this strategy and bargain accordingly.

Simply stated, a plea bargain is an agreement negotiated by the prosecutor and defendant, and approved by the court, in which the defendant agrees to enter a plea of guilty to certain charges on the condition that other charges be dropped and an agreed-to sentence be received.

Ramon was out of luck here. In many states, tighter rules do not allow plea bargaining in serious felony cases or in felony cases where the accused used a firearm. He either pleads guilty as charged and takes his chances on what the judge's sentence will be or he goes to trial. Ramon was going to trial.

Pretrial Conference

Prior to trial, the court and parties want to narrow the issues in contention and make one more effort at disposing of the case by a plea bargain. This is done at the pretrial conference, which is usually held a week prior to the scheduled trial. If a plea bargain is not reached, then sometimes the defendant will waive a jury and accept a court trial, and in return for this time-saving option the prosecution will dismiss the most serious charge and go to trial on a lesser charge.

Right to Speedy Trial

To protect a defendant from prolonged pretrial incarceration and possible loss of evidence or witnesses, a defendant has a right to go to trial without unreasonable delay (Sixth and Fourteenth Amendments). In most states defendants have a statutory right to be brought to trial within forty-five days for a misdemeanor or sixty days for a felony. This right can be waived by the defendant, and often is. Sheldon decided to waive time, but because the court was current on its cases, the trial proceeded on the scheduled date.

Preparing Witnesses for Trial

Only the naïve believe that attorneys don't prepare their witnesses for trial, and only incompetent attorneys don't prepare their witnesses. What ethical attorneys don't do is expect their witnesses to lie or even bend the truth. Attorneys usually are careful, however, that they ask questions that elicit answers that are helpful to their case.

Preparation of witnesses usually occurs at the attorney's office and includes explaining courtroom procedure, asking the witness some of the exact questions the attorney intends to ask in court and asking some of the same questions the attorney expects the opposing attorney to ask.

In preparing his client, the attorney-client privilege prevents the opposing attorney from asking the client what the attorney told him during the preparation. However, when an attorney prepares a nonclient to testify, he has to be careful what he says, because the opposing attorney can question the witness about what was discussed. Preparing a witness to tell the truth is acceptable. Tampering with a witness to slant or change his testimony is illegal.

Most defense attorneys have their private investigator conduct the initial interview and questioning of witnesses, but if the witness's testimony is crucial, the attorney will meet with them personally.

Because she was a crucial witness, Sheldon wanted to talk personally with the elderly lady who said she heard shots and saw the car speed away. However, because the crime was gang related, the woman was afraid of possible reprisals by gang members, so the district attorney had relocated the lady until after the trial. Sheldon reminded the district attorney that a state law prevented Sheldon from revealing the whereabouts of a witness to his client, and also the district attorney respected Sheldon and knew he would not do anything to jeopardize the lady's safety. Therefore the district attorney gave Sheldon the address of the lady so he could interview her.

During the interview, Sheldon learned that the woman was required to wear glasses for driving and she did have them on that night. He also determined that she had last had her eye prescription checked three months before, so her prescription was probably correct. She wasn't sure of the year of the car, but she was certain of the make, model and color. Sheldon decided her testimony would be quite believable to the jury.

Since the alibi witness in Ramon's case was so crucial to Ramon's defense, Sheldon spent over eight hours preparing her to testify. He discussed thoroughly her past, and even had his investigator verify what she told him. She had been a long-time friend of Ramon and his family, but she had no romantic interest in Ramon and didn't seem to have any reason to fabricate her story. He asked her the same questions over and over, sometimes with exactly the same words, other times varying the words. He pretended to be the prosecution, cross-examining her, sometimes standing right in her face and yelling at her, to see if she would crack. He accused her of lying to protect Ramon, of being forced to testify, of being promised money to testify, of having her family threatened if she did not testify, of wanting attention as a motive to testify and of being in love with Ramon and therefore willing to do anything for him, including perjuring herself and risking prison. She withstood his questioning well, and he believed she could handle any questions and tactics the prosecution would throw at her.

Witnesses' Obligation to Testify

If a witness is subpoenaed to testify, he usually must answer all valid questions. The exceptions are if he has a legally recognized privilege. Privileges include the attorney-client privilege, where the attorney cannot be forced to testify about what his client told him, the psychotherapist-patient privilege, where a psychiatrist cannot be forced to testify what his patient told him, and the husband-wife privilege, where spouses cannot be forced to testify against each other.

A witness can assert his Fifth Amendment right to not testify because his testimony may tend to incriminate himself. If the prosecution wants this witness's testimony, he can grant the witness immunity from prosecution, in which case the witness has to testify, since even if his testimony incriminates him he cannot be charged, so he has nothing to lose. A witness who is obligated to testify but refuses is guilty of contempt of court and can be placed in jail until he agrees to testify or until the trial is over, whichever occurs first.

The prosecution wanted Ramon's sister to testify that she was dating Joe Joe. She flat-out refused, out of loyalty to her family. The prosecution decided they would subpoena her to appear at trial and if she refused to answer the questions, the jury would probably assume she was dating Joe Joe, thus establishing the motive for the murder.

There Goes the Judge

Judges are assigned, usually by the presiding judge (PJ), to hear certain types of cases. Some presiding judges assign judges who are easy sentencers to the criminal calendar, so defense attorneys will have criminal cases tried by the court and not a jury, thus saving court time.

Defense counsel may want to disqualify a judge who has a reputation for harshness against defendants in the type of case at hand. Usually each attorney has one peremptory challenge, the right to disqualify a judge without giving a reason. Judges can also be challenged "for cause," which means the attorney has to state sufficient facts to justify disqualification of a judge.

Ramon's case was assigned to Judge Olsen. He was a former district attorney, but had mellowed over the years, and Sheldon felt he would be fair with his client. The prosecution accepted Olsen without objection.

Trial

After all the legal maneuverings, attempts to suppress evidence, thorough investigation, exchange of information and preparation of witnesses, the day of trial arrived. Sheldon arranged for Ramon to have a haircut and clean shave and shower, and Sheldon had his assistant drop off at the county jail a new black suit, white shirt and conservative tie for Ramon to wear to court.

On the morning of trial the prosecutor and Sheldon arrived at the courtroom, exchanged a few pleasantries (they had tried many cases against each other) and walked back to the judge's chambers. Friendliness between opposing attorneys is often misunderstood by the parties and the public. These are supposed to be adversaries, fighting to the death (sometimes literally, but the death of the defendant), yet here they are walking together into the judge's chambers, and then they come out talking, sometimes laughing like old friends. Instant skepticism and distrust are created, especially in the minds of those with the most at stake, the defendant and the victim (or the victim's family). The reality is that attorneys can fight tooth and nail with each other in court, yet go out afterwards, have a drink and be friends. Most trial attorneys are very competitive, but their competing doesn't mean they hate each other.

In chambers, prior to trial, after a little socializing and exchange of war stories, the attorneys and judge discuss the current case in general terms and discuss any trial motions, e.g., if one side wants to exclude anticipated evidence before opposing counsel presents it to a jury in open court. One side might request sanctions against the other side for failing to comply with discovery. Normally these motions should have been made prior to the day of the trial, but they can still be made here or, if denied in the past, can be renewed here.

Once these matters were resolved, Sheldon and the prosecutor and the judge discussed how long the trial would take (four days), reviewed each side's witness list and discussed the order in which witnesses would be called. Then the attorneys returned to the courtroom, the bailiff called for order, and the judge walked in and sat at the bench.

Some defendants will waive their right to trial by jury and instead have the judge try the case, called a "bench" or "court" trial. This is done if the defense feels the judge will be more sympathetic to the defendant than a jury would be. Some courts, to give a defendant the incentive to choose a time-saving court trial, will impose a lighter sentence when a judge finds the defendant guilty as opposed to after a jury finds the defendant guilty. Sheldon felt that Ramon's best chance was with a jury, hoping that at least one juror would not be convinced by the prosecution's case.

Jury Selection

Ramon has the right to trial by an impartial jury drawn from a representative cross section of the community. In felony cases, in most states and in federal court, the jury must be twelve persons and the verdict must be unanimous.

At the commencement of jury selection, the judge introduces himself and the attorneys, gives some general information about the case and jury selection procedures, and then asks general questions. The judge and attorneys usually have a list of the names and town of residence of each person on the jury panel. Most attorneys use a chart (see example page 149) to record information obtained as the jurors answer questions.

Ideal Juror

Many attorneys believe that a case is won or lost during jury selection, and most attorneys have an "ideal juror" in mind during the selection process. Opinions vary on what type of juror is more favorable to the prosecution or defense. Generally, peace officers and their families tend to assume the defendant is guilty. Military officers, white-collar workers and professionals tend to favor the prosecution. The socially, economically or educationally disadvantaged tend to sympathize with the defendant, as do lower-income people, disadvantaged racial minorities, older people, people who are married and people in the helping professions. Some defense attorneys like jurors who are teachers or parents with

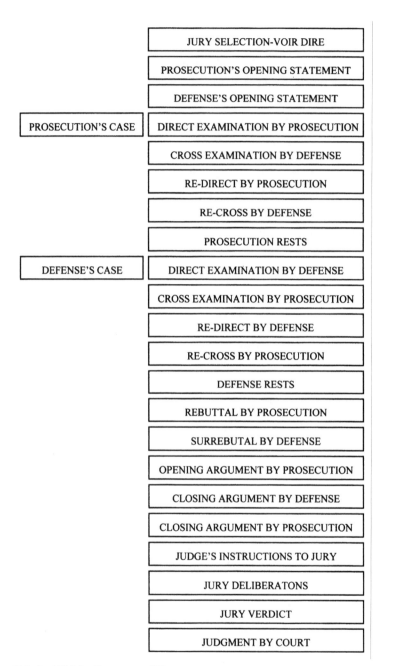

PROSECUTION'S CASE	JURY SELECTION-VOIR DIRE
	PROSECUTION'S OPENING STATEMENT
	DEFENSE'S OPENING STATEMENT
	DIRECT EXAMINATION BY PROSECUTION
	CROSS EXAMINATION BY DEFENSE
	RE-DIRECT BY PROSECUTION
	RE-CROSS BY DEFENSE
	PROSECUTION RESTS
DEFENSE'S CASE	DIRECT EXAMINATION BY DEFENSE
	CROSS EXAMINATION BY PROSECUTION
	RE-DIRECT BY DEFENSE
	RE-CROSS BY PROSECUTION
	DEFENSE RESTS
	REBUTTAL BY PROSECUTION
	SURREBUTAL BY DEFENSE
	OPENING ARGUMENT BY PROSECUTION
	CLOSING ARGUMENT BY DEFENSE
	CLOSING ARGUMENT BY PROSECUTION
	JUDGE'S INSTRUCTIONS TO JURY
	JURY DELIBERATONS
	JURY VERDICT
	JUDGMENT BY COURT

Criminal Trial—Sequence of Events

JUROR NUMBER	JUROR NAME	GENDER	AGE	MARITAL STATUS	CHILDREN	OCCUPATION	SPOUSE'S OCCUPATION	PAST JURY SERVICE?	VERDICT?	HUNG JURY?	IMPRESSION

Jury Selection Chart

grown children because they are used to hearing two sides to kids' stories before deciding who is right or wrong. Male jurors tend to be more tolerant of female defendants. Housewives are considered to be good jurors by either side, because they take their task seriously and conscientiously. Generally, jurors tend to sympathize with a defendant with whom they identify. Jurors with some legal knowledge, such as law students, may place undue emphasis on technicalities. A juror with some expertise in a particular field may try to dominate the jury deliberations if knowledge or expert testimony in that field is provided. Jurors who have served before may no longer find the proceedings novel or interesting and may pay less attention.

Sheldon decided that the ideal juror in Ramon's case would be a Hispanic-American female single parent with no more than a high-school education. He wanted someone who understood Ramon's culture, would relate to Ramon's alibi witness (his Hispanic-American girlfriend), would not be influenced by a husband at home, and had a history of caretaking. The prosecution's ideal witness was a Caucasian professional male, married, with a teenage son in college.

Attorneys watch for jurors who are anxious to be either chosen or excused. A juror who does not want to be on the jury may not listen carefully or take his job seriously, and can be antagonistic to the others during the deliberations and may push for a quick and simplistic verdict. A juror who is overly eager to be selected and gives all the "right" answers by saying how they can be objective, fair, impartial, open-minded and any other glowing quality they think the attorneys want to hear, may have a score to settle and want to take it out on the defendant or the prosecution.

Most attorneys have at least a basic ability to read a juror's body language. Folded arms indicate lack of openness, as does crossing of legs. Tapping of foot indicates impatience or boredom. Often body language speaks louder than oral answers, and sometimes the two are inconsistent. Usually the body language is trusted over the spoken answers. Courses on reading body language are taken by some attorneys.

Assistance in Jury Selection

If the defendant can afford it, specialists in jury selection will be hired. These people, usually with training and background in psychology and possibly law, study jurors' reactions and answers to determine how closely they come to the ideal juror. They may do a background investigation of the jurors, including economic, social, political and personal information, to further complete the juror profile.

Sheldon relied on his many years of experience in selecting the jury. He was skeptical how much help the so-called experts were in jury selection. The prosecution had a senior prosecutor sit in during jury selection to give additional reactions and input on which jurors would be best for their case.

Voir Dire

Voir dire, Latin for "to say the truth," is the procedure for determining which jurors are suitable to hear the case. Depending on the jurisdiction, the judge may conduct all the examination of prospective jurors (including questions submitted by the prosecution and defense), or the attorneys may conduct some or most of the jury questioning.

Depending on the nature of the case, jurors may be questioned while together as a group or in sequestration (out of the presence of each other) so questions won't embarrass the prospective juror in front of the others, and answers won't taint the other jurors.

The purpose of voir-dire questioning is to eliminate biased persons from the jury. Individuals who know the attorneys, the parties, the victim or the witnesses are routinely disqualified as being potentially biased.

In some cases, jurors may be asked to complete a questionnaire to provide the attorneys with some basic information prior to questioning.

An example of Sheldon's voir-dire questioning follows:

Q. Mrs. Johnson, have you heard anything about this case, either from family, friends or through the media?

A. Yes, sir.

Q. What have you heard?

A. I read a short newspaper article about the murder and the apprehension of the defendant.

Q. Have you formed any opinions about the guilt or innocence of the defendant?

A. No.

Q. Do you believe in our system of justice that says an accused is innocent until proven guilty?

A. Absolutely.

Q. Do you feel you can approach this case with an open mind and not form any opinions or conclusions until hearing all the evidence?

A. Yes, sir.

Q. Have you or any family member or close friend ever been the victim of criminal activity?

A. Yes, sir.

Q. What type of criminal activity was that?

A. Someone stole my husband's car at work.

Q. Was that person brought to justice?

A. Yes, he was.

Q. Mrs. Johnson, have you ever served on a jury before?

A. No, sir.

Q. Thank you, Mrs. Johnson. No further questions of this witness, your honor.

Challenges for Cause

Attorneys have an unlimited number of challenges of jurors "for cause." Cause means that, through the juror's answers to the judge's or attorneys' questions, the juror has shown that he cannot be impartial. Sometimes the reason for challenging the juror for cause is obvious, e.g., if they answer: "If the police arrested him, he must have done something wrong." When an attorney excuses this juror for cause there is no need to explain to the other attorney or judge why. However, if the reason is subtle, the attorneys may have a "sidebar" (approach the judge's bench and speak softly to him so the jurors do not hear) to explain the reason the juror should be excused.

An unsuccessful challenge for cause may antagonize a juror. A successful one may offend sympathetic fellow jurors. In small communities, jurors may be friends and want to serve together. Excusing one may cause hostility by the other who remains on the jury.

Peremptory Challenges

Attorneys have a limited number of peremptory challenges (no reason need be given for excusing a juror). Depending on the seriousness of the crime, the number can range from five in a simple misdemeanor case to twenty, as in Ramon's case, because the crime was punishable with death or life imprisonment. Attorneys cannot, however, use their peremptory challenges to systematically exclude jurors due to their racial, religious, ethnic, social, economic or political group. If one attorney believes the other is using his peremptory challenges to excuse jurors for improper reasons, he can ask for a hearing by the judge, out of the presence of the jury, and require the other attorney to explain the basis for his excusing particular jurors. If he doesn't have a good, nondiscriminatory reason, the judge will admonish him (warn him about his improper actions) and not excuse the juror.

When Sheldon used a challenge for cause or a peremptory challenge, he was very polite.

"Your honor, the defense thanks and excuses Mrs. Brownell."

Death-Qualification Process

Where the sentence includes the possibility of death, the jury must be qualified to sentence the defendant to death. If a juror has opposition to the death penalty that would prevent or substantially hinder him from sentencing the defendant to death, she can be excluded for cause. Potential jurors who would automatically vote for or against the death penalty must be excluded, since they would not be basing their decision on the facts presented. Here is an example voir dire on death qualification:

Q. Mr. Spencer, you understand that if the defendant is found guilty of the crime charged, the jury must decide whether he should live or die?

A. Yes, sir.

Q. The law requires that jurors approach this task with open minds and be guided by what they hear and see in court. Now with that in mind, I want to ask you if, in general, you have any personal or moral or religious views either in favor of or against the death penalty?

A. No, sir.

Q. Will you be able to follow the Court's instructions on the law that governs the issue of penalty and give your own fair and impartial consideration to all the facts and circumstances about the case involving the defendant?

A. Yes, sir, I believe so.

Q. Thank you, Mr. Spencer. No further questions, your honor.

Preparing the Jurors for the Case

Attorneys use voir dire to prepare the jury for their view of the case. An example is the following question asked by Sheldon:

"Mrs. Sampson, if the evidence indicates that a police officer planted evidence, specifically, a gun in the defendant's closet, would you believe what he said anyway?"

Sheldon was telling this juror that there is an issue of police misconduct in this case. So she was prepared to hear that evidence. It creates some expectation and drama in the proceedings.

Swearing In the Jury

Once twelve jurors and sufficient alternates (three in Ramon's case) were selected, they were sworn by the clerk to do their duty. They were then admonished by the judge not to converse with each other or anyone else on any subject connected with the trial, not to read or listen to the media and not to visit or view the place where the crime took place.

Opening Statements

My high-school speech teacher said to tell the audience what you are going to tell them, tell them and then tell them what you told them. The opening statement is telling them what you are going to tell them, in the form of evidence and witnesses' testimony. Although the jury already has general information about the case from the voir-dire questions, the opening statements formally introduce the jury to each side's theory of the case and the evidence that will be presented in support of those theories. Usually before the attorneys commence, the judge instructs the jury that opening statements are not evidence but only what each side expects the evidence to show.

In a criminal case the prosecution gives their opening statement first because they have the burden of proving that the defendant committed the crime. The defendant's attorney's opening statement follows the prosecution, although technically the defense can wait until the prosecution has presented its case before giving an opening statement. In practice this is seldom done because the defense wants the jury to hear that there is another side to the case before absorbing all the prosecution's evidence and possibly making up their minds before hearing the defense's version.

Opening statements are not to include argument, and if one side starts to argue the effect, meaning or proper interpretation of evidence, the other side can object and the judge will sustain the objection. Either attorney can request that witnesses be excluded so that the opening statements do not influence them.

In his opening statement, the prosecution said he would prove that Ramon had a motive for the murder, that a witness saw him at the murder scene when shots were fired, and that the murder weapon was discovered in Ramon's closet.

Sheldon, in his opening statement, said that Ramon was with someone the entire evening of the murder and that the alleged murder weapon had been planted in Ramon's closet, either by the police or someone else. Sheldon emphasized that, under our American legal system, the defendant is innocent until proven guilty and that the prosecution has the burden of proof beyond a reasonable doubt. He asked the jury to keep open minds until they heard all the evidence.

Direct Examination

After completion of opening statements, the prosecution calls its first witness and continues with the presentation of its case until it "rests." The prosecution usually wants to present evidence in a logical, often chronological order, to make it as easy as possible for the jury to follow and keep the evidence organized. Also, the prosecution wants to keep the jury's attention and interest. Jurors are usually more attentive first thing in the morning. Their attention wanes as the morning progresses. After lunch, their minds are usually dull while their bodies are digesting their meal. Late in the day they are usually tired and thinking about going home. Friday afternoon is the hardest time to keep jurors' attention and interest. Attorneys try to present dramatic or important evidence while the jurors are the most alert, and present mundane evidence (like technical lab results or the introduction of records from custodians) when jurors are less attentive.

In questioning a witness, the attorney usually wants to elicit the following information in the following order: Who the witness is (name, background, qualifications [if an expert witness]); how the witness is involved in the case (witness to the crime, heard threats from the defendant, found evidence); and what the witness saw, heard or did.

During direct examination attorneys usually must ask only direct questions. Examples of direct questions are:

Who did you talk to?

What did you see?

When did this happen?

Where did you go?

That's the old reporter's questioning guideline: Who? What? When? Where? (But not why? That's too open a question and it would allow a witness to go on for hours about why they did something.)

These are open-ended questions, allowing the witness to formulate the answer.

In contrast, leading questions, which are generally not allowed when questioning one's own witness, suggest the answer. Examples of leading questions are:

You saw the car in front of the house, didn't you?

Didn't you hear three shots?

Isn't it the truth that you heard him say, "I'll kill that son of a bitch"?

You saw his face, didn't you?

Then you called the police, correct?

With leading questions, the attorney, through his questions, is testifying, and just getting the witness to agree with him. Even if the witness disagrees, the attorney's questions sound like statements of fact, and may be mistakenly remembered as facts by some jurors.

If an attorney calls a witness who is "hostile" to his client's position, the attorney can ask the judge to allow him to treat the witness as a hostile witness and allow the attorney to ask leading questions.

The most basic rule in questioning a witness is: Never ask a question that you don't already know how the witness is going to answer. You ask every possible question during investigation or discovery, then at trial you pick and choose the questions to ask based on the witness's previous answers to those questions.

That way you control what the jury hears and avoid surprises.

Either attorney can request that witnesses be excluded from the courtroom during testimony to prevent them from hearing testimony and becoming educated about the case. Also, some witnesses may feel hesitant to testify if certain witnesses are present in the courtroom watching (glaring) and listening to their testimony. However, the victim generally has the right to be present. If the victim is deceased, then members of his family generally have the right to be present.

If the attorney wants the jury to listen to and accept what the witness is saying, the attorney will let the witness be the center of attention. Usually the attorney will stand at the far end of the jury box, essentially behind the jury when they are looking at the witness. The attorney is out of the jury's line of view and they will be undistracted as the witness testifies. If the witness is hostile, or to make a point, the attorney might move up into the jury's view to make himself the center of attention.

The prosecution's first witness was the county coroner, who testified about the autopsy and the cause of death being a .22 caliber bullet to Joe Joe's heart. The police officer that discovered the weapon in Ramon's shoe testified next. The prosecution then called their ballistics expert who testified that, based on his tests, there was a 99 percent chance that the bullet taken from Joe Joe's heart had been fired by the .22 caliber pistol found in Ramon's closet. The prosecution then had the elderly lady testify about hearing shots and seeing the car drive away. She even went further than expected and said that Ramon was the driver of the car.

Cross-Examination

After the prosecutor completes the direct examination of a witness, the defendant's attorney conducts his cross-examination. The cross-examining attorney's questions are limited to the scope of what was asked on direct examination. In other words, cross-examination is not the time to ask questions on topics not raised in the direct examination. To do that, the attorney must call the witness as part of his case, and conduct direct examination on those new topics.

There are several goals of cross-examination:

1. Impeach the witness with prior inconsistent statements. If the witness has testified at the preliminary hearing, then the defense attorney can obtain a copy of the reporter's transcript and use this sworn testimony as the basis for cross-examination. Here is an example:

"Mrs. Jensen, isn't it a fact that at the preliminary hearing in this case, when the prosecution asked you if you saw the face of the person who shot the decedent, you said, and I quote:

" 'It was very dark, I didn't get a good look.' "

"Yes, sir."

"Then I ask you, Mrs. Jensen, how you can testify today that my client is the person you saw the night of the murder?"

"Well, . . ."

Now the witness has to explain the apparent discrepancy in her testimony, and the jury will tend to disbelieve her, or so the defense hopes.

2. Discredit the witness's testimony on substantial issues. A witness may testify he overheard the defendant say he would kill the victim. During cross-examination, the defense attorney would want to try and show that the witness's hearing wasn't that good, that the witness was too far away to hear the conversation clearly, that the witness might have misunderstood what was said, that the comment may have been made in jest, or any other angle that would reduce the impact of the witness's testimony on direct.

3. Corroborate matters that are significant to the cross-examiner's case. A police officer might testify that, after the crime, he questioned the defendant. The defense attorney might want to have the officer testify that the defendant was calm during the questioning, cooperative and open in answering questions, thus inferring that he did not have a guilty state of mind and therefore, hopefully, the jury would conclude that he did not commit the crime.

4. Establish bias, interest or motive for the witness's testimony. A witness who is offered something in exchange for testifying, such as immunity from prosecution or leniency, has a motive to testify the way the prosecution wants. A defense attorney would want to establish this to undermine the credibility of the testimony, hoping the jury would think this witness had an incentive to exaggerate, if not outright lie, in return for what was promised.

When cross-examining a witness, attorneys have to be careful that they are not too aggressive with sympathetic witnesses. The jury may see the witness as the underdog, sympathize with him and give his testimony added value, just the opposite of what the attorney wanted to accomplish. Most attorneys are only aggressive if they know the witness is lying and the witness starts floundering and the attorney thinks he can break the witness down.

When he cross-examined the officer who found the .22 caliber pistol, Sheldon tried to get him to admit that he knew Ramon from previous contact and that he once told another officer that he "wanted to put Ramon away." The officer denied ever making any such statement. On cross-examination of the elderly lady, Sheldon got her to admit that she had not really seen the face of the driver of the car, and that the driver could have been a man or a woman, as far as she knew.

Re-Direct and Re-Cross Examination

The party calling the witness can ask more questions after cross-examination by the opposing attorney, to rehabilitate the witness. This is re-direct. The opposing attorney can then explore those matters by further cross-examination, called re-cross, and the attorneys can continue back and forth until they have no further questions of the witness.

Jurors' Questions

On rare occasions the judge will permit jurors to ask questions of witnesses. If a judge tells the attorneys he will allow this, the attorneys will usually request the judge to require any juror's questions be submitted in writing so that both attorneys can evaluate the question and make objections and obtain the judge's ruling, all out of the presence of the jury.

Judge's Questions

The judge may ask questions of a witness, but he must remain neutral and cannot align himself with either side. The attorneys can object to the judge's questions if they believe the question is improper or prejudicial.

Objections

Courtroom testimony is a great source of drama and conflict, and makes exciting reading and intense visual drama. Rules of evidence provide the guidelines for what are proper questions and what is admissible evidence. (See the sections on Rules of Evidence and Form of Questions in chapter seven, "Outline of a Civil Trial.") An attorney cannot use his right to ask a witness questions as an opportunity to harass or embarrass the witness, unless there is a legitimate reason. Also, the attorney cannot ask questions that elicit evidence that is not reliable.

Hearsay is a common objection. Hearsay is one person testifying as to what another person said, offered to prove that what the other person said is the truth.

The testifying person doesn't have direct knowledge of the facts that the other person talked about. This type of testimony is generally unreliable. It is much better to have the other person in court to see if he really said it and what facts he based it on, and to allow the other side to cross-examine him. Hearsay is admissible, however, in certain situations, such as if it is a statement made by the defendant (since he is in court and can testify regarding what is testified to), or statements made by a dying person regarding the circumstances of his death, such as "Joe killed me," since it is assumed that human nature causes us to be honest when we know we are about to die.

Many objections made in court are obvious as to their meaning:

"Asked and answered," means the question was already asked and answered, and it's not fair to keep asking the same question.

There are times that, technically, an attorney could object to a question, but for tactical reasons he won't. An objection calls the jury's attention to a question and may make it appear that the attorney doesn't want the jury to hear that information. Most attorneys use objections sparingly, only when they want to stop the line of questioning or when the answer will hurt their client.

A popular area for drama and conflict is the battle between attorneys as to what is proper questioning or treatment of a witness. Some attorneys like to test the limits of what a judge will allow or what the opposing attorney will let them get away with. If a trial attorney exceeds the proper bounds of conduct or questioning during trial, the opposing attorney can object to the misconduct, pointing out the specific misconduct being objected to, and request specific relief, such as an admonition, sanctions or a mistrial.

TIP: Watch Court TV for coverage of newsworthy trials, or go on the Internet to Court TV casefiles: *www.courttv.com/casefiles*. You can read transcripts from current or recent high-profile cases, including jury voir dire questions, opening statements, judges' rulings, direct and cross-examination questions and answers and more.

Defense Motions

After the prosecution rests, the defense may make a motion for dismissal of the charges against the defendant or request a directed verdict for acquittal, contending that the prosecution has failed to present sufficient evidence to prove beyond a reasonable doubt that the defendant is guilty of the crime charged.

These motions are commonly denied since the prosecutor's evidence is usually sufficient to raise questions that only the jury can decide.

Defense's Case
The defense now presents its witnesses and evidence. Sheldon called Ramon's girlfriend, who testified that Ramon was with her the night of the shooting. Sheldon watched the jury's reactions during this testimony. Although he felt the witness presented herself well, he saw, by the jury's body language, folded arms, bodies turned sideways and scowls on their faces, that the jury did not believe her.

Should the Defendant Testify?
One of most difficult decisions for defense counsel is whether or not to have his client testify. Some attorneys believe that the defendant should testify whenever possible because jurors find it difficult to acquit otherwise. Others believe the defendant should not testify unless he has an exceptionally good story and will perform well under cross-examination. The defense need not disclose ahead of time whether or not the defendant will testify, so the decision can be made at the last minute.

Because the jury was skeptical about the alibi testimony of Ramon's girlfriend, and since Ramon contended that he did not commit the murder of Joe Joe, Sheldon decided Ramon should testify. Sheldon spent eight hours over a four-day period preparing Ramon. Ramon made a good appearance as a witness and was able to, as he had practiced with Sheldon, look directly at the jury when he denied killing Joe Joe. During the prosecution's cross-examination, Ramon became angry and defensive when asked about some of his gang-related activities, but Sheldon objected and asked for a sidebar, which interrupted the prosecution's tempo and gave Ramon a chance to calm down and recompose himself.

Rebuttal and Surrebuttal
Rebuttal evidence is evidence put on by the prosecution after the defense has completed its case (rested). It is restricted to evidence made necessary by the defendant's case. Surrebuttal is evidence put on by the defense after the prosecution's rebuttal. It is restricted to evidence made necessary by the prosecution's rebuttal. Since the prosecution did not offer any rebuttal evidence or testimony, Sheldon had no surrebuttal.

Closing Argument (Summation)
Closing argument is the culmination of the attorney's efforts since the beginning of the case and the opportunity for the attorneys to show their eloquence and

passion for their case and client. Each attorney takes the evidence presented and weaves it into a logical, believable story that supports their theory of the case and their client's position. Most attorneys start preparing their closing argument prior to commencing trial.

Since he has the burden of proof, the prosecution argues first, followed by the defense, then the prosecution closes with a rebuttal to the defense's argument. The judge can set time limits, such as one hour, but in serious cases there is often no time limit.

The instructions that the judge will read to the jury are a good starting point for preparation of argument. The attorneys want to show the jury how the evidence supports the jury instructions, which is the law the jury must apply.

A basic rule of communication, understood by many lawyers, is that by communicating to several of the listener's senses, more will be remembered. So attorneys use the spoken word, visual items such as the tangible evidence, charts, diagrams and enlargements of jury instructions, and touch, by passing the evidence around to the jury.

Attorneys also focus on the discrepancies and weaknesses of the other side's case, e.g., what evidence was missing, which witnesses were not believable and which witnesses had a reason to lie.

The attorneys must believe in their case and convey that to the jury. Eye contact is crucial. Most attorneys will use an outline for their closing argument, glancing at it as necessary. Some write the entire argument out, but have to be careful to not read it and lose the interest and attention of the jury. Most attorneys attempt to appear spontaneous rather than rehearsed, and they use body movement and variation of tone to hold the jury's interest.

Experienced attorneys are careful not to use legal terms unless explained and big words that the jury may not understand. They know they must communicate in plain English and at a level appropriate for the jury. They also know that use of common experiences helps jurors relate to what is being said. A rule of thumb many attorneys use is to make several major points, then sit down. They avoid getting bogged down in detail and either boring or overwhelming the jury. They know that most people have a relatively short attention span.

The prosecution argued that the antagonism between the gangs and the violation of the "hands off" rule by Joe Joe dating Ramon's sister were strong enough motives for the murder. They argued that the defense's assertion that the murder weapon was planted was ludicrous, that no one had a motive to frame Ramon and that this was a desperate attempt by the defense to explain evidence that proved Ramon was the murderer.

Sheldon argued that Ramon would never kill his own sister's boyfriend, no matter what gang he belonged to, that Ramon had an airtight alibi for the night of the murder and that the prosecution witnesses' testimony was shaky at best and not sufficient to find his client guilty of murder beyond a reasonable doubt.

Jury Instructions

The judge instructs the jury on the law to be applied in the case being tried. It's up to the attorneys to submit to the judge the law they believe applies. The attorneys and judge usually meet, sometimes in chambers with the court reporter, sometimes in open court without the jury present, to discuss each attorney's selection of what law they think applies. The attorneys may file briefs citing cases and the reasons they believe a particular jury instruction should be given. If there is a disagreement over certain instructions, then the judge makes a decision and each side can state their position on the record to preserve their objections for appeal.

Most attorneys begin to think about and prepare their proposed jury instructions at the same time they begin thinking about and preparing their closing argument, which is the day they take the case.

The instructions are usually given at the close of evidence and after closing arguments, but they can be given at any time. Some attorneys request the jury be instructed on particular laws during the trial just before certain testimony is given. That way the jury can see how the testimony relates to the law.

Jury Deliberations and Verdict

After telling the jury the law they are to apply, the judge gives them directions on how to conduct their deliberations. These directions usually include the following:

"You are to act as twelve separate judges who must individually decide the case and should not be swayed by the opinion of the majority, but must also discuss the evidence and instructions with one another."

"You should approach your deliberations with open minds and not form a final opinion too soon."

"You are not to conduct any independent investigation concerning the case, and you are not to talk to anyone about the case until you have reached your verdict."

After giving these instructions the judge will have the clerk give verdict forms to the jury. The clerk, with the approval of the attorneys and the judge, usually prepares these forms. The jury is given two forms for each crime charged, one that says "guilty" and one that says "not guilty."

The bailiff is then sworn to take charge of the jury and he escorts them to the jury room, where they "retire" to deliberate. If authorized to take notes by the judge during trial, they may take their notes into the deliberations with them.

The jury's first task is to elect a foreman. The jury is kept together for meals, or meals are sent in to the jury room. They may ask for testimony to be reread, ask the judge to clarify instructions, ask to view the scene of the crime or other relevant locations, or to look at evidence or objects outside the courtroom. Attorneys use these requests to try to guess what the jury is thinking.

Jurors must confine their deliberations to evidence presented in court. They may not read newspaper accounts of the case, communicate with nonjurors about the case, consult with experts of their own about the case or conduct an unauthorized view of the crime scene.

If, during the deliberations, an alternate replaces a juror, the deliberations must start over.

If the jury does not reach a verdict the first day of deliberations, the bailiff escorts them back to the courtroom and the judge admonishes them to not discuss the case with anyone, to not read newspapers, listen to the radio or watch television regarding the case, and to return the next morning to continue deliberations. The judge then recesses for the day.

Usually one or both attorneys request the judge to sequester the jury so they are not subjected to newspapers, television or other media, or to friends or family who might want to discuss the case or might make comments about the case. The decision to sequester the jury is left to the sound discretion of the judge. If he does sequester the jury, the bailiff will escort the jury to dinner and to their hotel, then the next morning to breakfast and back to court.

The jury usually votes either to see how far apart they are or when they think they are close to a decision. The vote is usually by secret ballot, with each juror's vote written on a slip of paper, placed in a box and then tallied by the foreman or other designated person. Most states and the federal courts require unanimous verdicts in criminal cases.

When the jurors reach a verdict or if they believe they cannot reach one, they tell the bailiff, who notifies the judge, who notifies the attorneys, who return to court. During deliberations, the judge may be hearing other cases and the attorneys may wait in the courthouse if they believe the verdict will come within a reasonable time; otherwise they may return to their offices or visit a local restaurant or bar, cellular phones on and ready for the call from the court clerk that "the jury is in."

Once the attorneys are back in the courtroom, the judge reconvenes court and the bailiff then escorts the jury into the courtroom.

The foreman speaks for the jury. If he states that the jury cannot reach a verdict, the judge will inquire if there is a reasonable possibility that the jury can reach a verdict if they return to the jury room and deliberate further. If the judge determines that there is no reasonable possibility that jurors will agree on a verdict, or if the prosecution and defense consent, the judge will discharge the jury and declare a mistrial.

If the jury has reached a verdict and completed the appropriate verdict form and signed it, the foreman gives it to the bailiff who gives it to the judge, who usually reads it to make sure it is properly prepared. He then gives it to the clerk or back to the foreman, who reads it out loud.

If the verdict is "not guilty," the court clerk enters the acquittal in the court's minutes and the defendant is discharged. If the verdict is "guilty," the defendant, if already in custody, is usually returned to jail pending sentencing. However, the judge may set bail or release the defendant on his own recognizance (OR) pending sentencing.

The judge usually then thanks the jury for their time and instructs them that they are free to talk to anyone about the case. It is not uncommon for the attorneys or their investigators to interview at least the foreman and sometimes all the jurors to learn how they evaluated the evidence, how their deliberations progressed, and to determine if anything improper occurred during the deliberations that might form a basis for appeal.

In Ramon's case, the jury deliberated for three hours and found Ramon guilty of murder in the first degree. When Sheldon later interviewed the jury foreman, he said they did not think the police or anyone else framed Ramon by putting the gun in his closet. They thought it was his gun and that linked him to the murder sufficiently to prove that he was guilty. They understood the elderly woman wanting to help convict Ramon by saying she saw his face then changing her testimony, but they thought her testimony on the make, model and color of the car established that at least Ramon's car was there that night, and probably it was Ramon driving and firing the fatal shot into Joe Joe's heart.

Communications Between Judge and Jury

There should be no private communications between the judge and the jury. Such actions would impinge on the defendant's constitutional rights to the assistance of an attorney and to be personally present at all trial proceedings. If a juror tries to communicate with the judge, the judge should notify both attorneys and explain the circumstances and how the judge handled the matter.

The evening before the jury in Ramon's case started their deliberations, a juror saw the judge in a local store and commented to him that he "had his hands full." The judge made no return comment and the next morning before court started he called the attorneys into his chambers and told them about the juror's comment. Neither attorney thought it was significant enough to question the juror further, and later that day before the lunch recess, the judge admonished the jury, telling them that there should be no communications between him or the attorneys and the jury outside the courtroom.

Motion for Mistrial

It's every defense attorney's dream to have a mistrial declared for his client, as long as it is not because of the defense attorney's misconduct. Some attorneys make a motion for mistrial when the prosecution does any little thing out of line. This is usually to preserve their client's rights on appeal (the attorney must make the motion for mistrial when the objected-to event occurred, otherwise he cannot raise it on appeal).

The motion for a mistrial is a request to terminate the trial before a verdict. The judge will grant the motion if the prejudice that occurred to the defendant by the objected-to conduct or incident cannot be cured by instructions to the jury to disregard.

Misconduct by the prosecutor or jury or a jury deadlock, or the jury's inability to reach a verdict because of an accident, illness or other physical cause beyond the court's control, are all basis for a mistrial. For example, if there were three alternate jurors, but four of the original jurors had to be excused because of illness, they would be one juror short and, unless the attorneys agreed to an eleven-person jury, a mistrial would occur.

If a mistrial is granted, it delays the case, increases the chances that important evidence to prove the prosecution's case will not be available at trial, and usually forces the prosecution to reconsider a plea bargain to dispose of the case. However, if a mistrial is declared, no jeopardy attaches, which means that the defendant can be retried. The second trial on the same charges is not double jeopardy.

Prejudgment Motions

If the defendant is found guilty, before he is sentenced the defense attorney can make several motions. The most common is a motion for new trial. Some of the grounds for a new trial are:

1. Jury misconduct: If, in interviewing the jury, the defense attorney learns of something improper, e.g., a juror said he had a similar gun and he ran some tests to prove that what the defendant said happened could not have happened, the attorney would obtain declarations from willing jurors of this misconduct and submit them to the judge as the basis for the motion.

2. Prosecutorial misconduct: If the defense attorney believes the prosecution used improper methods to influence the jury, e.g., an appeal to passion or prejudice or arguments unsupported by evidence, then this will be the basis for the motion. The alleged jury or prosecutorial misconduct must have been prejudicial, i.e., it must be "reasonably probable" that a result more favorable to the defendant would have occurred had the jury or prosecution refrained from the misconduct alleged by the defense attorney.

3. Errors of law: Examples include the judge admitting certain evidence that should not have been admitted, or instructing the jury on the wrong law to apply to the case.

4. Insufficiency of the evidence: If the defense attorney believes the verdict is contrary to the law or evidence, he can ask the trial judge to make an independent review of the evidence. In conjunction with the motion for a new trial, the defense attorney can make a motion to modify the verdict to a lesser offense or lesser degree.

5. Newly discovered evidence: If the defense could not have reasonably obtained the evidence prior to or during trial, and it is reasonably probable that a different verdict would result if the newly discovered evidence had been available

during trial, then the defense attorney might succeed with this motion.

6. Loss of trial transcript: To appeal, a transcript of the trial (written record of the questions and answers and objections and court rulings) must be available. If it is lost, then the defendant is probably entitled to a new trial.

"It is exceedingly rare for a judge to change a jury's verdict, but sometimes justice requires it," said one experienced judge. "In twenty-two years I've done it twice, once in a criminal trial and once in a civil trial. I have to go through serious soul searching to change a jury's verdict. By nature, judges are not inclined to second-guess juries. Ninety-nine percent of the time the tendency is to uphold the findings of the jury because judges have a great deal of respect for the collective wisdom of twelve jurors. But on rare occasions it is the judge's duty to set aside a jury verdict. It doesn't matter which way it goes, you are going to be criticized. But that goes with the territory. A judge is there to make tough decisions. We are not there to win friends and influence people."

STORY IDEAS

Hours after watching his difficult verdict reduced, one juror who convicted a woman of murder only to see her set free called the judge's decision "a complete injustice." The man said he felt like he was "having a heart attack" when the judge announced he was reducing the woman's sentence from life in prison to the 279 days she had already spent in jail.

Sheldon made a motion for a new trial on the basis that there was insufficient evidence to find Ramon guilty. The judge took the motion under submission and issued his ruling two days later, denying the motion.

Death-Penalty Cases

Trial of a death-penalty case is divided into two phases, the guilt phase and the penalty phase. At the penalty phase, evidence in aggravation and mitigation of the sentence is introduced. The jury considers the evidence and decides if the sentence should be death or life without possibility of parole. The penalty phase has the same basic structure as the guilt phase, i.e., opening statements, introduction of evidence, direct and cross examination, final arguments and jury instructions. If the defense raises a sanity defense, then trial of the sanity phase comes between the guilt phase and the penalty phase. It is usually the same jury for all three phases.

Prior Convictions

The prosecution can file allegations that the defendant has committed prior serious or violent felonies. The court has discretion to dismiss these priors if it would be in the interests of justice.

A defendant found to have prior convictions of crimes has established himself as a person who is a continual threat to society and who has been unsuccessful in efforts at rehabilitation. Prior convictions ("priors") can enhance the defendant's sentence by lengthening his prison term, establishing a mandatory minimum sentence, making otherwise innocent conduct criminal (an ex-con with a gun), elevating a misdemeanor to a felony, making a "wobbler" (a crime that can be charged either as a misdemeanor or a felony) into a straight felony and eliminating probation as a sentencing option. The defendant can ask the court in its discretion to dismiss priors so the judge does not have to impose as severe a sentence.

Prior felony convictions, if they involve moral turpitude (defined as a "readiness to do evil," i.e., crimes of violence) may be admissible to impeach the defendant after he testifies. Impeaching means that, because of this prior conduct, the defendant is more likely to lie, and therefore his testimony should be given less weight than someone without prior felony convictions.

Ramon had several priors, one for auto theft and one for assault, which were introduced at the penalty phase of his case. Also during the penalty phase, the jury heard evidence that Ramon and his sister had been beaten and abused by their parents, who were alcoholics, and that Ramon had become the protector of his sister. They decided he was acting from that worthy but misdirected motive when he had killed Joe Joe, and so they decided he should get life in prison without the possibility of parole rather than a death sentence.

Sentencing Hearing—Nondeath Cases

In nondeath-penalty cases the judge determines the sentence. Like every other phase of the case, there are time periods, such as not less than six hours but not more than five days after verdict, for sentencing. However, the defendant can waive these time periods and usually does for sentencing so the probation department can prepare a presentencing probation report. The probation department, which usually has sixty days to complete the report, acts as the eyes and ears of the court by interviewing the defendant, his family members, the victim or victim's family, and other people involved with the defendant, such as employers, friends and past probation officers, if any. The prosecution will give the probation officer any relevant information, such as the defendant's priors, threats against the victim or witnesses and the defendant's performance on probation in other cases.

The defendant's attorney will usually suggest to the probation officer a sentence tailored to fit the defendant and the crime. Judges have the authority to impose a variety of innovative sentences, including volunteer programs and home detention. Because of jail overcrowding, judges are particularly amenable to jail alternatives.

After the probation officer has completed his report and usually made a sentencing recommendation, the court receives the report and the sentencing hearing proceeds. At the hearing, the defendant can speak and have others speak on his behalf. The victim, victim's family and attorney may speak. This testimony can be presented in person or by letter, audio or videotape. No one is placed under oath and there is no cross examination.

The judge has certain sentencing guidelines for each crime committed, with the primary consideration being protection of society. Misdemeanors are usually punished by fines and county jail time. However, the choice of sentence is within the discretion of the judge as long as he is acting within prescribed statutory limits. The defendant can be released from jail to go to work or school, or time in county jail can be served on weekends, or through restitution or community service. Jail time can be reduced by good conduct and work time. It can also be served through an electronic monitor-home arrest program. Felonies are punishable by fines and prison time. The defendant can be sentenced for a determinate term, an indeterminate term or a combination. Within the statutory minimum and maximum sentencing guidelines, the judge can sentence at the lower, middle or upper term depending on mitigating or aggravating circumstances. The trend is toward increasingly strict sentencing requirements, including three-strikes provisions that take away the judge's discretion in sentencing and make sentencing increasingly uniform and mechanical.

The judge has the choice of imposing concurrent or consecutive sentences. If the defendant is found guilty of two offenses, each punishable with a six-month sentence, and the judge imposes them concurrently, the defendant will serve six months. If he imposes them consecutively, the defendant will serve one year. In deciding, the judge may consider the nature and circumstances of the offense, the defendant's appreciation of and attitude toward the offense, and his character as shown by his behavior and demeanor at the trial. The defendant will receive credit for time served, which is the time spent in county jail from first being taken into custody until being sentenced.

Probation

Rather than imposing jail time, the judge can, if the offense did not involve a gun or is not a forcible or serious felony, suspend the imposition or execution of a sentence and order the conditional and revocable release of the defendant into the community on probation. The defendant can be under the supervision of a probation officer, considered formal probation, or of the court, considered informal probation. Probation usually lasts for up to five years for a felony and up to three years for a misdemeanor.

If the defendant violates a condition of his probation or commits another crime, then the probation officer or the district attorney can file a motion to revoke probation, and the defendant will be taken into custody and returned to jail.

Appeal

A defendant found guilty at the trial-court level still has hope of overturning the decision at the appellate-court level. Every jurisdiction allows at least one appeal as a right after a conviction, and some allow two. An attorney to handle the appeal is usually provided, free of charge, for the first appeal. However, 90 percent of all convictions appealed by defendants are affirmed in full with no modification. There is only a 10 percent chance the appellate court will make any changes to the trial court's decision.

If the appellate court reverses the trial-court decision, it is considered an order for a new trial unless the appellate court orders otherwise, such as dismissal of the case because the error made in the trial court is so serious that a new trial would be unjust.

Appeals must be filed within certain time periods, usually thirty calendar days from judgment for a misdemeanor and sixty calendar days from judgment on a felony. To file an appeal, the appealing party, usually the defendant, obtains the clerk's transcript (a chronological overview of the trial-court proceeding including a list of the various exhibits introduced at trial) and the reporter's transcript (the questions and answers of all the witnesses). The trial-court exhibits and physical evidence are provided to the appellate court if they request them.

> ### STORY IDEAS
>
> *A man convicted of murder five years ago will get a new trial because his attorney and his wife were having an affair during the first trial. A judge ordered the man returned from prison so a new trial could be scheduled.*

The appealing party, called the appellant, submits an opening brief, which is a statement about the case including the charges, pleas, motions, court rulings and a brief summary of the trial, verdict and sentence. The appellant includes a statement of the facts that form the basis for the appeal along with the supporting law.

Within usually thirty days of the appellant filing his brief, the respondent, usually the prosecution, files the respondent's brief, with his view of the case and the law he thinks should apply to support the action taken in the trial court, why there was no error and why the trial court's decision should be upheld.

Appellant then has usually twenty days to reply to the respondent's brief, and the matter is then before the appellant court, which will review and decide the case, sometimes requesting oral arguments from the attorneys.

Although Sheldon thought there might be a basis to appeal Ramon's conviction, Ramon and his family did not have sufficient money to pay Sheldon to pursue the appeal. They decided to seek the assistance of a state public defender, provided free of charge, to pursue the appeal.

Federal Habeas Corpus Review of State-Court Convictions

After state court appeals are exhausted, the defendant can file a habeas corpus petition in federal district court alleging he is being held in state custody in violation of his federally guaranteed statutory or constitutional rights. If the federal court grants the petition, the case will usually go back to the trial court for a new trial.

Juvenile Proceedings

If a minor is suspected of committing a crime, a police officer can temporarily detain him. Before the officer can question the youth, he must advise him of his Miranda rights. For less serious offenses, the officer might issue a citation for the minor to appear before a probation officer. Alternatively, the officer might request a petition be issued and the child and parent will be contacted by a

"It's an important concept of our criminal justice system. We are not really there to determine if the person is guilty or innocent—that would be a nice way of looking at it. But the real job of a jury is to determine whether the prosecution has proven guilt beyond a reasonable doubt. I do a better job for my client if I keep in mind that that is the standard the law provides. That is what the judge is going to tell the jury. So we are not going out to try to prove that our client is innocent. We usually can't do that. But we want to see what all the problems with the prosecution's case are. The holes in it that might amount to a reasonable doubt, so we can argue to the jury that the prosecution's case has not been proven beyond a reasonable doubt. Also, the vast majority of cases are not 'who done it' cases, they are mostly what did this person really do and what were the mitigating circumstances and what were the crimes actually committed."

TOM WORTHINGTON, ATTORNEY, CRIMINAL LAW SPECIALIST

probation officer. If the officer decides to confine the minor, he must place him in a juvenile facility, not in the adult jail. The officer must immediately notify the minor's parent that the child is being detained. The minor is usually allowed to make one or more completed phone calls. At the juvenile facility, a probation officer will interview the minor ("intake"), investigate the alleged offense and determine what is in the child's best interest. Options typically include counseling and releasing the minor and closing the case, referring the minor to a nonjudicial agency or community program and closing the case, placing the minor under informal supervision to keep track of his behavior, or referring the case to the prosecutor for filing and either releasing the minor to his parents or retaining him in custody.

If the minor requests an attorney, the juvenile-court judge must appoint one, usually the public defender or a court-approved counsel experienced in handling juvenile cases. The attorney represents the minor, not the minor's parents, even if the parents hire and pay him.

If a detention hearing is to be held it must occur within forty-eight hours of the minor being taken into custody. At the hearing the attorney for the minor receives the police report, probation report and any other documents that were available to the probation officer. The prosecutor usually submits the matter to the court on the basis of the police report and the oral or written recommendation of the probation officer. The attorney for the minor can cross-examine the probation officer, the police officer and anyone else who prepared reports regarding the minor or the incident. The minor has the right to confront witnesses and cross-examine them, and the right to assert a Fifth Amendment privilege against self-incrimination.

If the juvenile-court judge decides that the minor violated the law, he can make the minor a ward of the court and the minor will be detained. An arraignment is held, usually at the detention hearing, and the minor, through his attorney, enters a plea and negotiation of the charges can occur, the equivalent of plea bargaining for adults. If the prosecution wants the minor treated as an adult, a fitness hearing will be held to determine if the minor is or is not fit for the care, treatment and training programs of juvenile court. If the minor remains in the juvenile justice system, a jurisdictional hearing is held, the equivalent of a trial in adult criminal court. The hearing is conducted in the same manner as a court trial in adult court, with opening statements, questioning of witnesses, motions and closing arguments. If the judge finds that the allegations in the petition are true, he declares that the minor comes within the provisions of the juvenile-court statutes. Then a dispositional hearing is held, the equivalent of the sentencing hearing in adult court. In sentencing a minor, the juvenile court puts the emphasis on treating and rehabilitating the minor in addition to protecting the public.

At all juvenile-court hearings the minor and his parents and the minor's attorney are entitled to be present. However, the hearings are closed and confidential unless the judge opens them to the public. Unlike in adult court, the minor has no right to bail, no right to a jury trial and no preliminary hearing. Juvenile court is considered a civil rather than a criminal court, even though it determines violations of criminal laws by minors. There is no finding of guilt and no convic-

STORY IDEAS

A juvenile-court judge ruled that a sixteen-year-old accomplice charged in the shooting of a jewelry store owner will not stand trial as an adult. The judge said the girl lacked criminal sophistication and was under the influence of an older man who took advantage of her naiveté. He also said the girl is a good candidate for rehabilitation in the juvenile justice system. The district attorney filed first-degree murder charges against the girl and man, who were allegedly robbing the store when the owner was killed. The ruling means the girl will be tried in juvenile court. If convicted, the girl will remain in custody with the state youth authority a total of eight and a half years.

STORY IDEAS

An eleven-year-old boy was ordered to stand trial as an adult on murder charges in the sniper slaying of a man outside a convenience store. The sixth grader would become the youngest person ever to be tried as an adult for murder in the state. He could get life in prison.

---

tion in juvenile court. If a petition is filed and the juvenile is found to come within the provisions of the juvenile code, then the state steps in and assumes control over the minor. To be considered a minor, the person must be under eighteen at the time the crime was committed. However, for detention purposes, most states provide that their juvenile courts have jurisdiction until the minor is twenty-five years old.

CHAPTER SIX

Civil Law

"See, that's what court is. The court doesn't exist to give them justice. Court exists to give them a chance at justice.

"Are they going to get it?"

"They might. They might. See, the jury wants to believe what the jury wants to believe. It is something to see. I've got to go down there tomorrow and pick out twelve of them. All of them, all their lives, hear it's a sham, it's rigged, you can't fight city hall. But when they step into that jury box, I can just barely see it in their eyes . . . maybe . . . maybe."

—"The Verdict," screenplay by David Mamet

L aw can be broadly divided into criminal law and civil law. Government prosecutors enforce the criminal law and violations are punishable by fine, jail or prison. Private individuals and businesses enforce the civil law, and violations are dealt with by awarding money as damages. Civil law includes a number of categories.

Personal Injury and Property Damage (Tort Law)

The law requires people to act and manage their property reasonably so other people and their property are not injured. A person who fails to meet this legal duty has committed a civil wrong (called a "tort," from the French word "wrong") and the law provides the injured party with a remedy for the injury to their person and property. Depending on the act, the wrongdoer may be liable under a theory of intentional misconduct, negligence or strict liability.

Intentional Misconduct

Intentional acts are those we reasonably know or should know will follow from actions we purposefully engage in.

Assault and Battery

Assault is a deliberate act that causes a person to fear that she is in imminent danger of being struck. She must be aware of the act. So if Joe runs up behind Mary with a baseball bat raised and ready to strike, but stops short and puts the bat on the ground before Mary turns around and sees him, no assault has occurred, since Mary was not aware of Joe's actions. But if she saw his reflection in the mirror and believed he was about to hit her with the bat, Joe has assaulted Mary and she is entitled to sue for damages for the fear she experienced from the imminent attack.

Battery occurs when a person deliberately hits or touches another without permission. If Joe stumbles down the stairs and knocks Mary over, no battery has occurred, since Joe did not deliberately knock Mary over. But if Joe intentionally brushes up against Mary so he can run his hand across her buttocks, he has committed a battery. However, if Mary is Joe's girlfriend and it was OK with her that he brushed his hand across her buttocks, no battery occurred, since Joe had her permission, either expressed or implied, from their relationship.

Assault and battery are crimes as well as torts. Mary could file a complaint with the police for Joe's assault and battery. She can also file a civil suit against Joe for the assault and battery and recover monetary damages for her upset and any physical injury that resulted from Joe's actions.

> **STORY IDEAS**
>
> *Three former altar boys who accused a former priest of sexual assault will receive $7.5 million as part of a settlement. The Catholic Diocese agreed to pay $3.1 million and two insurance companies, Lloyd's of London and Interstate, will pay the remaining $4.4 million.*

False Imprisonment

Intentionally confining someone against their will is false imprisonment. The confinement need not be done by direct physical force. It can be accomplished by using words or actions that place a person in fear of leaving.

Mary's boss accused her of taking money from the cash register. He told her she could not leave until she signed a confession. Mary was afraid to leave because her boss was standing over her in a threatening manner. Her boss is liable for false imprisonment. False imprisonment is also both a crime and a tort.

Intentional Causing of Emotional Distress

If a person intentionally or recklessly acts in an outrageous manner that he should recognize is likely to cause emotional suffering, he is liable for this tort.

While tenants were out of town, the landlord, with no prior notice to the tenants, removed their belongings and rented their apartment to someone else. When the tenants returned and found their belongings gone and their apartment occupied by someone else, the wife became hysterical and suffered a miscarriage. The landlord was liable for intentional infliction of emotional distress.

Malicious Prosecution

Making a criminal complaint or filing a civil lawsuit against someone from a malicious motive and without reasonable grounds is malicious prosecution.

A nightclub owner ejected a patron from the club. The patron returned and asked for a refund of his cover charge. The nightclub owner ordered his bouncers to beat up the patron while the nightclub owner called the police and filed charges against the patron for being drunk and creating a disturbance. The nightclub owner was liable for malicious prosecution since he filed the charges to discourage the patron from bringing a civil action for battery.

Abuse of Process

In abuse of process, the lawsuit is justified but the person uses the court's power to achieve an impermissible result. Debtor owed creditor $300. Creditor sued debtor and attached debtor's automobile worth $5,000 and debtor's bank account with $3,500 in it. Creditor's attachment of excessive property of debtor was abuse of process.

Defamation—Libel and Slander

Defamation is a false statement that tends to diminish another's reputation so that other people think less of him and don't want to associate with him. Libel includes more permanent forms of expression such as writings, pictures and images. Slander is spoken words. The libel or slander must be unprivileged and false and it must expose the person to hatred, contempt or ridicule, or cause them to be shunned, avoided or injured in their occupation.

Joe prints a flyer with an emaciated picture of Fred and the letters "HIV" under it. He leaves a pile of the flyers at the local post office. Fred does not have HIV. As a result of people seeing the flyer, they avoid Fred. Joe has committed libel. If Fred was a public figure and Joe put a question mark after HIV, his flyer probably would not have been libel, since he has the privilege to comment about public officials, and he is just raising a question, not making a statement. If Fred really had HIV, truth would be a defense and Joe would not be liable for libel, though he probably would be liable for invasion of privacy.

STORY IDEAS

A prominent plastic surgeon has filed a libel and slander lawsuit against two former associates he claims spread allegations, now being investigated by the state medical board, that he fondled and ridiculed sedated patients and abused drugs.

Invasion of Privacy

People generally have a right to be left alone to live their lives privately without being subjected to unwanted publicity. Susan called 911 when her husband had a heart attack. A news camera crew arrived with the 911 personnel and filmed the unsuccessful efforts to revive Susan's husband. The film appeared on the six o'clock news. Susan was never asked for permission. The news camera crew invaded her privacy.

Trespass to Land

Unlawfully interfering with a person's possession of their land is trespass to land. Neighbor's trees have grown across the property line and hang over Jim's house. Neighbor, by means of his trees, is trespassing on Jim's property.

Conversion of Personal Property

Taking or destroying personal property is the tort of conversion. Joey and Timmy break into Dan's house and take a stereo. They have converted Dan's personal property, and Dan has the right to have the stereo returned or to recover the full value of the stereo from Joey and Timmy. Conversion is also a crime, usually classified as robbery, burglary or theft.

Interference With Domestic Relations
Some states still allow suits for alienation of affections of husband or wife. Boss seduces his secretary, who is married. Secretary's husband could sue the boss for alienation of his wife's affections.

Interference With Business Relations
Inducing someone to break their business relationship with another can form the basis for this tort. Helena, a rock singer, had an exclusive contract to sing only at the Jackpot Casino in Las Vegas. James, aware of this contract, talked Helena into performing at his casino in Vegas. The Jackpot Casino has the right to sue James for interfering with their business relationship with Helena.

Fraud
Intentionally telling a person something that is untrue, knowing they will rely on the untruth in making a decision that results in their loss, is the tort of fraud.

Robert tells Helen that if she lends him $80,000, he will invest it in his new check-cashing business and she will receive one-half of the profits. In fact, Robert has no intention of investing the money in his business but instead intends to use the money to buy a new Porsche to impress his girlfriend. Helen relies on Robert's representation that her money will be invested in the business and she will receive one-half of the profits, so she gives Robert the money. Robert never gives Helen any money back or any income from his business. He has defrauded Helen.

Negligence
Negligence is failure to do what a reasonable person would have done under the circumstances. Jerry is driving down the road talking on his cellular phone and not paying attention to traffic ahead. The car ahead stops and Jerry runs into the rear of it, damaging the car and injuring the driver. The law says that a driver of a car must act reasonably, which means he has a duty to maintain a proper lookout for traffic ahead and to drive at a safe distance so he can stop if traffic ahead stops. Jerry failed to act reasonably so he was negligent, and he is responsible for the damage and injury his negligence caused.

Note that in negligence, there is no intent to cause the injury. It's just a failure to act reasonably under the circumstances. If Jerry had intentionally driven into the car ahead, he would have committed the tort of battery, and possibly assault if the driver ahead saw him coming.

If the car ahead had come to a sudden and unexpected stop for no reason, then the driver of that car may have been negligent for stopping unnecessarily when there was a car behind. The driver of the car ahead would have contributed to the accident and in some states he could not recover for his damages and injuries. However, in most states his negligence would have been compared to Jerry's negligence in determining fault. They might each be found equally liable for the accident.

> **STORY IDEAS**
>
> *A woman who suffered a severe head injury when a wind-driven balloon in the Thanksgiving Day parade knocked part of a lamppost onto her has taken the first step in filing a $95 million negligence lawsuit against the city. The woman spent almost a month in a coma after fierce winds sent the balloon out of control. She has filed a notice of claim against the city, the first step toward a lawsuit.*

Negligent Causing of Emotional Distress

Some states allow a person to sue even if there was no physical impact with them, if the other person's negligence caused such a degree of fright that it resulted in physical injury or illness. A speeding car flips through the air and lands two feet in front of Sam, who is standing on his front porch. He suffers a heart attack out of fright that the car was going to hit him. He has a cause of action for negligent infliction of emotional distress against the driver of the speeding car.

> **STORY IDEAS**
>
> *A devout Hindu is suing a Taco Bell that he claims served him a beef burrito. The suit contends that eating a single bite of forbidden beef instead of the bean burrito he had ordered emotionally damaged the man. Hindus hold cows sacred and believe beef is unclean.*

Medical Malpractice

If a doctor is negligent (does not act as a reasonable doctor under the circumstances) in diagnosing or treating a patient's condition and as a result of the doctor's negligence the patient suffers injury, the doctor is liable for malpractice. The problem for many years was getting one doctor to testify against another, since the law requires an "expert" doctor to give his opinion that the defendant doctor's conduct fell below the standard of the profession. Out of fear of ostracism by their colleagues or medical societies, most doctors engaged in a "conspiracy of silence" by refusing to criticize each other. However, there are more doctors now who have a greater allegiance to the proper practice of medicine than to protecting their negligent colleagues, so plaintiffs' attorneys can usually locate a doctor who will testify when negligence occurs.

Henry sees Dr. Goof and complains about pain in his left arm. The doctor takes a glance at the arm and says it's probably just a sprain. He sends Henry home with some pain medication. That night Henry goes into full cardiac arrest and is rushed to the hospital, where he is treated for a heart attack. Since pain in the left arm is one symptom of a heart attack, and since a reasonable doctor would conduct various tests to determine if Henry was having a heart attack, Dr. Goof was negligent in not having the tests performed, and he is liable for malpractice.

STORY IDEAS

A woman whose psychiatrist diagnosed her with 126 personalities, including Satan and a duck, accepted a $2.4 million settlement in a malpractice case against the doctor who was accused of falsely convincing her she had multiple personalities. The woman came to the psychiatrist because she was depressed, but after six years of treatment she was left suicidal, haunted by false memories and believing she was, among other things, an angel who talked to God. She said the doctor implanted false memories through hypnosis, convincing her she had been raped, pushed into an open grave and had an abortion. As a condition of the settlement, the doctor admitted no wrongdoing.

Wrongful Death

When a person's negligence causes the death of someone else, he is liable for the tort of wrongful death. The deceased person's spouse, children and possibly parents and siblings have a cause of action for wrongful death. They can sue for the loss of the financial support of the deceased, along with the loss of his comfort, companionship, advice and training.

> **STORY IDEAS**
>
> *The family of a teen boy fatally stabbed by another student on high school grounds is filing a wrongful death claim against the school district. Their claim alleges the district should have known that the school was understaffed and without the proper supervision to protect their son and his classmates from the number of "seriously emotionally disturbed students."*

Wrongful Birth

Some states recognize a cause of action if a doctor fails to perform a proper vasectomy, sterilization or abortion and, as a result, a woman gives birth to an unplanned-for child. Mary and Bob had three children and didn't want any more. Bob had Dr. Snip perform a vasectomy. Mary and Bob engaged in sexual intercourse with no other form of birth control, believing, as Dr. Snip told them, that there was "no way" Bob could father a child. In fact, the vasectomy was not performed properly and Bob did father a child. Mary and Bob have a claim against Dr. Snip for wrongful birth, and their damages are the cost of raising the unwanted child.

> **STORY IDEAS**
>
> *A federal jury rejected a "wrongful birth" claim against an obstetrician by the parents of a Down's Syndrome child. The parents contended that the doctor failed to perform prenatal testing that would have revealed their unborn child's disability. The parents said they would have opted for an abortion had they known the unborn child's condition, and therefore would not have incurred the costs of caring for their son.*

Strict Liability

If an individual engages in certain dangerous activities that pose a great likelihood of harm to others and someone else is injured as a result of that activity,

The "deep pocket" concept is that a plaintiff's attorney wants to find some way to include in the suit a defendant who has plenty of money. The best defendants are people with insurance and large corporations. If a defendant has insurance, then the claim against that defendant must be covered by his insurance policy. For example, I currently have a case against a man who was arrested for driving under the influence. During the booking process, he turned and slugged one of the police officers in the jaw, seriously injuring him. I represent the police officer and have filed suit alleging assault and battery (intentional torts) and negligence. The assault and battery is a no-brainer—we would win. But the man has homeowner's insurance that covers certain negligent acts by him, but does not cover intentional acts. I don't want this defendant's actions to be intentional. I want to show that he was so intoxicated that he could not form the necessary intent to commit an intentional tort. He was just acting negligently when he hit the officer. Tough case, but if I succeed, the insurance will pay. If a jury decides it was not negligent, but was intentional, then I have to try to collect against the defendant directly, not an easy thing to do.

the person engaging in the activity is liable for the injuries or damages, regardless of fault. In other words, it doesn't matter if they were negligent or not, they are liable strictly.

Ultrahazardous Activities

Blasting with explosives in a thickly populated area, using dangerous or toxic substances such as crop dusting or fumigating with deadly poisons, or working with gas, electricity or fire pose an undue risk of harm to members of the community. Anyone who conducts such activities does so at their own risk, and is responsible for any injuries caused to others, even if there was no negligence involved.

Jerry, who is a crop duster, sprays a field on a clear, calm morning. A sudden, unexpected wind arises and blows the chemicals into a shopping center two miles away and several people require medical attention from the fumes. Because many courts consider crop dusting an ultrahazardous activity, Jerry is liable, even though he could not have foreseen the unexpected winds.

Dangerous Animals

People who keep dangerous animals are strictly liable for any injuries the animals cause. Generally all animals that are usually considered wild animals are considered dangerous, such as lions, bears, wolves, chimpanzees and snakes.

Bruce, who has raised a wolf since it was born, takes the wolf over to a neighbor's house to visit. The neighbor's child runs up to the wolf to pet it. The wolf nips the child on the hand. Bruce is strictly liable for the injury.

STORY IDEAS

A downstairs tenant sued the owner of a twelve-foot python after the snake apparently turned on a faucet and caused the bathtub to overflow. The man left the snake soaking in the tub at his upstairs apartment while he watched the Super Bowl at a neighbor's house. The amount of water damage was unspecified.

Product Liability

Manufacturers are strictly liable for personal injuries caused by defective products. The person injured can bring an action against the party that designed, manufactured, sold or furnished the product. The injury can be from a design defect, manufacturing defect or inadequate warnings or directions. The rationale for this law is that the manufacturer can pass along the expense of this liability to the consumer by increasing the price of each unit sold.

Acme Ladder Corporation manufactures stepladders. Joe, their lead designer, comes up with a plastic ladder, which the company starts to sell. Joe failed to properly test the ladder and it turns out that after repeated use in the sun, the plastic weakens and the steps can break. Tom falls and breaks his leg when one of the ladder's steps breaks. Acme Ladder is strictly liable for a design defect. Also liable are the wholesaler and retailer of the ladder.

Class-Action Lawsuits

When a large number of people have a common interest they may sue as a class to prevent multiple lawsuits. Class-action suits are usually brought in federal court since plaintiffs and defendants often live or conduct business in different states. Sally developed an infection and became sterile because of the contraceptive device she was using. She joined with thousands of other women in a class-action lawsuit against the manufacturer of the device. She received part of the class settlement.

Contracts

A contract is a voluntary agreement between competent parties (usually at least eighteen years of age) to do or not to do something that is legal. There must be something of value (called "consideration") exchanged for the promise. Some contracts must be in writing to be enforceable, e.g., the sale of real estate, a contract that cannot be completed within one year or a promise to be responsible for someone else's debt. Otherwise, oral contracts are just as enforceable as written ones. It is just harder to prove what each party agreed to.

The usual contracting steps are: One party makes an offer, which states the subject matter, quantity and price; the other party accepts the offer. If the other party changes the terms, e.g., they want to pay $10 less, it is considered a counter-offer and the original offering party can accept or reject the counteroffer. A contract can have one or more conditions, e.g., I will buy your car if my mechanic says it's in good condition. If the mechanic says it's in good condition, the contract is binding. If he says it is not, the condition has not been met and there is no contract.

Courts will not enforce contracts for illegal acts such as a promise to sell illegal drugs or a contract entered into under duress, e.g., sell me your car or I will beat you up.

If one party breaches the contract, the other party is no longer obligated to keep his side of the bargain. His remedy for the breach is to receive the "benefit of the bargain," which usually is the item bargained for or the amount of money he would have received if the other party had not breached the contract.

Mike negotiates to buy a car from Ted for $3,500, and then Ted refuses to turn over the car to Mike when Mike produces the money. Mike can sue for specific performance, a court order requiring Ted to deliver the car to Mike in exchange for the $3,500. If Ted cannot do this (he sold the car to someone else), and Mike has to pay $4,200 for a comparable car, Mike is entitled to the difference between the $3,500 and $4,200, or $700, from Ted, the loss of the benefit of the bargain he had with Ted.

Business Law
Forms of Business
The way a business is organized depends on its size, financial success, tax considerations and potential exposure of investors to liability from its operation.

Sole Proprietorship
One person, as the name implies, owns a sole proprietorship. It is the simplest form of business organization and the most common form of business in the United States. It can have employees. The major disadvantages are that the owner is personally liable for debts and other obligations of the business, and it has less stability than other forms of business because it usually is dissolved or sold when the owner dies.

Partnership
A partnership is two or more people who co-own a business conducted for profit. In a general partnership all partners are equally liable for acts of the business. In limited partnerships (at least one general partner and one limited partner) the limited partner's liability is limited to the amount of his investment. The general partners are personally liable for debts and other obligations of the partnership. This form of business is also less stable because the partnership usually is dissolved or sold when one partner dies.

Corporation
A corporation is formed by one or more people (incorporators) who file articles of incorporation, usually with the secretary of the state where the business operates. Owners of the corporation own shares of stock and are generally not liable for the actions and debts of the corporation, though they may lose the money they invested in the stock. The advantages of a corporation are the limited liability of its investors (their personal assets are not at risk) and that the corporation usually continues to exist even if owners or managers die. People are generally more willing to invest in corporations because of this increased security, and

because they can sell their stock if they want to liquidate their investment. The principal disadvantage of a corporation is it is subject to two levels of taxation, first on the profit made and second on the dividends distributed to investors. A corporation is an entity separate from its owners and managers, and it can buy, sell and own assets in the name of the corporation.

Limited-Liability Company

A fairly recent development is the limited-liability company. It is an unincorporated business organization that provides the limited liability of a corporation but no double taxation, since profits are taxed as ordinary income to the owners. It is formed by filing articles of organization with the secretary of state.

Workers' Compensation

An employee injured at work is entitled to medical treatment for the injury and compensation for lost wages (temporary disability) resulting from the work-related injury. It matters not how the injury occurred or whether or not anyone is at fault. It is a form of no-fault or strict liability. Each state has its own procedures and dollar amounts for compensation for on-the-job injuries. An injury that occurs on the way to work or while going home is usually not covered unless the employee was conducting business (making a delivery, for example) for his employer at the time. The usual types of work-related injuries are slip-and-fall, strains, injuries from machinery or equipment, and repetitive-motion injuries, e.g., carpal tunnel syndrome from keyboarding. The amount of temporary disability is usually 50 to 60 percent of the employee's regular salary. If the injury is permanent, the employee is entitled to compensation for his reduced earning ability due to the disability and vocational training for a job he can do with his disability. If the employee is killed on the job, his family is entitled to a death benefit.

Michael was working on a machine that cut sheets of metal into straps. One piece of strapping snapped back and punctured Michael's eye, resulting in blindness. All his medical bills were paid, along with 50 percent of his lost salary while he was unable to work, and he received $10,000 in permanent disability for the loss of the eye. He also received the right for any future medical care needed for the injury.

Employment Discrimination

Various federal laws prevent discrimination in hiring or firing employees because of their race, color, religion, sex, national origin, age or physical or mental disabilities. Some federal laws apply to all employers. Some apply only to employers that employ at least fifteen or twenty employees. The Equal Employment Opportunity Commission (EEOC) enforces some federal laws. Others have to be enforced by the individual affected through a civil lawsuit. Most states also have laws that prevent discrimination in employment and many apply to employers with fewer than fifteen employees.

Sharon, a black female, applies for a job at Hunter Corporation, which has over 250 employees. At the interview she is told they are downsizing and not hiring anyone at the current time. The next day she learns from Ted, a white male, that Hunter Corporation hired him that morning. She believes she has been discriminated against either because she is a female or black. She can file a complaint with the EEOC and they will investigate and attempt to reach a settlement with Hunter Corporation, such as an agreement to hire Sharon and to stop discrimination in hiring practices.

STORY IDEAS

The Supreme Court left intact a federal rule that requires airline pilots to retire when they reach age sixty, turning away pilots' arguments that they are being victimized by age discrimination. The justices, acting without comment, rejected a challenge by pilots to the Federal Aviation Administration regulation, which was justified as necessary since the FAA cannot ensure that pilots over age sixty will not be incapacitated by a heart attack or suffer from a subtle loss of their mental capabilities.

Sexual Harassment

Sexual harassment, sometimes called gender discrimination, at the workplace is any unwelcome sexual advance or conduct that creates an intimidating, hostile or offensive working environment.

Examples of sexual harassment include sexual references, off-color jokes, vulgar or lewd comments, obscene or sexually suggestive cartoons, pictures or posters, inappropriate or unwanted physical touching, and suggestions to engage in sexual conduct. A single outrageous act (telling a female employee she must sleep with the boss if she wants to keep her job) or frequent subtle acts (moaning whenever a female employee walks by) may be sufficient to constitute sexual harassment.

The law usually requires the worker to file a complaint with the Equal Employment Opportunity Commission (federal) and the state agency that enforces fair employment practices prior to filing suit in court.

STORY IDEAS

A $3.5 million damage award against the world's largest law firm for failing to protect a legal secretary from sexual harassment by a managing lawyer was upheld by the state appeals court. A succession of female employees complained to supervisors about the attorney's conduct, but virtually nothing was done about it. Besides the $3.5 million in punitive damages, the court upheld $225,000 in punitive damages against the attorney personally and $50,000 in damages for emotional distress. The secretary worked for the firm for three months, including one month for the attorney. After lunch he dumped M&M's in a breast pocket of her blouse, touched her breast through the blouse, pulled her arms back from behind and said, "Let's see which one is bigger." The attorney resigned from the firm several months later.

Wrongful Termination

Most employments are considered employments "at will," which means the employer can fire an employee without giving any reason, and the employee is free to quit without giving any reason. However, the employer is still subject to not discriminating against an employee and cannot fire an employee because of race, gender, age, national origin or sexual orientation. Union employees are usually covered by a collective bargaining agreement, and civil service employees are usually protected by laws that require "just cause" for firing. Also, many high-level management positions are governed by written employment contracts that specify the requirements for termination of employment.

Intellectual Property Law
Patent
A patent is a right granted by the U.S. Patent and Trademark Office (PTO) to an inventor for the exclusive right to make, use and sell his invention for a specified period of time (fourteen to twenty years depending on the type of invention).

STORY IDEAS

A federal court jury has awarded $903,000 to a black refinery worker who said his employer shredded his complaint of race discrimination and fired him in retaliation. The man was awarded $298,000 for lost wages, $105,000 for emotional distress and $500,000 in punitive damages. The man, a pipe-fitter mechanic, took supervisory classes but was not allowed to supervise company crews afterward, unlike white graduates of the classes. He said he was later denied an overtime request that was granted to white employees and was treated with hostility by supervisors when he complained. He said he was eventually fired in retaliation for his complaints about discrimination.

There are three types of patents: utility patents (which include a process, a machine, a manufacture, a composition of matter or an improvement of an existing idea already in one of these categories); design patents (innovative, nonfunctional but part of a functional article, e.g., a new shape for a perfume bottle); and plant patents (plants or flowers that are novel and non-obvious).

Patent infringement (violation of a patent right) usually results in the holder of the patent filing suit requesting a court order that the violation stop (an injunction) and that damages be awarded.

Inventions can be protected in other countries by filing applications with the PTO for foreign-patent rights.

Trade Secret

Trade secrets are information or know-how not generally known in the industry, that give the user an advantage over competitors. Trade secrets are protected from others improperly acquiring and using them as long as the owner was diligent in keeping the information secret.

The formula for the syrup used in Coca-Cola is a trade secret. It was never patented (which would have required its disclosure), and purportedly only five people in the world know its ingredients.

Trademarks

A trademark is a name, design, logo, slogan, symbol or other device used by a business to identify its products or services (sometimes called service marks) and distinguish them from others. There is no time limit on ownership of a trade-

As a strategy, many attorneys, when they file suit on behalf of a client, will include as many different "causes of action" as they can think of. The same act by a defendant may be considered a breach of an agreement, fraud, intentional infliction of emotional distress and negligent infliction of emotional distress. Suing on all four theories provides more weight to the lawsuit to scare or intimidate the other party and to use for negotiation purposes in settlement. This is the same strategy district attorneys use when they file multiple charges against a defendant, knowing they can bargain away some of the charges in exchange for a guilty plea on the remaining charges. In civil cases some defense attorneys will counter with a threat to file suit for malicious prosecution against the plaintiff and his attorney, alleging that there is no reasonable basis for suing for some or all of the causes of action. The plaintiff's attorney may have to reconsider the basis for each cause of action, and he may dismiss one or more to avoid the potential of being sued himself, or having his client sued for the improper actions of the attorney.

mark. Application is made to the Patent and Trademark Office for registration of a trademark or service mark. Improper use of a trademark can cause dilution of the value of the mark.

Speedshoes has trademarked its name and uses it on high-quality running shoes. Copy Corporation manufactures cheap shoes but puts the Speedshoe name on them. Runners buy the cheap imitations that fall apart, and they then think Speedshoe has downgraded their quality and runners stop purchasing the real Speedshoes. Speedshoe can file suit against Copy Corporation for trademark infringement, obtain an injunction requiring Copy Corporation to stop using Speedshoe's name on their cheap shoes, and obtain money damages for the loss of business resulting from Copy Corporation's trademark infringement.

Copyright

Copyrights protect all types of original creative expression, such as works produced by authors, artists, composers and designers. The creator has the sole right to publish and sell the work, usually for the life of the creator plus fifty years. The creator can grant or sell the rights to anyone else.

Commercial Law

Commercial law deals with the sale and lease of goods, promissory notes and checks, letters of credit, bulk transfers, transportation of goods, security interests in real estate, and stocks, bonds and securities. It provides rules and guidance for the smooth functioning of commerce.

Labor Law

Labor law, primarily contained in the National Labor Relations Act, regulates legal relationships between employers, employees and labor unions. Labor law guarantees employees the right to organize and form or join labor organizations to bargain collectively through representatives they select. Labor law usually comes into play when a union organizes employees and attempts to get the employer to recognize the union as the employees' bargaining representative. It also provides rules and guidelines for the negotiation of collective bargaining agreements with employers and the interpretation of bargaining contracts, workplace safety and compliance with government regulations.

Antitrust Law

To promote competition and production of goods at fair prices, federal and state law regulates businesses to prevent unlawful restraints of trade, price fixing and monopolies. The Sherman Anti-Trust Act and amendments, enforced by the Federal Trade Commission and the U.S. Department of Justice's Antitrust Division, investigates and prosecutes violations and can impose fines and prison terms.

Top executives from Fat-Cat Corporation and Big-Bucks Company meet and agree they will divide the market for their similar products so they do not compete with each other. They then both raise their prices by 20 percent since there is no competitor that manufactures their products. They have formed a cartel to restrict competition between them and violated the Sherman Anti-Trust Act. They are subject to fines and imprisonment.

Types of Damages

A person found liable for a tort or for breach of a contract is liable for the damages caused.

Nominal Damages

Nominal damages are awarded when a person wins his case by proving that the other party violated one or more of his rights, but the damages caused by the violation are minimal or nonexistent. Courts award nominal damages to reaffirm the person's legal rights.

Compensatory Damages

Compensatory damages are meant to compensate the injured person for the injury suffered by restoring her as much as possible to her former position (before the breach or wrong occurred) or giving her some monetary equivalent for the injury she suffered.

Liquidated Damages

Liquidated damages are often written into contracts. They are an amount that fairly estimates the damage each party would suffer if the contract were breached. They serve to let the parties know in advance what it will cost them and what they will receive if the other side breaches the agreement.

Consequential Damages

Consequential damages are the damages and losses suffered as a result of the wrongful act. If Joe runs into Mary with his car, he is responsible for Mary's injuries. Also, if Mary goes to the hospital and the doctor commits malpractice in treating her, Joe is also responsible for Mary's injuries from the doctor's malpractice because the courts have held that it is reasonably foreseeable that a person requiring medical attention after an accident may be further injured by a doctor's improper treatment.

Punitive Damages

Punitive damages are awarded to punish wrongful, fraudulent, intentional or malicious acts that cause damage to others. Where a defendant's conduct has been outrageous, punitive damages (also called exemplary damages) are meant to punish him and deter him and others from such conduct in the future.

STORY IDEAS

A couple's $145 million damage award against insurer State Farm was sliced to $25 million by a judge who castigated the company but said the jury's verdict was excessive. The punitive award plus $2.6 million in compensatory damages was won by the couple as a result of the company's failure to protect them after they were sued over a fatal car accident. They claimed the company's corporate policy was to cheat customers in order to pursue profits.

Costs

Usually the winning party in a lawsuit is entitled to have their costs paid by the losing party. Costs usually include court filing fees, witness fees, jury fees, reporters' fees for depositions, and sometimes the costs of expert witnesses.

Attorney Fees

Generally parties are not entitled to receive compensation for their attorney's fees. The exceptions are if a contract provides for payment of attorney fees by the losing party and if a law provides for attorney's fees in the specific type of case.

The big money for a plaintiff (and a plaintiff's attorney) is in punitive damages. Juries have returned verdicts in the hundreds of millions of dollars in punitive damages to punish large corporations for their intentional acts that injure people. Whenever the facts justify it, a plaintiff's attorney will allege wrongful, fraudulent, intentional or malicious acts by the defendant, justifying punitive damages. Also, when suing a defendant with no insurance coverage for his actions, most attorneys will try to allege fraud, because if a judge or jury decides the defendant acted fraudulently, the judgment cannot be discharged by the defendant by filing bankruptcy. That way, at least the plaintiff has a chance of collecting some of the judgment from assets owned by the defendant.

Debtor-Creditor

When someone becomes overindebted and is unable to pay their credit cards, medical bills, car or house payment, they will soon hear from a debt collector. It may be the collection department of the same company who extended the credit (the lender or creditor), or the lender may turn the bill over to a collection agency that specializes in collecting past-due debts. Late or nonpayment of debts is usually reported to a credit bureau that maintains records of people's payment history and supplies this information to other lenders checking on credit histories. Such information may remain on a credit report for up to seven years. Collection agencies are regulated by the Federal Fair Debt Collection Practices Act, which is enforced by the Federal Trade Commission. Most states have laws regulating collection practices by lenders and collection agencies. The collection agency may contact any person to locate the debtor, but they cannot tell the person the purpose of their call. Once located, the collection agency can contact the debtor during reasonable hours, usually after 8:00 A.M. and before 9:00 P.M.

If the debtor instructs the collection agency in writing to cease and desist from contacting the debtor, or to communicate with the debtor only in writing, the collection agency must follow the debtor's request. If an asset such as a car, house or merchandise secures the debt, the creditor can repossess those items. But in collecting a debt, the debt-collection agency cannot harass, oppress or abuse the debtor or any other person. If the debt remains unpaid the creditor or agency can file suit to obtain a judgment for the amount owed, plus attorney fees and costs, and proceed to collect the judgment by garnishing the debtor's wages or seizing bank accounts or other specified assets.

Some people seek bill consolidation loans to simplify monthly payments. Others live on or finance new business ventures on their credit cards. Some are successful, while others find they have used up all the credit on their cards by cash advances and cannot make the monthly payments, and they may then consider bankruptcy.

Bankruptcy

The most common type of bankruptcy is Chapter 7, or straight bankruptcy. Under this method, the creditor usually gets rid of the debts that are dischargable, e.g., most credit-card debt and medical bills. However, some debts may be nondischargable, e.g., some taxes, child support and alimony, certain student loans, debts incurred by fraud and debts or obligations incurred due to drunk driving. The debtor can keep certain specified assets, called exemptions, e.g., a certain amount of equity in a home and car, household items and tools of one's trade up to a certain value. If a debtor wants to keep an asset that he owes money on, he can "reaffirm" the debt, agreeing with the lender to continue to pay the debt in exchange for being able to keep the asset. If the debtor owns assets that are not exempt, the assets must be turned over to the bankruptcy trustee, who will sell the assets and apply the money to the debtor's debts. A record of the debtor filing bankruptcy is placed on the debtor's credit record for ten years, and many creditors will not extend credit for part or all of that period of time, or if they will, they will charge a higher interest rate.

The second most common type of bankruptcy is Chapter 13, also called "wage-earners" bankruptcy. Under this plan, the debtor who has a regular income agrees to make monthly payments for between three and five years and those payments are applied to his debts. The creditors may receive anywhere from a few percent up to 100 percent of what is owed to them. This plan is commonly utilized by debtors who own more assets than can be protected under

Chapter 7, because they get to keep all their assets, even nonexempt ones, or who have sufficient income to apply some of it to their debts after paying all their living expenses.

The other two common forms of bankruptcy are Chapter 11 bankruptcy, which is for businesses that are reorganizing, and Chapter 12 bankruptcy, for farmers experiencing economic difficulty. They agree to pay creditors from profits from future crops.

The moment a debtor files bankruptcy, an automatic stay is issued by the bankruptcy court, which orders all collection efforts to stop immediately.

Joe and Mary are overextended on their credit cards and they have some medical bills from Mary's illness. They cannot make their monthly payments. Collection agencies are calling and threatening to sue them and attach their wages. They file for Chapter 7 bankruptcy. All creditors must stop contacting them and stop all collection efforts. Joe and Mary agree to reaffirm the loan on their car and they continue that monthly payment and get to keep the car. All their other assets are exempt and, four months later, all their debts are discharged. They start fresh with no debts other than their car loan.

Real Property

Real property (also called real estate) law includes sales, exchanges, financing, development, zoning, construction, remodeling and foreclosure of real property. It also involves title insurance, property use and rights, building codes, easements, liens, water rights, methods of taking title, condemnation, nuisances and disputes between neighbors. The most common real-estate dispute is between landlords and tenants.

Landlord-Tenant

The landlord, usually the owner of the property, rents (usually a month-to-month agreement) or leases (usually an agreement for one or more years) the property to the tenant. The rental agreement (contract) may be oral (usually in month-to-month agreements) or written (usually required for agreements over a year). The landlord agrees to give the tenant use of the property and the tenant agrees to pay rent each month to the landlord. Disputes most commonly arise when the tenant gets behind on the rent or when the landlord refuses to maintain the property in reasonable condition and the tenant then withholds rent to try to force the landlord into maintaining the property. These disputes often lead to the landlord starting eviction proceedings to legally remove the tenant.

Eviction begins with the landlord giving the tenant notice to either pay the rent or move out. If the tenant does not pay or move out within a certain number of days (usually three), then the landlord files a lawsuit for eviction. If the tenant files an answer to the lawsuit, a judge decides the case. If the tenant does not file an answer, then the landlord can take the tenant's default. If the judge decides in the landlord's favor, a judgment for possession is entered and the sheriff will enforce it by moving the tenant out after a few days' notice. If the tenant wins at trial, he usually can remain on the premises and the judge orders correction of whatever triggered the suit, such as payment of rent and correction of defects on the premises.

Though many landlords would like to (and some still do), turning off the tenant's utilities or changing his locks prior to eviction is illegal. The landlord must go through the necessary legal steps to obtain a court order to remove the tenant. Otherwise the landlord can be subject to a lawsuit by the tenant.

Nuisance

Certain kinds of activities on one's land that interfere with other's enjoyment of their rights may amount to a nuisance. If the activity interferes with the rights of the general public, it is a public nuisance. If it interferes with the rights of a private individual such as a neighbor, it is a private nuisance. The government seeks to stop public nuisances, while the individual affected stops private nuisances. In deciding if a nuisance exists, the court balances the benefit of the activity with the harm it causes.

> **STORY IDEAS**
>
> *An engineering professor whose house and yard are packed with rotting food, newspapers, old cars and junked appliances was ordered to pay $146,000 to neighbors for the nuisance. The professor showed up to court five minutes after the court proceeding was over and demanded to be heard, but the judge ruled against her by default.*

Family Law
Premarital Agreement

A couple considering marriage can agree in writing prior to marriage what their rights will be in property owned prior to, during and after marriage, and what their obligations will be for spousal support during and after marriage. A valid premarital agreement (also known as a prenuptial agreement) requires that each party fully disclose their assets and debts to the other party prior to entering into the agreement. Agreements regarding child custody must be in the best interests of the child, and agreements regarding child support must be fair to the child.

Common-Law Marriage

If a couple has not been formally married, but agree to be husband and wife, live together as if they are husband and wife and represent themselves as husband and wife, about a quarter of the states recognize their relationship as a common-law marriage. Most other states will recognize the couple's common-law marriage if they met the requirements of a state that allows it, then move from that state to a state that does not have common-law marriage.

Dave and Linda lived together in Texas. They considered themselves husband and wife although they had neither obtained a marriage license nor had a wedding ceremony. They told everyone they were husband and wife and they filed joint tax returns as husband and wife. Texas recognizes common-law marriages and Dave and Linda would be considered husband and wife in Texas. They then moved to California, which does not allow common-law marriages. But California will consider Dave and Linda legally married, since they met the common-law marriage requirements of Texas before moving to California.

Marriage

Once a couple is married, whether by common law or formal ceremony, they are subject to state law regarding their property and their obligations to each other and their children. If they decide to end their marital relationship, they must do so according to the laws of the state where they divorce.

Annulment

If certain conditions exist at the time of marriage, then either or both spouses may obtain a court order annulling the marriage, which means the marriage never occurred. Annulments may be granted if one of the parties was underage, or already married and not divorced, or the marriage is between two people too closely related, or because either party cannot engage in sexual relations, or because of fraud by one party, such as not disclosing the only reason they are getting married is to obtain a green card. Most marriages, however, are not terminated by annulment. They are ended by divorce.

Divorce

Divorce, also called dissolution of marriage in some states, is a court decree that the marriage has ended. All states have no-fault divorces, which means neither spouse needs to prove it was the other's fault for the divorce, they need merely say that they had "irreconcilable differences" or a similar problem. Some states still retain fault (e.g., adultery, cruelty or desertion) as an alternative grounds for divorce, allowing parties to air their dirty laundry in court if they choose.

Divorce can be as simple as totaling up all the property, dividing it in half (in community-property states) and each party going their separate ways. But because of the emotional component of marriage, divorce can be as complicated as fighting over what each party contributed to the marriage, the value of businesses and property, the right to and amount of spousal support or child support, and the ever-popular who gets the kids. Though courts have progressed in removing or keeping in check the emotional component of divorce, angry or revenge-seeking spouses will find a place in the legal proceeding to ventilate their emotions.

Separation

A couple becomes separated when they no longer intend to live together as husband and wife. A legal separation is a court order declaring that the couple is separated, and the order usually provides for division of property, spousal and child support and child custody. Most people eventually amend their legal separation to a divorce.

Marital Property

Forty-one states and the District of Columbia are separate property states, and nine states are community-property states. Originally in separate-property states, which spouse got what on divorce depended on where the money to buy each asset came from. Everything each spouse earned or received (gifts or inheritance) during marriage was his or her separate property, and anything bought with those earnings was that spouse's separate property. If the family home was purchased and paid for with the husband's earnings, at divorce it was his. Strict application of the separate property law frequently led to unfair results, so the rule of "equitable distribution" was developed. Under this rule the judge considers the total assets of the couple, the length of their marriage and each party's contributions to the marriage. The judge then divides the property fairly. If a divorce was granted because of one spouse's fault, the judge could adjust the division of the marital assets as a form of punishment against the party at fault.

Joe engaged in repeated extramarital affairs and finally Sally filed for divorce, raising Joe's infidelity as the basis for the divorce. Because the divorce was considered Joe's fault, the judge awarded Sally 70 percent of the property and a significant amount of alimony.

In community-property states the earnings of each spouse during marriage are considered community property, and whatever is purchased with those earnings is considered community property. On divorce, each spouse receives an equal share of all community property.

Alimony

Alimony, also called separate maintenance or spousal support, is paid by one spouse, usually the higher income earner, to the other spouse for a period of time. It is usually based on the need of one spouse and the ability to pay of the other spouse and, depending on the length of the marriage, usually continues until the receiving spouse's earning ability increases to a certain level or that spouse remarries, lives with someone else or dies.

Julie and Bob were married twenty-six years. Julie works in a gift shop earning $6 an hour. Bob is in top management with a large corporation and earns $150,000 a year. Bob will pay alimony to Julie, probably for the rest of her life, unless she remarries or lives with a man who helps to support her.

Child Custody—Visitation—Support

Divorcing couples with children must make arrangements for the care and support of their minor children. They decide (stipulate), or the court orders, if they will share the care (joint custody) or one parent will primarily be responsible for the care (sole custody). The court looks to the "best interests of the child" in determining the custody arrangement, and the paramount best interest of the child is usually to have regular and frequent contact with both parents.

Although there is supposed to be no gender preference between parents, usually small children go with the mother. Custody has two components, legal custody and physical custody. Legal custody is who has the say over major decisions, e.g., health, education and religion. Physical custody is who has say over day-to-day activities.

S ome parents (usually the father) think that if they quit their job or take a lower paying job, they won't have to pay child or spousal support. Wrong! The courts, in such cases, will determine what the parent's earning capacity is, based on education and past earnings, and assign or impute that amount of earnings to the parent and order him to pay support as if he were earning that amount. It is then up to that parent to work or not, but if they do not pay the support ordered by the court they can be held in contempt and placed in jail as punishment for not paying.

The parent who does not assume the primary care of the child usually receives visitation with the child. The usual arrangement ordered by the court is every other weekend and one night during the week, and alternating holidays and two to six weeks in the summer. However, many couples are able to agree on their own visitation arrangement.

Most states have guidelines for determining child support based on the usual cost of raising a child. The income of the noncustodial parent (in some states) or the income of both parents (in other states) and the amount of time each parent spends with the child are considered in determining the support figure.

STORY IDEAS

Fifty-nine days in jail was enough for an accused deadbeat dad to see the error of his ways. After writing a repentant letter to the judge, he pleaded guilty to a felony charge of failing to pay more than $34,000 in support payments for his three children. "Being in jail is quite an experience," the man wrote to the judge. "If your intention was to punish me and teach me a lesson, you have certainly accomplished your goal. Never in my life have I associated with or met such people, and I certainly know how I don't want to spend my life." The judge released the man and delayed sentencing on the felony conviction to allow the man time to get a job and begin making payments to his ex-wife.

Adoption

Licensed private and state agencies assist couples in adopting children. In the case of a newborn, the agency may supervise the care of the biological mother and then place the baby with qualified parents. Some adoptions are handled privately, often through an attorney who specializes in arranging private adoptions. Biological mothers who want to give up their babies and prospective parents who want to adopt contact the attorney. He then matches babies with parents. Parents can pay for medical expenses and incidental costs, but they cannot legally pay specifically for the baby. If they did pay for the baby, it would be considered a black-market adoption, a crime. Upon adoption of a child, the legal rights and duties of the biological parents are terminated and new rights and duties are created for the adopting parents.

Paternity

Paternity is the determination of the biological father. Usually the mother knows exactly who the father is or has a good idea which of several men is the father. If she chooses to initiate a paternity action, she can file the necessary papers in court and the prospective father(s) have to submit blood for DNA comparisons with the mother's and child's. If testing determines a particular man is the father, he is obligated to support the child and he has parental rights of custody and visitation if he chooses to assert them.

Name Change

An individual can change his name by petitioning the court. Some states allow a person to change his name just by consistently using the new name. The purpose of a name change cannot be to defraud someone or escape obligations. Petitioning the court for a name change is more formal and the person receives a court order authorizing the change, which makes it easier to change one's name on legal documents, e.g., driver's licenses, passports and credit cards.

Freddy Flush, a convicted child molester, must register his residence address with the local police. He decides to change his name to Bobby Jones so he doesn't have to register. His name change is invalid since it is done to avoid a legal obligation.

STORY IDEAS

A man who has lived as a woman for twenty-two years but can't afford a sex-change operation won the right to legally change his name to Lisa. "As Tammy Wynette so aptly observed, sometimes it's hard to be a woman. This is especially true in this case," the judge wrote in his ruling allowing the name change to occur.

Estate Planning

Many people are uncomfortable acknowledging they will die, so they prefer not to plan for their own death. Less than one-half of all adults have a will. Those who do accept the inevitability of their death have a variety of estate-planning tools available.

Will

A will is, in almost all states, a written expression of the person's wishes of how his property will be dealt with upon his death (a few states recognize oral wills). Also, a guardian can be nominated in the will to take care of the decedent's minor children. Holographic wills are handwritten wills. Formal wills are typed or printed and signed by the party and witnesses. To execute a valid will, the person creating it (testator) must be competent, able to understand what he is doing, must intend the document to be his will, and the will must meet certain requirements, e.g., witnessed by two disinterested people.

Intestate

When a person dies without a will, their estate (property) is distributed intestate—according to the laws of the state. These laws usually provide that the person's property is divided between the spouse and children. If no spouse, then all the property goes to the children. If no children, then all goes to the spouse. If no children or spouse, then the property goes to the deceased's parents and siblings, and if none, then to more distant relatives. If the deceased had no relatives, then the state gets the property.

Probate

Probate is a court procedure where the executor or personal representative of the estate gathers the estate assets, inventories and values them, applies some to pay debts, taxes and the expenses of probate, and then distributes the remainder to the heirs specified in the will, or pursuant to state law if there is no will. If there is a will the court determines its validity. Some states have simplified probate procedures for estates under a certain value, typically $100,000.

Durable Power of Attorney

A durable power of attorney is a document where the person creating it, called the "principal," grants certain authority to another person, called "the agent" or "attorney in fact," to act on behalf of the principal. The power can be specific, to do a single act, or general, to do anything the principal can do. Durable powers of attorney remain valid even if the principal becomes mentally incapacitated. The durable power can become effective upon signing, or "spring" into effectiveness on the happening of a certain event, typically when the principal becomes incapacitated. Most powers provide that two doctors must determine incapacity. Durable powers can be for financial decisions or for health-care decisions.

Living Will

A living will is written instructions to any health-care provider stating what treatment individuals do or do not want if they are not able to express their preference at the time, usually because they are terminally ill or in a permanent coma. Many durable powers of attorney for health care include the information contained in a living will.

Conservatorships and Guardianships

A guardian (usually appointed for children) or conservator (usually appointed for adults) is someone who is appointed by the court to make personal and/or financial decisions on behalf of another person who the court determines is unable to make those decisions. The person appointed is usually a relative. The court usually requires an annual accounting of actions taken on behalf of the person. If the person does not think he needs a guardian or conservator, he can oppose the petition.

Trusts

A trust is a legal instrument used to hold and manage property. Property is transferred from personal ownership to ownership by the trust.

A living trust (also called "inter vivos trust") is an arrangement where a person transfers some or all of his property to the trust during his lifetime. The person creating the trust is called the trustor, grantor or settlor. The person who manages the property transferred to the trust is the trustee. The trust is for the benefit of one or more people, the beneficiaries. Typically the trustor and trustee are the same. The person transfers his property to his living trust, and he then manages the trust property for his own benefit during his lifetime. Upon his death, the successor trustee assumes management and usually transfers the property to the named beneficiaries, and the trust is terminated. If the trust is revocable, the trustor can cancel the trust at any time and transfer the property out of the trust back to himself. If the trust is irrevocable, the person who created it cannot remove the property from the trust.

Will Contests

Siblings unhappy with how their parents left their estates can challenge the will by filing suit and alleging that their parents didn't know what they were doing (lacked testamentary capacity), forgot to include them (mistake), were improperly influenced by someone else (undue influence) or whatever other grounds they can come up with to have the will declared invalid.

Taxation Law

People or businesses that want to organize their finances to minimize their local, state and federal tax liability usually consult with an attorney who specializes in tax law. Many of such attorneys are also CPAs or have master's degrees in taxation.

Environmental Law

Environmental law deals with the impact of man on his natural surroundings. Federal and state laws now regulate emissions into the air and water, hazardous waste, the wilderness and endangered wildlife. Because the government has limited resources to enforce these regulations, many public-interest law firms monitor and file suit to enforce the various laws and regulations meant to protect our environment.

STORY IDEAS

One of the country's largest mining companies has agreed to spend $50 million for environmental improvements and pay a $6 million fine to settle pollution charges concerning two facilities in Arizona and Montana, the Justice Department announced. The company agreed to clean up toxic contamination at the two sites and to establish a new pollution-management program at all thirty-eight of its facilities in seven states.

Immigration

Foreigners (called "aliens") who wish to immigrate to the United States usually first obtain an immigrant visa to legally enter the country. Some visas are subject to numerical limitations based on a certain number of citizens of each country or a certain category of immigrants being allowed into the U.S. each year. Visas not subject to numerical limitations are reserved for immediate relatives of U.S. citizens and certain other categories of applicants.

Once a resident alien, the individual can apply for citizenship through a process called "naturalization." They must meet certain requirements, including having resided continuously in the United States for five years as lawfully admitted permanent residents. Upon successful application, demonstration of good moral character and passing a literacy and education test, they can be granted citizenship after taking an oath of allegiance to the United States. An alien who becomes undesirable, e.g., by committing criminal offenses, can be deported from the U.S.

International Law

International law deals with the laws and courts of other countries and laws and treaties that govern trade and relations between nations.

Air and Space Law

Air and space law deals with international treaties governing activities in the air and outer space.

Administrative Law

Many activities in our daily lives are regulated by administrative agencies, e.g., driver's licenses, Social Security benefits and building permits. If a right granted by one of these agencies is either denied or revoked, there are administrative procedures for hearings and appeals, e.g., a hearing if a driver's license is suspended or Social Security benefits are denied.

Admiralty/Maritime Law

Admiralty and maritime law deal with the law of the sea and shipping.

Appellate Law

Appellate law deals with cases after trial, where one or both parties are unsatisfied with the outcome and therefore seek review by a higher court.

Insurance Law

Attorneys who represent insurance companies in the defense of claims against their insureds are often called insurance defense attorneys. Though they technically represent the person insured, the insurance company pays them. They only represent the insured up to the amount of liability insurance the insured carries. If the insured has $100,000 in automobile liability insurance but caused injuries and potential claims of $300,000, the insurance lawyers must notify the insured in writing that they only represent him up to the $100,000 in liability and that he should retain his own personal attorney to represent him for any claims in excess of the $100,000.

Outline of a Civil Trial

Seven weeks of jury trial after a year of preparation, and it all came down to what was written on that piece of paper.

"Will you please read the verdict, madam clerk," the judge said, observing courtroom etiquette. The clerk unfolded the paper.

Larry had schooled me ahead of time.

"No matter what the decision, don't let on any emotion. If you look happy, the defense attorneys will figure you would have been happy with less and they will file a motion for a new trial and try to bargain us down. If you look sad, you look like you failed and we don't want to convey that impression."

I sat stone-faced, having locked my emotions within, and held a pencil over a yellow legal pad to write down the verdict and help me stay focused.

"We the jury find for the plaintiff, in the amount of one million two hundred fifty thousand dollars."

We had won! Larry, an experienced trial lawyer, and myself, a new attorney fresh out of law school working on my first case. The two of us against three defense attorneys from the biggest insurance defense firm in the county, against three experienced trial attorneys and all their assistants, staff and money.

Larry had mortgaged his home to finance the case. I had tried the case alone for one week when Larry became ill. Our client had been living in a rundown apartment with his girlfriend taking care of him since the accident, hoping for the day he would receive some money to buy a better wheelchair, to have a kitchen with counters remodeled down to his chair level so he could prepare meals, hoping to be able to buy a modified van with a ramp and hand controls so he could drive himself around and not be dependent on others. But in my naiveté, I didn't realize that we and our client were still years away from seeing one cent of the jury's verdict.

—Reflections on my first jury trial—the author

You've read the headlines:
"Jury gives woman who spilled cup of coffee in her lap $2.86 million." "Public cries out for jury reform."

Newspapers want to sell their product so they print facts together in a way that is sensational and emotionally evocative. Seldom do they go into detail and explain how a jury of twelve average people reached their decision.

The reality is, in twenty-two years of trial work, I have never represented an injured person who would not, in a heartbeat, give back the money they received if they could be rid of the injury they suffered that got them the money.

Neck injuries, back injuries, scarred faces, burned bodies, lost eyes, nonfunctional limbs, brain damage and paraplegia. For most of us, our physical health and well being, the proper, pain-free functioning of our bodies is more precious than any amount of money.

Personal-injury cases, whether auto accidents, defective products or medical malpractice, involve great drama. A driver is not paying attention, a product fails, a doctor bungles an operation. In the blink of an eye lives are irreparably changed. A person is seriously injured or killed while another is wracked with guilt or defiant with denial. Personal-injury cases are civil cases involving tortious (wrongful or negligent) conduct by one or more individuals that causes injury to another person.

The following is based on my first jury trial. An older, experienced plaintiff's personal-injury attorney who represented a young man injured in a motorcycle accident had hired me to assist him with the biggest case of his career.

Facts of the Case

It was a spring Sunday morning. The foliage in the mountains was bursting forth new life as Joe Curley maneuvered his Honda 250 motorcycle along the curving tree-lined road on his way to his girlfriend's house. As he came around a gentle right-hand curve, he saw a logging truck ahead making a left turn onto the highway from a side road on the right. Joe let off on the accelerator and started

```
┌─────────────────────────────────────┐
│         CIVIL WRONG OCCURS          │
│   (TORT OR BREACH OF CONTRACT)      │
└─────────────────────────────────────┘

┌─────────────────────────────────────┐
│          INJURED PARTY              │
│       HIRES AN ATTORNEY             │
└─────────────────────────────────────┘

┌─────────────────────────────────────┐
│            ATTORNEY                 │
│      INVESTIGATES FACTS             │
└─────────────────────────────────────┘

┌─────────────────────────────────────┐
│   ATTORNEY ATTEMPTS TO SETTLE       │
│   CASE WITH DEFENDANT OR            │
│      INSURANCE COMPANY              │
└─────────────────────────────────────┘

┌─────────────────────────────────────┐
│  IF NO SETTLEMENT, ATTORNEY         │
│   FILES & SERVES COMPLAINT          │
└─────────────────────────────────────┘

┌─────────────────────────────────────┐
│           DEFENDANT                 │
│         FILES ANSWER                │
└─────────────────────────────────────┘

┌─────────────────────────────────────┐
│           DISCOVERY                 │
│   (EXCHANGE OF INFORMATION)         │
└─────────────────────────────────────┘

┌─────────────────────────────────────┐
│     CASE SET FOR TRIAL OR           │
│         ALTERNATIVE                 │
│      DISPUTE RESOLUTION             │
└─────────────────────────────────────┘

┌─────────────────────────────────────┐
│   IF NOT RESOLVED BY ADR            │
│           SET FOR                   │
│    SETTLEMENT CONFERENCE            │
└─────────────────────────────────────┘

┌─────────────────────────────────────┐
│        IF NOT SETTLED               │
│        GOES TO TRIAL                │
└─────────────────────────────────────┘

┌─────────────────────────────────────┐
│         VERDICT OF                  │
│       COURT OR JURY                 │
└─────────────────────────────────────┘

┌─────────────────────────────────────┐
│          JUDGMENT                   │
│      ENTERED BY COURT               │
└─────────────────────────────────────┘

┌─────────────────────────────────────┐
│            APPEAL                   │
└─────────────────────────────────────┘
```

Civic Case—Sequence of Events

210

to feather his foot brake to slow and pass behind the truck as it completed its turn and cleared the roadway. Joe was wearing a motorcycle helmet and was known as a careful driver. The tail of the truck cleared the right lane ahead and Joe proceeded toward the open road, intending to pass by the truck. Suddenly the truck stopped and started backing up, blocking the open roadway that existed a moment before. Joe applied his foot and hand brakes fully as he had learned in a motorcycle safety class and the bike started to skid but remained on a straight path. Joe realized he was going to run into the side of the truck, and he bent his head down so the helmet would protect his head. His front wheel struck the left rear tire of the truck and Joe flew forward, striking his head on the bottom log on the bed of the truck. His body landed next to his bike against the rear tire. Joe was unconscious for fifteen minutes. When he came to, fire personnel were strapping him onto a backboard and bracing his head with a cervical collar and head blocks. Joe had no feeling in his body below his chest.

Joe's dad knew attorney Larry Burke because Larry had represented him in a minor fender bender five years before. He called Larry and arranged for Larry to meet Joe at the spinal care unit of the local regional hospital.

Evaluating the Client

The moment he meets a potential client the attorney is evaluating him for the impression he will make on a jury. Larry liked Joe immediately. Joe was a tall, good-looking young man with a healthy outlook on life even as he was coming to terms with having a severed spinal cord and never being able to walk again. Larry felt that a jury would like him too, and would want to help him if the facts and law allowed.

Evaluating the Case

Investigation

After visiting Joe in the hospital, Larry met with Tom Redding, a private investigator who had helped him on previous cases, and together they visited the accident scene. There was still debris from the motorcycle lying on the side of the road. They gathered this up and placed it in a large box and marked it with the date, time and location. They took a series of still photographs as the accident scene would look from Joe's point of view as he rounded the corner and approached the side road from where the truck had been entering the highway. They located the motorcycle at a towing yard and photographed it. Tom went to the highway patrol office and obtained a copy of the accident report, and then interviewed the officer who prepared the report. He also obtained a copy of the ambulance records.

With this initial information Larry evaluated how the facts supported the three elements of a personal-injury case.

1. Negligence

There must be a basis to find that the defendant was negligent, which means he did not act as a reasonable person under the circumstances. Larry knew that some trucking companies used "spotters," individuals sent down the highway a distance to warn oncoming traffic that a truck is crossing the highway. Since the logging company had not used a spotter the morning of Joe's accident, he felt this made them negligent. Larry also felt that Joe did what the average person would have done in the situation. He assumed the truck crossing the highway was going to continue forward and make room for him to proceed behind. He never expected the truck to stop and back up across the highway.

2. Causation

The negligent act of the defendant must have caused the injury to the plaintiff. Causation was clear in Joe's case. The trucking company's failure to warn Joe of the crossing truck caused him to continue forward and run into the side of the truck.

3. Damages

The plaintiff must have suffered damages that were caused by the negligence of the defendant. Joe had clearly suffered damages, including medical bills, loss of income, pain and suffering, and future medical expenses and loss of earning capacity.

Attorney Fees

Most attorneys take personal-injury cases on a contingency fee. If they succeed in recovering money for their client, then they receive a percentage, usually one-third or 40 percent. If they are unsuccessful, they receive nothing for their time and effort. Larry agreed to represent Joe and advance all the expenses of the case and in return, if they won, Larry would be reimbursed for his expenses, then receive one-third of the balance if the case was settled without trial, or 40 percent if the case went to trial.

Managing the Case

Once an attorney assumes representation of a client, he wants to be in control of all information that goes to the defendant or the defendant's insurance company. Larry sent a letter to the logging company putting them on notice that he was representing Joe in this accident and to direct all further communications and correspondence to him and to refer the letter to the logging company's insurance company.

The attorney wants to make sure his client gets the treatment needed from competent doctors. Most attorneys suggest the clients see their family doctor and let the family doctor make any necessary referrals to specialists. Some attorneys know reliable doctors and will refer clients to them. Some crooked attorneys know crooked doctors who will provide unnecessary treatment to inflate medical bills.

Some attorneys tell their clients to go about their lives as if there were no lawsuit and no possibility of obtaining money for their injuries. They want their clients to get back to work as soon as possible, knowing this will make the most favorable impression on a jury.

Larry encouraged Joe to work hard in physical therapy and rehabilitation and to eventually seek whatever employment was available.

Settlement Efforts With an Insurance Company

The full value of a case cannot be determined until the plaintiff has either recovered from his injuries or his condition is stable enough to evaluate. Then a settlement demand is presented to the insurance company. The demand includes a summary of the facts and law showing why the insured is liable, and presents documentation of the plaintiff's injuries and damages, including medical records, reports, bills, lost wages and pain and suffering. The settlement figure is based on what the attorney would expect a jury to award if the case went to trial.

Larry had some initial correspondence with the logging company's insurance carrier, but the insurance company was taking the position that the accident was all Joe's fault. They said that, based on their investigation, if Joe had been driving within the speed limit and watching for traffic ahead, he had sufficient time to stop before reaching the truck. Larry knew this case would have to go to trial.

Litigation

Depending on the state, a personal-injury lawsuit has to be filed within one or two years from the accident date. Because of the attitude of the insurance com-

M any people think that if they refuse to accept the summons and complaint, or don't touch it, or don't answer the door when the process server shows up, or keep moving and staying one step ahead of the process server, they can avoid being served and thus won't have to deal with a lawsuit. All of these tactics have been tried many times in the past, and states have alternative methods of serving refusing or absent defendants.

If someone won't answer the door, the summons and complaint can be left at the front door, sometimes tacked to the door, followed by the mailing of a copy to the address. That is effective service.

If someone refuses to accept or avoids touching the summons and complaint when the process server confronts them, the documents can be dropped at their feet and that is effective service.

If someone keeps moving, trying to stay one address ahead of the process server, the summons and complaint can be mailed to their last known address and published in the local newspaper four weeks in a row, and that is effective service.

Once served the defendant usually has twenty or thirty days to file a response, usually an answer, to the complaint. If the defendant does not file an answer or other response within the required time period, his default is taken and the plaintiff receives whatever he requested in his complaint. Defendants who have insurance inevitably send the summons and complaint to their insurance carrier, who hires insurance defense attorneys to file the appropriate response. Although outwardly these attorneys are representing the defendant, they really are representing the insurance company, since it's the insurance company that pays their fee and that will pay the settlement or verdict.

When an insurance defense firm is hired the attorney assigned to the case prepares an "initial case analysis" (ICA). The ICA contains a summary of the facts, a legal opinion on liability, evaluation of the damages, a recommendation concerning future discovery and a recommendation for alternative dispute resolution (ADR). It also has an evaluation of the opposing counsel, recommended further investigation by the insurance company and how soon the case could be either settled or taken to trial.

The insurance company for the logging company hired a defense firm with sixty-four lawyers. They immediately assigned three attorneys to the case. They filed an answer denying any liability and commenced discovery.

pany, Larry filed suit six months after the accident. He had the summons and complaint served on the logging company.

Discovery

The attorneys on each side of a case want as much information as possible about the other side's client, witnesses, evidence and contentions. The defense attorney wants details about the plaintiff's background, injuries, treatment, loss of wages, employment history and version of the accident. The plaintiff's attorney wants information about the defendant's background, version of the accident, witnesses and other evidence. The rules of civil procedure provide four primary methods of discovery:

Interrogatories: Written questions prepared by one side that the other side must answer under oath.

Request for Production of Documents and Things: In our case the defense wanted to inspect our client's motorcycle. We had to make it available at a specified time and location for the defense attorneys and their experts to inspect it.

Depositions: In-person testimony, under oath, usually held at the requesting attorney's office with the other attorney present. The party or witness being deposed must answer questions about the accident, injuries and any other information that may lead to evidence admissible at trial. The questions and answers are recorded by a court reporter who types them into a deposition booklet, which is available, for a fee, to each attorney. Some depositions are now being recorded on videotape, especially if the witness may not be present at the trial.

Subpoenaing of Records: A subpoena (court order) is served on the custodian of records, such as the treating doctor or employer, to make the records available for copying.

The defense attorneys in Joe's case took the depositions of everyone from the ambulance driver and paramedic who responded to the accident scene, to the emergency room doctor and nurses, all of Joe's treating doctors, Joe's former employers and two of his co-workers, and Joe's girlfriend and parents.

We took the depositions of the truck driver, his supervisor, two other truck drivers and the owner of the property the truck was exiting from when the accident occurred.

Law and Motion

The inevitable disagreements between plaintiff and defense counsel over what questions are proper, what documents must be turned over and what records are subject to subpoena are resolved by the judge hearing the law-and-motion calendar.

The defense attorneys wanted details about Joe's sex life prior to the accident, since we were claiming that his inability to engage in sexual relations was part of the damages. We refused to answer interrogatories that asked for intimate details. The defense attorneys filed a motion requiring us to answer, we filed opposing papers and we all appeared in law and motion and argued our positions.

The judge provided guidelines on what had to be disclosed, specifically, frequency but not partner's names.

It can be quite entertaining to sit in a session of law and motion and listen to the points argued and watch the various personalities of the attorneys and judge. Call your local court and ask the civil clerk when civil law-and-motion matters are heard. (Most courts hear these matters at 9:30 A.M. on Fridays.)

Alternative Dispute Resolution

We completed discovery and were ready to prepare our case for trial. In many states and jurisdictions, there is such a backlog of cases that the courts encourage or require alternative dispute resolution (ADR), either mediation or arbitration. It was not a requirement in our county so our case proceeded toward trial.

Jury Trial vs. Bench Trial

Although trial by jury is a right in many cases, it is not required. The parties can either "elect" to have a jury or "waive" the jury. Bench trials are usually quicker since there is no time spent on jury selection or deliberations. We definitely wanted a jury trial, feeling they would be sympathetic to Joe and his injuries.

Preparing for Trial

The court notified us of our trial date four months in advance. My task was to prepare written summaries of each deposition. We would use the summaries to prepare questions for witnesses and to determine if their trial testimony was consistent with their testimony at their depositions.

Larry developed the overall strategy for presenting the case. He wanted Joe to be the young, healthy, all-American kid who was just at the beginning of his life when he was injured because the logging company couldn't take ten minutes to have a spotter walk down the road and warn oncoming traffic about the exiting truck. The witness who would help us the most was the logging truck driver. At his deposition he came across as angry and defensive. He kept his arms crossed, answered our questions in an abrasive manner and looked at us with contempt. He displayed no remorse about the accident or Joe's injuries. We hoped he would do the same at trial, for no jury could like this guy.

Focus Groups and Mock Trials

It's easy to talk yourself into what a great case you have. To obtain some objectivity, most attorneys discuss their cases with their spouses, friends, colleagues and almost anyone who will listen. They watch for reactions and elicit questions to gain another perspective on the facts, knowing that a jury may have similar thoughts. Because ours was a significant case, we had a marketing firm locate and hire six individuals who were representative of our potential jury. We spent two days presenting an abbreviated version of our case, with testimony from Joe and several other witnesses, reading parts of the deposition of the truck driver, and Larry's closing argument. The people hired, called a mock jury or focus group, then deliberated just like a jury, except their deliberations were video-taped so we could study their thoughts and reactions to our case. Although we had shown the mock jury an aerial photograph of the accident scene and a drawing of the highway done by a graphic artist we had hired, the jury did not have a good sense of how the roadway looked to Joe. We decided that we needed the real jury to visit the accident scene to see for themselves the road, curve and logging truck driveway to appreciate distances and what Joe saw on the day of the accident.

Organizing Trial Materials

Orchestrating and conducting a trial properly requires a great degree of organization. Some attorneys have trial assistants or paralegals whose only function is to keep all materials organized, indexed and readily accessible. Computers are used by some to store and quickly access materials. We had seven boxes of materials, including depositions, medical records, our notes, pleadings and discovery documents. Larry prepared a trial notebook containing his overall plan for the case and summaries of materials. Since he would be conducting all the questioning of witnesses, I organized the exhibits, depositions, records and other materials so I could hand them to him as he needed them.

Trial Brief

A trial brief summarizes the facts of the case, the applicable law and the points of contention between the parties. It is the attorney's first chance to inform and gain the support of the judge for his client's case. We kept our brief to three pages, knowing that busy judges often are unable to read long legal documents. The defense attorneys submitted a twenty-eight-page brief. We knew they were getting paid by the hour.

Trial Subpoenas

As the trial day approached, I prepared subpoenas for our witnesses. A subpoena is a court order to appear at a certain date, time and courtroom to be available to testify in a particular case. A subpoena duces tecum requires the witness to bring requested records, books, documents or other items stated in the attachment to the subpoena.

Although some of our witnesses would have voluntarily come to trial on the date and time we requested, most experienced trial lawyers subpoena all witnesses, even friendly ones, and even their own experts. Once subpoenaed, if a witness fails to appear the attorney can ask for a continuance and the judge should allow it. Also, subpoenaing all witnesses makes it more difficult for the opposing attorney to suggest bias of a witness who comes in voluntarily to help your case.

Preparing the Client to Testify at Trial

Usually in a civil case your client is the most important witness. In preparing a client to testify, you have to analyze his personality and have him make adjustments where necessary. The toughest witness I ever had to prepare was a client involved in an auto accident. He was twenty-two years old. He had been abused and beaten by his father as a child. He was a former drug addict. He was tough and articulate. He watched me like a hawk. The feeling I got was that if I made any mistake, he would leap across the desk and choke me to death. He also was eager to get money for his injuries. I dreaded the impression he would make on the attorney for the insurance company. I imagined him getting into a verbal and possibly physical battle with the attorney. But I thought of an approach that turned my client's attitude around. In preparing him to testify, I told him that the other attorney was the one who would write the settlement check. And the more he liked my client, the bigger the check would be. This got through to him. He laughed, his mood lightened. As we practiced for his cross-examination he started saying; "Yes, sir" and "No, sir." He smiled. It worked. The opposing attorney commented to me after the trial what a friendly, reasonable person my client was. If he only knew.

Direct Examination

On direct examination you are asking the questions, so you want the witness to give information to help prove the case. Your questions only serve to help the witness tell his story. We practiced with Joe, asking him open-ended questions such as Where were you going? What were you going to do there? How fast were you driving? What did you see? What did the truck do? What did you do? We wanted him telling his story in logical, sequential order that could be easily understood by the jury.

Cross-Examination

In preparing a client to be cross-examined by the opposing attorney, you want him providing as little information as possible in response to the opposing attorney's questions. To prepare Joe, we told him the following:

"You want to listen carefully to the question. If you don't understand the question or any word in the question, say so and the attorney has to rephrase the question. The attorney has to ask a clear question that you understand before you have to answer."

"If you understand the question, then pause a moment to prepare your answer."

(You emphasize the importance of the pause because you don't want your client to get swept up into a rapid dialogue with the other attorney, where they may blurt out something unexpected or get emotionally stirred up and become antagonistic or defensive.)

"The best answers are the shortest answers, and the two shortest answers are 'yes' and 'no.' If you can answer the question with a yes or no, do so and stop. Let the attorney ask you another question."

"The other two good answers are 'I don't know' and 'I don't remember.' The difference between the two is that 'I don't know' means you never knew at any time, like, what is my mother's maiden name? You don't know, so that's your answer. 'I don't remember' means you knew at one time but you don't remember today. An example is: 'What was your first grade teacher's name?' You knew at one time but you just don't remember today."

"It's OK not to know or not to remember. Don't feel like you have to have an answer to every question, because if you do, the other attorney will ask you questions he knows you could not know the answer to just so you will make something up. Then he'll show you couldn't know, and that maybe you're making up the rest of your answers too."

"Most questions require more than a 'yes' or 'no' answer. They require you to give some information. For those questions, listen carefully for what information is requested, give only that information and stop. Don't volunteer any additional information. If you do, you're providing information the attorney did not ask for, giving him ideas for more questions and helping him."

"Some questions call for answers about time, speed and distances. Unless you had a stopwatch, a speedometer that you were watching without interruption and a tape measure, you probably won't have exact answers to these questions. So make sure you don't give exact answers. If you do, the other attorney will have an accident reconstructionist plug your answers into a formula and inevitably they will have you traveling way over the speed limit when the accident happened. So always approximate, estimate, say 'somewhere around,' leave yourself some leeway in your answer. Give a range, but avoid exact numbers unless you're absolutely certain."

"If during your testimony you realize you made a mistake, stop and correct yourself."

"Look at the attorney asking you questions when you answer. Don't look at your own attorney because it may look to the jury like you are being coached."

"If an objection is made to a question, don't answer. Stop and wait for the judge to make a ruling whether the question is proper or not and whether or not you can answer."

"Do not become hostile, defensive or antagonistic with the other attorney. Remain calm and pleasant. Don't try to match wits with him—he has a lot more practice at it than you do."

"Don't adjust your answers so they make a more favorable impact on the jury. Just give the facts. It's up to me, as your attorney, to take the facts and create the most favorable picture for your case. Leave the advocacy to the attorneys."

We had Joe study the questions and answers from his deposition. If he answered a question at trial differently than he answered in his deposition, the defense attorney would impeach him with the inconsistencies in his own testimony, which would undermine his credibility on all his other testimony.

We practiced the questions we expected the defense attorneys to ask. We acted the way we expected the defense attorneys to act, e.g., abrasive, condescending, caring, angry, so that Joe could experience and practice his response to this behavior prior to the real thing.

The week before trial we took Joe shopping and helped him pick out a dark gray suit, white shirt and dark blue tie. He looked conservative, clean and believable. We were almost ready.

Settlement Conference

Courts schedule a settlement conference one to two weeks prior to the trial date in an effort to settle the case and avoid the time and expense of trial. By then all parties and their attorneys usually have evaluated the strengths and weaknesses of their cases and, hopefully, become realistic about the probable outcome at trial.

The attorneys and insurance adjuster (the person with the money) usually meet with the judge in his chambers and discuss the case in general. Then one side goes outside and the judge speaks confidentially with the other side to see what their bottom line is. He then does the same with the other side and determines how close they are. He may continue to work back and forth trying to bring the parties together in a settlement.

Larry sent me to the settlement conference. He didn't think the defense's settlement offer would even be close to what he thought the case was worth. He was right. The defense "indicated" they "may" be able to get $500,000 to settle the case. Since we were looking for twice that amount, the case did not settle and we continued our preparation for trial.

Trial Day

Finally the day set for trial arrived. Larry had so much anxiety built up that he couldn't sleep the night before. He finally got up at 4 A.M. to review his notes one last time.

Larry and I reported with Joe to the presiding judge's department at 8:30 A.M. The other attorneys were already sitting in the courtroom. As often happens, the presiding judge sent us to an available judge for one last settlement effort. The court's file, which contained the complaint, answer, all other pleadings filed by each side, rulings on law-and-motion matters and the minute order showing the results of the previous settlement conference, was handed by the presiding judge's clerk to Larry and we carried it to the courtroom where the case was sent.

We met in chambers with the settlement judge. He listened to each side's version of the case and asked where we were in settlement efforts. We said we would take $1.5 million. The defense said they would pay $500,000, maybe a little more. The judge said it didn't look like a settleable case and he sent us back to the presiding judge. The PJ then sent us to Judge Conners' department for trial.

Assignment to a Trial Judge

You usually take the luck of the draw in assignment to a particular judge for trial. I have heard stories of attorneys who routinely bribe calendar clerks with generous Christmas gifts, and in exchange their cases are assigned to their favorite trial judge.

Even in a jury trial it helps to know the judge's background and biases to decide whether or not to "paper" the judge. Each side is usually entitled to one peremptory (no reason need be given) challenge of a judge. "Papering" the judge means you have a boilerplate pleading entitled "Peremptory Challenge of Judge" and you just fill in this particular judge's name. Some courts do not even require a written challenge—the attorney can just tell the presiding judge he exercises his peremptory challenge, and the presiding judge will assign the case to another judge. You can also challenge a judge for cause if you think he cannot be fair and impartial by explaining the basis for your belief.

Information about judges and their backgrounds is available from publishing companies in some states, and information about their biases can usually be obtained from other attorneys who know the judges personally or have tried cases in front of them.

Judge Conners was a new judge, a political appointment from a local law firm. He seemed like a lightweight, which meant the attorneys would run things in the courtroom and he would not. Larry and I decided he would be fine since he had no apparent previous dealings with the defense attorneys or their firm.

Pretrial Conference in Chambers

Prior to the attorneys walking into his courtroom with the file, the trial judge generally knows nothing about the case. He usually has the attorneys come into his chambers to meet them informally and to have them familiarize him with the case. It's also a chance for the judge to tell the attorneys how he runs his courtroom.

Judge Conners told us court would start each morning at 9:00 A.M. We would take a fifteen-minute recess about 10:30, resume until noon, break for lunch for one and a half hours, resume at 1:30, take another break at around 3:00 and finish each day at 4:30. He wanted us to meet with his clerk each morning before the trial resumed to mark any exhibits we intended to use that day. (Traditionally the plaintiff's exhibits are marked in sequence with Arabic numbers, 1, 2, 3, 4, etc., and the defendant's exhibits are marked with letters of the alphabet from A to Z followed by AA to ZZ.) At the end of each day he wanted us to disclose to the other side the witnesses we would be calling the next day so the other side could be prepared for cross-examination.

Motion In Limine

In pretrial discovery the defense had obtained information from an acquaintance of Joe's that he had seen Joe smoke marijuana about two years prior to the accident. There was no evidence that he had smoked marijuana near the time of the accident. To avoid the possible prejudicial effect of the defense bringing out this remote evidence, we made a Motion in Limine.

"In Limine" (pronounced in Lim-in-e) is Latin for "at the very start." These motions are used to obtain rulings on evidentiary issues usually before the trial begins. There's a popular saying in the law, which is: "You can't un-ring a bell." That means that once an attorney or witness has said something in front of a jury, it's very hard to get the jury to pretend they never heard it. So we requested an order that the defense could not bring out this information because its prejudicial effect far outweighed any value it had. The judge agreed and granted our motion.

If the defense had violated the judge's order excluding this evidence (they didn't), they would be subject to contempt and sanctions and their conduct could serve as the basis for a mistrial if sufficient prejudice had occurred.

The defense requested that all witnesses be excluded from the courtroom until they were called to testify, a fairly routine request to prevent witnesses from listening to each other and, consciously or unconsciously, adjusting their testimony to be consistent with the other witnesses' testimony.

Courtroom Etiquette

Awareness and observation of courtroom etiquette is important to show respect for the judge (the courtroom is his domain, and some judges are more possessive and controlling about their territory than others) and to avoid a severe rebuke in front of the jury for a violation. If unfamiliar with a particular judge's courtroom rules, most attorneys will learn about them from other attorneys who have tried cases in front of the judge, from the judge's clerk or from the judge directly during one of the conferences in chambers. Following are some judges' rules I have come across over the years:

1. The attorneys must ask for permission before they walk up close to a witness, usually to hand them an exhibit.

"May I approach the witness, your Honor" is a common and proper request. Some judges don't require that request, finding it wasteful of time.

2. The area of the courtroom between the judge's bench and counsel's table is known as the "well." Many judges do not want attorneys to walk in the well. Instead, the attorneys are to walk around behind the counsel tables.

3. Some judges have rules regarding putting briefcases on the tables—they want them only on the floor.

4. Some judges, particularly in federal court, require attorneys to stand at a podium for their questioning of witnesses and not walk around the courtroom.

5. Attorneys are officers of the court and they must maintain respect for the court and legal system. They cannot mislead the court on the law or facts. They generally cannot communicate with the judge during a trial unless the opposing attorney is present.

A breach of any of these rules by an attorney can constitute misconduct. The judge usually will admonish the jury to disregard the misconduct. If the misconduct is serious, the judge may cite the attorney for contempt, impose sanctions, declare a mistrial and refer the matter to the state bar for further disciplinary action.

The judge's conduct is also regulated by various rules usually contained in state law. They too must be courteous to the attorneys, parties, witnesses and jurors. They must be open-minded and impartial.

Attorneys must object to judges' misconduct when it occurs; otherwise the conduct is considered waived and cannot be considered on appeal.

"Your Honor, I respectfully object to your Honor's remarks and assign them as error, ask that the remarks be stricken from the record and that the jury be admonished to disregard your Honor's remarks."

If the judge's misconduct is prejudicial and cannot be cured by an admonition, the attorney can move for a mistrial.

Judges too can be sanctioned by their regulatory body, and even removed from the bench for severe misconduct.

Judge Conners was quite relaxed about procedures in the courtroom, which allowed the attorneys to exhibit their own style throughout the case. He was courteous, as were all the attorneys, which allowed us and the jury to focus on the facts of the case.

Jury Selection

The selection of jurors can be the most decisive part of the trial. Contrary to the ideal and popular myth of blind justice, justice is decided by a judge or a jury, individuals with their own backgrounds, ideas and biases. One juror can sway a jury or undermine the jury's work. One juror can result in a hung jury. Two or three jurors who are outspoken and forceful can convince the remaining jurors and thus determine the outcome of the case. In most states, a civil jury is composed of twelve jurors, and agreement by nine or ten decides the case (unlike a criminal trial, which requires a unanimous decision). In some civil cases, especially in federal court, six- and eight-person juries are common.

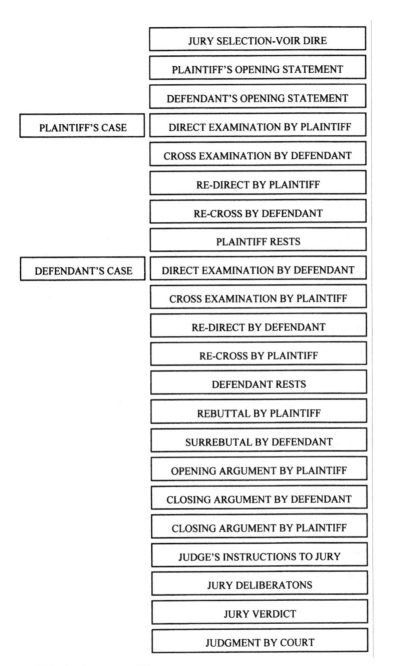

JURY SELECTION-VOIR DIRE

PLAINTIFF'S OPENING STATEMENT

DEFENDANT'S OPENING STATEMENT

PLAINTIFF'S CASE — DIRECT EXAMINATION BY PLAINTIFF

CROSS EXAMINATION BY DEFENDANT

RE-DIRECT BY PLAINTIFF

RE-CROSS BY DEFENDANT

PLAINTIFF RESTS

DEFENDANT'S CASE — DIRECT EXAMINATION BY DEFENDANT

CROSS EXAMINATION BY PLAINTIFF

RE-DIRECT BY DEFENDANT

RE-CROSS BY PLAINTIFF

DEFENDANT RESTS

REBUTTAL BY PLAINTIFF

SURREBUTAL BY DEFENDANT

OPENING ARGUMENT BY PLAINTIFF

CLOSING ARGUMENT BY DEFENDANT

CLOSING ARGUMENT BY PLAINTIFF

JUDGE'S INSTRUCTIONS TO JURY

JURY DELIBERATONS

JURY VERDICT

JUDGMENT BY COURT

Civil Trial—Sequence of Events

Jury Panel

We took our seats at our respective tables. By tradition, the plaintiff's attorneys sit at the table closest to the jury box and the defense attorneys sit at the table furthest away from the jury. We all wanted to be organized and settled before the judge's clerk called the jury commissioner to request a jury panel be sent to the courtroom. First impressions are important and attorneys generally like to look competent.

Our jury panel consisted of forty potential jurors. They each handed their juror card with their name to the bailiff and then took a seat in the back of the courtroom. When they were settled the bailiff told them there would be no eating, drinking, talking or gum chewing in the courtroom, and he then called court to order and Judge Conners took the bench. He introduced himself and thanked them for coming and fulfilling their civic duty. He told them they would be asked a number of questions, not meant to upset them or invade their privacy, but asked to help the attorneys select an impartial jury. He asked the clerk to give them the oath.

"Do each and every one of you agree to answer the questions asked of you honestly and fully to the best of your ability?" and the jurors in unison answered, "I do."

The judge read a short summary of the case prepared by the attorneys, stated the names of the attorneys and parties, read a list of witnesses and told the jurors the case was expected to last seven weeks. He then had the clerk, who had placed the jurors' name cards in a container (much like the device that holds bingo numbers) rotate the container and pick cards and call jurors. As each name was called, the juror came forward and sat in the jury box, until all twelve seats were occupied. I wrote down each juror's name on my jury chart. We sized up each juror, looking at their clothing and jewelry, reading material, walking and talking style. We watched for aggressive or opinionated jurors who might dominate or antagonize the other jurors. We watched for jurors with leadership abilities who might unduly influence the jury. We watched for jurors with expertise in an area of the case, such as the operation of motorcycles or large trucks.

Although we choose not to do it, primarily because of the cost, some attorneys will have investigators do a background check on each juror, obtaining lists of assets and debts, credit records and any criminal records.

We had our preference in jurors. Generally jurors who favor the plaintiff in personal-injury cases are in the helping professions such as teachers, psychologists, psychiatrists and nurses. Jurors who favor the defense are usually owners of businesses, managers and accountants. Race could also be a factor, for Black and Hispanic jurors tend to be plaintiff-oriented, Oriental jurors tend to be defense-oriented. The younger generation tend to be more plaintiff-oriented, and the older generation tend to be more defense-oriented.

Voir Dire

The plaintiff and defendant have a right to trial by an impartial jury. The only way to determine if a potential juror has a bias or prejudice that would prevent him from being fair is to ask him. Of course, most people will not come right out and say they are biased. The truth is, few of us think we are. So it's the attorney's job to ask questions about the juror's background, beliefs and life experiences and from her answers determine if the juror can be fair and impartial, or better yet, be partial in favor of your client.

Further, by asking questions that reflect the facts, theories and approaches of the case, the attorneys hope to precondition the jury to decide in their client's favor. For example, in our case, we asked the jurors if they would have any difficulty awarding a significant sum of money to the plaintiff if the law and facts supported such an award. This let the jury know that we were looking for a large sum of money, and it got them thinking in those terms.

There is certain information that a plaintiff's attorney would love to put in front of the jury, the primary one being that the defendant has liability insurance that will pay what the jury awards. However, it is misconduct and possibly reversible error to ask jurors questions about insurance or to indicate that the defendant is insured. The truth is that most people on a jury know that most defendants are insured and that an insurance company will end up paying the verdict.

Some courts (particularly federal courts) require the attorneys to submit to the judge all questions they want asked of the potential jurors, and the judge does the questioning. This gives the court control over the questioning and prevents the attorneys from asking improper questions.

Most state judges ask general questions of potential jurors and then allow the attorneys to ask their own questions. Most attorneys prefer this because it gives them a chance to address the jurors individually and develop rapport. The first impressions the attorney makes during voir dire are important and usually lasting. Most attorneys try to project an image of fairness and trustworthiness.

In some cases, usually involving complex issues or unusually sensitive matters, juror questioning is done outside the presence of other potential jurors. Usually questionnaires prepared by the attorneys and approved by the judge are given to the prospective jurors to either fill out before going into the courtroom, or to take home and complete and return for the attorneys to review before questioning them. This not only saves time in court, but prospective jurors will usually reveal more intimate information in the privacy of a written question, rather than having to state it publicly in front of other jurors and the judge in open court.

If as the questioning proceeds, the judge, who has a duty to ensure a fair and impartial jury, believes that a person is biased or prejudiced, he will thank and excuse that person. If, after questioning by the attorneys, one attorney believes that a person is biased or prejudiced, he can challenge the person "for cause" and ask the judge to excuse her. If the judge agrees, he will excuse the person. There is no limit on the number of jurors who can be challenged for cause.

Once there are no further challenges for cause, the attorneys can use their peremptory challenges. Each side usually has six. No reason need be given for excusing a person under a peremptory challenge. However, peremptory challenges cannot be used to discriminate against and exclude a certain group of jurors by race, ethnic background, religion or gender. If one attorney thinks the other is excusing jurors for discriminatory purposes he can object and, usually out of the presence of the jury, state why he believes his opponent's move was discriminatory. The judge will then ask the excusing attorney to explain his reason for excusing a juror. If he doesn't have a nondiscriminatory reason, the judge will probably refuse to excuse the juror and warn the attorney about his conduct.

"We would like to thank and excuse Mrs. Martin," Larry said as we utilized our first peremptory challenge.

As a juror is excused he is replaced with another from the jury panel, who is questioned and can then be challenged for cause. The use of peremptory challenges then continues. When each side passes consecutively or all peremptory challenges are exhausted, the jury is sworn to render a true verdict according to the evidence.

If the trial will last more than a few days, several alternate jurors are chosen the same way, to replace a regular juror who might become ill or have an emergency before the case is over. If there is no alternate left when a regular juror is excused, the parties can agree to proceed with a smaller number of jurors; otherwise a mistrial is declared and the case has to be tried over again. If a juror is replaced after deliberations begin, the judge must instruct the jury to begin deliberations from the beginning to include the new juror's views.

228

During the voir-dire process attorneys usually are looking back at the jury panel remaining in the courtroom to get a sense of who might replace a juror that they challenge.

Some attorneys use no challenges to make it look like they have such a strong case that any group of people would decide in their favor. Then if the other side uses any challenges it makes it look like they are afraid some jurors will see through their case.

In the end, attorneys often use their hunches or intuition. We had a middle-aged woman on our jury who smiled at us when she was called to sit in the jury box, and smiled at us during our questioning. Larry didn't trust her and asked me what I thought. She looked OK to me. Larry left her on the jury. After the case was over and we interviewed some of the jury, they told us that this lady was the one holding out for the lowest verdict for our client. Larry should have trusted his instincts and excused her.

After three hours of questioning and challenges, we had our jury of twelve people and three alternates. We were comfortable with the jury and thought they would give Joe a fair shake.

Jury Management

Larry thought it was unrealistic that the jurors could remember all the important evidence in a seven-week trial. He asked Judge Conners to give the jurors pads and pencils to take notes during the trial. The defense attorneys were afraid that while jurors were taking notes, they might miss important evidence. They were also concerned that jurors might take inaccurate notes that would sway other jurors. Judge Conners ruled that the jurors could be given notepads but they had to be left in the courtroom at night and they would be collected and destroyed after the trial.

The judge told the jury that before each break and lunch and before recessing for the day, he would admonish them not to discuss anything about the case with each other or anyone else, not to form or express any opinion about the case until it was submitted to them, to avoid news coverage of the case and to not make any independent investigation into the facts of the case.

Opening Statements

The attorney for each side gives an overview of his case and what the evidence will prove. The plaintiff's attorney, since he has the burden of proof, goes first, followed by the attorney for the defendant. In rare cases the defendant's attorney may choose to wait and give his opening statement after the plaintiff has presented his entire case.

The simplest opening statement is a chronological summary of the facts and what each witness will testify to. A second, more dramatic and emotionally stirring approach, and the one that Larry used, is to wrap the facts around "rights and duties."

"We are here to affirm our rights, as drivers of vehicles, to travel down a highway safely. We are here to reaffirm the duty of a company operating logging trucks to not cause a hazard on the roadway, or if they do cause a hazard, they must warn approaching drivers of the hazard."

Some attorneys develop a case theme and come back to the theme throughout the trial.

"This is a case about a young man who will never walk again, and whose gift of a normal life and a bright future was taken from him forever."

Some attorneys give the jury an overview of the trial process itself, explaining about opening statements, presentation of evidence, closing arguments, instructions on the law from the judge, and the jury's duty to deliberate and decide based on the evidence.

In their opening statement, the defense wants to halt any momentum developed by the plaintiff's opening statement. They want to develop skepticism and doubt about the plaintiff's case and present an affirmative theme of their own.

"On March 4 Joe was out enjoying the scenery and not paying sufficient attention to the roadway ahead."

The defense wants to emphasize the jury's need to keep open minds so they won't make a decision before the defense has a chance to present its case.

The judge, and sometimes the attorneys, will remind the jury that opening statements are not evidence. They are just what each attorney thinks the evidence will prove.

Here are one judge's comments about opening statements:

"In my experience, jurors tend to believe attorneys who are relaxed, natural, confident and friendly. Attorneys who patronize or lecture the jury are hurting their case. Introduce yourself and your client and just be conversational and do your best to make the presentation of your case interesting. Emphasize important points by varying your tone of delivery, making subtle gestures and moving slightly closer to the jury box. But don't crowd the jury. Don't intimidate them. That's why some judges require attorneys to address the jury from behind a lectern or from the counsel table."

Rules of Evidence

There are hurdles that must be leaped and potholes that must be avoided to get your evidence before the jury, and they are packaged in the rules of evidence. The general purpose of these rules is to make sure that the evidence the jury receives is fair and trustworthy. Here are a few examples:

Foundation: The source of the evidence must be established to show it is reliable. To introduce a document you must show who prepared it, when it was prepared and that the contents are reliable.

Hearsay: A statement made by someone outside of court, which is now offered in the courtroom to prove the truth of what they said, is hearsay. For example, if a witness testifies that Mary said that Joe was drinking the night before the accident, this would be hearsay. The basic rule is that hearsay is inadmissible because the other side cannot cross-examine the original person (in this example Mary) who made the statement, since they are not on the witness stand. There are numerous exceptions to the hearsay rule, however. Admissions made by a party outside the courtroom are admissible since the other attorney can call the party and ask them about the statement.

Privileges: Otherwise relevant evidence can be excluded to protect certain relationships where confidential communications are assumed. The most common is the attorney-client privilege. A client cannot be questioned about what his attorney told him, nor can an attorney be questioned about what a client told him. Other privileges include physician-patient, psychotherapist-patient, penitent-clergyman and newspaperman-source. Also, spouses cannot testify against each other or about marital communications.

Relevancy: Only evidence that might help prove or disprove a disputed fact in the case is relevant and therefore admissible. The fact that Joe received a speeding ticket on his motorcycle two years prior to the accident is not relevant to prove that he was speeding at the time of our accident. It might be relevant if he was speeding along the same stretch of highway where the accident occurred and his custom and habit was to always speed on that stretch of highway.

Form of Question

An attorney's questions have to be clear so that the witness and opposing attorney know what is being asked, and the question has to be fair. Typical objections to the form of a question are:

Leading: A leading question suggests the answer. They are generally not allowed on direct examination except for preliminary matters to save time. For example: "You work as an accident investigator?" to get right to the point, rather than asking, "What type of work do you do?"

Narrative: Questions have to call for specific factual information, not long-winded narrations of what occurred. For example, the question "What happened in this accident?" is objectionable because once a witness starts on a roll of telling his story, the opposing attorney has little idea what he is going to say, and thus cannot object to his saying things that may be inadmissible. Questions have to be broken down into segments so the opposing attorney knows what is coming and can raise any objections. For example, "What time did you get up?" is OK, but "What did you do that day?" is too general. "What did you do next?" is a common way to lead the witness through the story step by step and avoid narrative answers.

Vague, Ambiguous, Indefinite, Unintelligible: If it's not clear what information the attorney is seeking by his question or the question could be interpreted several different ways, then it is objectionable and the attorney will have to rephrase it so it is clear what he is asking.

Assumes Facts Not in Evidence: If the question states information that has not been introduced into evidence, such as "Isn't it a fact that you were smoking marijuana the night before the accident?" and there is no evidence to that effect, then the question is objectionable.

Speculative: If the witness has no personal knowledge of the information asked, such as "Do you think his brakes were not working correctly?" then the question asks the witness to guess or speculate and it is objectionable.

Argumentative: This type of question takes issue with the witness's previous answer. An example is "How can you say the other driver was speeding when you had not looked at your speedometer?"

Asked and Answered, or Cumulative: An attorney cannot ask the same or similar question over and over to emphasize a point.

Sometimes attorneys know their questions are objectionable, but they ask them anyway, leaving it up to the opposing attorney to be attentive and object. If they fail to object, they got the information they wanted in.

Plaintiff's Case

After the defense completes its opening statement, the judge usually turns to the plaintiff's attorney and says:

"Call your first witness."

Now it's up to the plaintiff's attorney to prove his case through the testimony of witnesses and the introduction of tangible evidence.

Burden of Proof

In a civil case the plaintiff has the burden of proving his case by a preponderance of the evidence (as opposed to beyond a reasonable doubt required in criminal cases). We had to prove that it was "more likely than not" that the trucking company and their driver were negligent, that their negligence proximately caused Joe's injuries and damages, and that all the damages we claimed were a result of the defendant's negligence. Preponderance of the evidence means the slightest tipping of the scales in favor of the plaintiff.

Direct Examination

We chose not to call Joe as our first witness. We wanted to lay some foundation about the accident and injuries, and we wanted to show the demeanor of the truck driver before having Joe testify. And we wanted to personalize Joe, develop the story of what happened to him in the accident and what his life was like before the accident and how it had been drastically changed by the accident. We wanted the jury anxious to hear from him and to be sympathetic to his injuries when they finally heard his testimony.

Our first witness was the investigating officer, who testified about the location of the vehicles after the accident, the skid marks from Joe's motorcycle and the marks on the side of the logging truck at the point of the impact.

Preparation for Questioning Witnesses

Most attorneys plan their questioning of witnesses with an outline of the subjects they want to cover. This allows them to keep on course during the heat of the courtroom battle but allows flexibility to respond to unexpected answers. Some attorneys need the security of an exact script and thus write out every question and ask them in order, never deviating from their list. This prevents responding to a witness's answers and demeanor with follow-up questions appropriate to the moment.

Generally, short, precise questions that elicit short answers are best because the jury more easily remembers small bits of information. Long-winded, complex questions, often meant more to demonstrate the attorney's eloquence or knowledge, only bore and confuse the jury. Some attorneys repeat themes during questioning, thus providing the jury with a thread of continuity throughout the trial. Visual aids can help jurors remember since they are both hearing and seeing the information.

We called the paramedic, who was first on the scene, to describe how Joe was lying on the ground with no feeling below his chest, how he was loaded on and strapped to a backboard, then set on a gurney and placed in the ambulance.

Then we called the truck driver and let him display his abrasive, defensive attitude in response to our questions. He reminded me of a kid who had been caught doing something wrong and then crosses his arms, sulks and denies he did it, even though you just saw him do it. In retrospect, I don't understand why the defense attorneys didn't work with this man and get him to feel some remorse for the accident and sympathy for Joe's injuries. If he had conveyed that on the witness stand, I am sure the verdict would have been much less. But his attitude offended the jury, as we learned later interviewing them, and since he seemed like he did not care about what had happened to Joe, the jury felt they needed to demonstrate their caring by the size of their verdict.

Attorney's Style and Demeanor

Some attorneys try to imitate the style of famous and successful attorneys. Jurors can usually see through these imitations and tend to distrust the attorney. Those attorneys that develop their own style are usually the most credible.

Here are a few guidelines that some attorneys follow:
1. Don't act overly friendly or familiar with witnesses.
2. Don't attack a sympathetic witness.
3. Don't ask misleading questions.
4. Don't act disappointed if a witness doesn't give the expected answer.
5. Don't start out by saying you have "just a few questions," and then go on and on.

Next we called the doctors who treated Joe. They testified about the severing of his spinal cord, the absence of any hope he would ever have for feeling or function of his body below his chest. They explained about the need to have a catheter and urine bag for the rest of his life, and his inability to have normal sexual relations and the unlikelihood of fathering a child.

We called the physical therapist who had helped Joe with his rehabilitation, who testified how hard Joe worked to strengthen his arms and shoulders, to learn how to operate his wheelchair and how to transfer himself from his chair to the bed, to the toilet and to a car.

G erry Spence relates in his book, *How to Argue and Win Every Time*, the following regarding treatment of witnesses:

"When I was a young lawyer feeling my power, my strategy in a certain case was to attack and destroy every witness the other side put against me. I took on the witnesses; old men with watery eyes who I knew were but company syco-phants trying to keep their jobs. I took on the experts, scholarly actors who I knew were but paid witnesses attempting to earn their fees rather than reveal the truth. Cut them up, shredded them, pulverized them. The jury was out only fifteen minutes before it returned a verdict against my client. I was devastated. Hadn't I won every battle? Hadn't I destroyed the witnesses? Hadn't my power on cross-examination been overwhelming?"

"As the jury was filing out of the courthouse, one of the women approached me. She looked up at me with tears in her eyes. It had obviously been hard for her to turn my severely injured client out of a court of justice with nothing."

" 'Mr. Spence,' " she said quietly, " 'why did you make us hate you so?' "

We called his previous employer, who testified that Joe was a hard worker, dependable and cooperative.

We called an accident reconstructionist we had hired, who testified that based on the skid marks, the co-efficient of friction for the road surface and the impact damage to the motorcycle and truck, the speed of the motorcycle at impact was 28 mph. He further testified that, working back from that impact speed, based on Joe's description of the accident, he was traveling between 49 and 54 mph when he first saw the truck. These figures were critical and helpful since the speed limit was 55 mph and this put Joe below the posted speed limit.

Preparation of Expert Witnesses

Expert witnesses (those who are qualified to express opinions) have to be care-fully prepared. Our primary accident reconstruction expert, because of a busy schedule, could only meet with us the evening prior to his testimony. We spent four hours together, bringing him up to date on all the previous testimony so he could incorporate it into his calculations and reasoning in reaching his opinion.

The value of experts can be mixed. In interviewing the jury afterward they found the experts who were the most technical and formal to be the least believ-able. They found our one accident reconstructionist, who himself was a motorcy-cle rider and came across as an ordinary guy, to be the most believable.

Because expert witnesses usually have testified in many cases, they are vulnerable to attack if the opposing attorney has access to copies of previous depositions and transcripts of former court testimony. It's important for an attorney to review his expert's prior testimony to make sure he is not contradicting himself in the current case.

We called an economist to testify what Joe's loss of earnings would be over his expected lifetime, due to his injuries and inability to engage in many forms of employment.

We then called Joe's girlfriend, who talked about how Joe's life had changed because of his injuries, his inability to engage in sports, which he loved, to go for walks, hikes, to the beach. Basically, he was restricted to where his wheelchair could go, which were hard, gradually sloping surfaces. And she talked about his moods, how he had been fun-loving and optimistic before the accident, and depressed and pessimistic after.

With all this talk about Joe, we could feel that the jury could hardly wait to hear from him. Even though they saw him every day in the courtroom, they had yet to hear him speak. So, as our final witness, we called Joe.

Up to this point Joe had been sitting in his wheelchair in the gallery, behind the bar. We had previously measured the opening in the railing and determined that Joe's wheelchair was too wide to fit through. But we didn't let that on. The morning he was to testify, we stood and called him. He wheeled up slowly to the opening and bumped first one side, then the other side, trying his best to get the wheelchair through. We went over to help, looking puzzled how to fit the wheelchair through too narrow an opening. It soon became apparent to everyone in the courtroom that our efforts were hopeless. Finally the judge stood and said we could wheel Joe outside the courtroom, down the hall, into the back door to his chambers and back around into the courtroom through the door the court personnel used. We loved it. Everyone was eager to get Joe to the witness stand. Everyone saw the limitations people confined to wheelchairs suffer, such a simple thing as being unable to travel twenty feet from the gallery to the witness stand, something every other witness did with ease but something that became a major difficulty for Joe and his chair.

By the time Joe testified the jury was sympathetic to him and listened with open minds and hearts to his story. He told how he had been out for a drive that Sunday to enjoy the scenery and fresh air on his way to see the girl he hoped to marry one day. He had been driving carefully and within the speed limit. When he first saw the truck, he assumed it would complete its crossing of the highway in one maneuver. He slowed but did not see any need to make an emergency stop, not, that is, until the truck stopped dead in front of him and started to back up. At that point he applied full brakes, pressing evenly on the front and back brakes as he had learned was the proper way to achieve full braking power on a motorcycle. He testified he realized he was going to hit the side of the truck, and so put his head down so as not to hit his face. He didn't remember anything after the impact until the paramedics arrived, and he then had no feeling below his chest.

The jury listened with their complete attention. We realized our strategy had succeeded. Now we just had to minimize the impact of the defense's cross-examination and witnesses.

Cross-Examination

An attorney has two goals in cross-examining the other attorney's witnesses:
1. Obtain facts favorable to his client.
2. Discredit witnesses by showing that their testimony on direct examination was untrue, biased or based on faulty memory or perception.

Some attorneys believe they must cross-examine every witness in order to fulfill their self-image of an effective trial lawyer. Other attorneys will not cross-examine a witness who has not harmed their case or client. Others think that no cross-examination makes a witness look strong and not challengeable, so they will ask a few general questions and then sit down.

Some attorneys adopt a hostile or rude demeanor in cross-examination, acting as if the witness is lying, even if they cannot prove it. This can often backfire because if there is no evidence of lying, the jury will tend to sympathize with the witness who is being attacked unjustly and question the credibility of the attorney instead.

The easiest way to attack a witness on cross-examination is with the witness's own prior inconsistent statements, usually given during their deposition. The setup is as follows:
1. You confirm with the witness the testimony they gave on direct examination.
2. You confirm that they previously testified at a deposition.
3. You read into the record the question and answer from the deposition that is inconsistent with their current testimony.
4. You sit down, leaving the inconsistency hanging with the jury.

Some attorneys ask one too many questions at this point, such as: "Now which testimony is true?" Inevitably the witness will explain which is correct and why the other was not really what he meant, which tends to blunt the effect of the inconsistency.

Most drama in witness questioning occurs during cross-examination. That's when the attorney can take maximum control and lead the witness by suggesting the answers and just elicit the witness's agreement on the facts stated by the attorney. The form of the question determines how much leading is occurring. Here are some examples of leading questions, from slightly leading to extremely leading:

Questions beginning with words such as: Do, Did, Are, Is, Was, Were. Example:

"Were you driving at 70 mph just before this accident?"

This question suggests the answer but gives the witness an even-handed chance to admit or deny.

Questions beginning with words such as: Don't, Didn't, Aren't, Isn't, Wasn't, Weren't. Example:

"Weren't you driving at 70 mph just before this accident?"

This question not only suggests the answer, it assumes that the information asked is true and almost accuses the witness of wrongdoing.

Questions beginning with: Isn't it a fact; Isn't it correct; Isn't it true; Won't you agree. Example:

"Isn't it a fact that you were driving at 70 mph just before this accident?"

This question emphasizes even more strongly that the information is true and factual, requiring the witness to strongly deny the assumed fact.

Questions followed with: Right? Correct? Isn't that true? Isn't that correct? Isn't that right? Example:

"You were driving at 70 mph just before this accident, correct?"

Again, this states the assumed information as fact and merely asks for the witness's agreement.

Usually the more the attorney thinks he can push the witness around (the weaker or more unsure the witness is), the more aggressively the attorney will try to lead the witness.

When cross-examining Joe, the lead defense attorney started gently, but soon got to the question we knew was coming and had prepared Joe for:

"Now Joe, you were driving faster than 54 mph before this accident, weren't you?"

Joe came right back with the answer we had rehearsed many times. Looking the defense attorney straight in the eyes, he said:

"No sir, I was driving 50 mph before I saw the truck."

The defense attorney took our bait and asked the next question:

"How can you be sure you were driving exactly at 50 mph before this accident?"

"Because I had just glanced down at my speedometer before I entered that last curve."

The jury was satisfied and the defense attorney was smart enough to change the topic. He had made no headway on cross-examination on this crucial point, and had only allowed Joe to emphasize and expand on the testimony he gave on direct.

Re-Direct

After cross-examination the attorney who called the witness has the right to ask further questions on re-direct examination. The scope of re-direct is limited to questions to explain any inconsistencies or confusion that arose during cross-examination.

Re-Cross

After the inconsistency or confusion has been explained, the cross-examining attorney can re-cross-examine the witness to try to show that some inconsistency or confusion still remains or cannot be explained.

Defendant's Case

Once the plaintiff has completed calling all of his witnesses, the plaintiff "rests," which means he has completed his case. It is then the defendant's turn to call witnesses.

Direct Examination

The defense's job is to shoot holes in the plaintiff's case. The lead defense attorney called two other truck drivers that worked for the logging company. They testified that they felt they never needed a spotter when exiting that particular side road. He called a physician expert on spinal cord injuries who testified that paraplegics could still have sex, they just needed their mate to provide all the stimulation and they could probably maintain an erection long enough for penetration. He then called an economist who testified that Joe could probably now earn more money than he did before, because, statistically, he was less likely to change jobs or careers.

Cross-Examination

We asked very few questions on cross-examination of the defense witnesses. We felt most of them did not hurt us and, in fact, some of them helped us.

Rebuttal and Surrebuttal

After the defense completes their case, they rest and the plaintiff can call additional witnesses to rebut, that is, to contradict or explain any new evidence the defense presented. The defendant can then call additional witnesses under surrebuttal to rebut plaintiff's rebuttal witnesses. Both rebuttal and surrebuttal are usually very brief, if they occur at all.

Expedited Methods of Introducing Evidence

To save time, the rules of evidence allow several shortcuts to introduce evidence:

Judicial Notice: Either party can ask the court to take judicial notice of laws, rules and regulations; the common meaning of English words, phrases and legal expressions; court records; and matters of common knowledge. We asked the judge to take judicial notice of the weather conditions on the day of the accident by offering newspaper weather reports for that day. This saved us from bringing in a meteorologist to testify.

Admission: Either party can voluntarily concede the truth of any matter during the course of discovery or trial. This saves the other party the trouble of introducing evidence to prove the matter.

Stipulations: The attorneys can agree that particular facts or matters are true and therefore not in dispute between the parties. No evidence need be offered on the stipulated matter.

Motions During Trial

Motions are generally presented in writing because they carry more weight with the court and provide a better basis if an appeal is necessary. They are usually made out of the presence of the jury to allow the court and attorneys to speak freely without concern for prejudice to the jury. Some judges excuse the jury to the jury room and allow the attorneys to present their motions in the courtroom. Other judges have the attorneys and reporter come into their chambers to argue motions. Here are the most common motions:

Motion for Nonsuit: If, after the plaintiff's opening statement, or after the presentation of the plaintiff's evidence, the defense believes the plaintiff has failed to establish a prima-facie case, they can make this motion. The motion concedes the truth of the plaintiff's proposed or admitted evidence and any inferences reasonably drawn from the evidence, but contends that those facts, as a matter of law, are not sufficient to prove the plaintiff's case. In other words, if the plaintiff's case has no merit then there is no need for the defendant to present his case. If granted, part or all of the plaintiff's case is dismissed.

Motion for Directed Verdict: If either party believes the opposing party has not offered sufficient evidence to support a verdict for their client, they ask the judge to direct a verdict in their favor. The judge may grant a directed verdict on some or all issues.

Motion for Continuance: Continuances are not favored by courts either before or during trial because the courtroom, judge, reporter and other resources have been committed to resolving this case. They are granted only if an unforeseeable emergency arises, such as the death or serious illness of an attorney or key witness. Usually attorneys ask for recesses for several hours or a day to deal with most unexpected events that occur during trial.

Motion to Reopen Case: If either side inadvertently neglected to offer key evidence during the presentation of their case, or if they have been surprised by evidence offered by the opposing side, they can request the opportunity to reopen their case and present the evidence.

Motion for Mistrial: If an error, irregularity or prejudicial event too substantial to correct by an admonition to the jury occurs during the trial, then the party who feels they cannot receive a fair trial can move for a mistrial.

Motion to Amend Pleadings to Conform to Proof: If the pleadings allege one thing and the evidence proves another, then an attorney can request this motion be granted.

Closing Argument

Closing argument is the attorney's chance to show his best skills. He uses the evidence and any reasonable inferences from the evidence to weave, hopefully, a compelling argument why the jury should decide in favor of his client.

Like an opening statement, a closing argument can simply summarize what each favorable witness said. A more sophisticated closing argument will discuss the demeanor of witnesses, talk about human motivation and appeal to fairness, reasonableness and common sense. It will talk about qualities and values we strive for and how reaffirming those values is now in the jury's hands.

Some attorneys will try to guess who will be elected as the jury foreman and then tailor their argument to that person's interests and motivations, hoping that if that person is convinced, they will try to convince the other jurors during deliberations.

If the attorney has developed and carried a theme throughout the trial, closing argument is the time to show how all the evidence supports the theme.

During their argument, some attorneys will watch the jurors closely and read their body language. Are the jurors sitting attentively or stirring uncomfortably in their seats? Are they leaning forward and nodding approval as the attorney speaks, or are they sitting back, cross-armed, keeping out what is being said? The attorneys will watch the jurors' eyes to see if they are paying attention or getting bored, comprehending or getting confused. And the attorney will try to adjust his argument, his pacing, his choice of words, his distance from the jury and his demeanor to try to recapture the jury's attention and acceptance.

Plaintiff's Argument

The plaintiff has the burden of proof so he goes first in his closing argument (sometimes called the plaintiff's "opening argument").

Larry argued that Joe had a right to drive down the highway safely and not have that right infringed on by the defendant's actions. He also argued that Joe had the right to pursue his life and work without injury and how, because the defendant had violated that right, Joe now would spend the balance of his life looking at the world from a wheelchair.

Like all the rest of the trial, there are rules and guidelines as to what is proper and improper in a closing argument. The plaintiff cannot mention that the defendant has insurance. He cannot argue the "golden rule," which is, "how much would you, members of the jury, take to suffer what the plaintiff has suffered?" Obviously there's no amount of money most people would take to be confined to a wheelchair the remainder of their lives.

The plaintiff's attorney will let the jury know that the plaintiff is entitled to economic damages, including reasonable medical expenses, future medical expenses, wage loss and loss of future earnings. Most plaintiffs' attorneys will emphasize to the jury that this is the plaintiff's only chance in court, he cannot come back later and ask for more. If he does not receive fair compensation today, he won't ever receive it.

When a jury awards money for the plaintiff's pain and suffering, there is no precise measuring stick. The jurors must use their own judgment as to what amount is reasonable based on the evidence. However, to help the jury decide the plaintiff can use the "per diem" argument, which Larry presented as follows:

"Joe is entitled to recover for his pain and suffering. I believe a reasonable figure is $50 a day. He has a life expectancy of 40 years, that's 365 days times 40 years, which is 14,600 days of life left, times $50 a day, which equals $730,000 for his pain and suffering."

Some attorneys are hesitant to mention an exact figure for pain and suffering, fearing that some jurors will think them greedy and afraid that other jurors will not award more than the attorney asks for. So the attorney argues a range, such as between twenty and one hundred dollars a day.

Defendant's Argument

The defendant goes next with his closing argument. The defendant inevitably argues that his side has no liability and therefore the jury should decide in favor of the defendant. But most defense attorneys will add a caveat, as they did in Joe's case, which is, "If you should decide my client is liable, then $200,000 for pain and suffering is more than sufficient to compensate the plaintiff for his injuries." They offer this lower figure so that if the jury finds for the plaintiff, they don't just blindly accept the plaintiff's figure.

Plaintiff's Final Argument

The plaintiff then has a brief concluding or rebuttal argument, which is limited to countering points raised by the defendant in his closing argument. The plaintiff is not supposed to raise new issues in his concluding argument since the defense has no opportunity to respond.

Jury Instructions

Following completion of closing arguments, the judge instructs the jury what rules of law are to be applied in the case. But it's the attorneys who select the law they believe is applicable. The federal courts and most states have books of approved jury instructions. Each side exchanges their proposed jury instructions before the case begins, but they usually don't discuss them until all evidence is introduced, usually right before closing arguments.

The defense had rested late in the day, so Judge Conners had all attorneys meet with him in chambers early the following morning to discuss jury instructions. This can be a critical part of the case. Most instructions are obvious: the law of negligence, the legal definition of proximate cause and preponderance of the evidence, what damages are legally recoverable. But there usually are one or two instructions that one side wants and the other side believes are improper.

In our case, we wanted the instruction that a driver on the highway has the right to assume that all other drivers are acting reasonably and obeying the law. We wanted to argue that the logging truck driver and his company were not acting reasonably by not having a spotter on the highway. This instruction would provide a legal basis for that argument. The judge decided our requested instruction was proper.

Jury Deliberations

After being instructed on the law, the jury retires to the jury room to deliberate. Typically, the bailiff is sworn by the court clerk to take charge of the jury. His duties include:

1. Escort the jury to the jury room.
2. Stay with them if they break for lunch.
3. Escort them back to court when they have reached their decision.
4. Keep others from speaking or communicating with them during their deliberations.

The jury usually deliberates during normal working hours unless they are close to a verdict. Before any breaks in the deliberations, the judge will admonish the jury to not discuss the case with anyone until they reconvene in the jury room.

Attorneys read much into the length of deliberations. In a personal-injury case, if the jury returns quickly, it probably means a defense verdict. If a jury decides in the plaintiff's favor, they usually require an hour or more to agree on the dollar amount.

Many juries will delay telling the bailiff they have reached a verdict so they can at least get a free lunch (the losing party pays for the lunch).

There is no set length for deliberations—it just depends on the complexity and strength of the facts of each case. The jury in our case deliberated for nine hours over two days. We were pretty sure after the first four hours that they were going to decide in Joe's favor. After six hours the jury requested a reread of the jury instruction on compensation for pain and suffering. We then knew for sure that they were adding up the money.

It is misconduct and the basis for a mistrial if jurors conduct their own experiments or obtain evidence outside of court, like going to the accident scene themselves or seeing how far it takes for a motorcycle to stop. The jury must reach their verdict by discussion and agreement. They cannot flip a coin, nor can they reach a "quotient verdict" (average the amount of damages each person believes should be awarded).

If the jury indicates they cannot reach a verdict, the judge usually asks if further deliberations might result in a verdict. If the jury says yes, he asks them to deliberate further. If they say no, he will declare a mistrial and the case will have to be tried again.

If the bias of a juror comes out during deliberations ("I hate all motorcycle drivers"), it can form the basis for a mistrial. If juror bias or misconduct comes out after the verdict, usually during interviews with jurors, it can form the basis for a motion for a new trial.

Finally on the afternoon of the second day of deliberations the jury foreman notified the bailiff that they had reached a decision. All attorneys were called back into the courtroom, the judge returned, then the jury was escorted in and took their seats. The scene described at the beginning of this chapter then followed.

Verdicts

Typically the jury is given a verdict form at the beginning of their deliberations. The form can be as simple as: "Did the plaintiff prove his case, yes or no?" "If yes, how much does he get?" This is a general verdict.

A more complex verdict form is a special verdict, which asks a series of questions.

"Was the defendant negligent? Yes or No."

"If yes, was the defendant's negligence the proximate cause of the plaintiff's injuries? Yes or No."

"If yes, did the plaintiff's conduct contribute to his injuries? Yes or No."

"If yes, by what percentage? _____"

"How much should the plaintiff receive before deducting for his own negligence?"

"How much should the plaintiff receive after deducting for his own negligence?"

Once the required number of jurors, usually three-quarters in a civil case, agree, the jury has reached a verdict and they record it on the verdict form, the foreperson signs it and the jury delivers the verdict form to the court.

Once the clerk reads the verdict, the judge usually asks the jury if that is their verdict, and those that voted for it say yes. Either attorney can ask that the jury be polled, which means each juror is asked if this is their verdict.

The clerk then enters the verdict into the court minutes.

In our case all twelve jurors voted for the verdict; we had a unanimous decision.

Once the court has received and recorded the verdict, the jury is thanked and excused.

Judge Conners told the jury that some of the attorneys may want to talk with them later, and it was up to each juror if they chose to speak to us. All the attorneys stood in respect as the jury left, and some of them walked over to Joe and shook his hand and wished him good luck. It was a very emotional moment.

Judgments

Usually after the jury leaves the judge states, on the record, that judgment will be entered in accordance with the jury's verdict. Then the clerk types up a judgment form stating that judgment is entered for plaintiff against the defendant in the amount of $1.25 million, the judge signs it and it is entered, depending on the county, in the county judgment book or in the register of actions or onto microfilm or into the court's electronic data processing system. This all occurs usually within twenty-four hours of the jury's verdict.

Once the judgment is entered, interest at the legal rate starts accruing on the judgment and the plaintiff can take steps to enforce the judgment, which means collect the money from the defendant, and the clock starts running on making post-trial motions and filing an appeal.

In our case the lead defense attorney asked the judge if the enforcement of the judgment could be stayed for thirty days. The judge granted the request. That meant that we could not take steps to collect the money for that period of time. It also meant that the defense intended to make a motion for a new trial.

The American legal system generally does not provide for recovery of attorney fees unless there is a contract allowing them or a statute authorizing them. We would be paid by receiving 40 percent of the jury's verdict. Since we were the prevailing party, we would recover, over and above the jury's verdict, certain costs from the defendant, including our filing fee, costs of depositions and subpoena fees, witness fees and jury fees.

Motions After Trial

In large verdict cases, you can count on various post-trial motions.

Motion for a New Trial: If either party believes that a miscarriage of justice has occurred by the jury's verdict, they can make a motion for a new trial. Essentially what they are asking is, "Let's do it all over again because the jury's decision was out of line."

Five days after the trial, while we were still basking in our victory, we received defendant's written motion for a new trial, the basis of which was that the jury's finding of only 10 percent fault on Joe's part was not supported by the evidence.

Other motions that could have been made after the trial are:

Motion for Judgment Notwithstanding the Verdict: If the losing party believes there is no substantial evidence to support the jury's verdict, he can make this motion. If granted, the judge enters judgment for the losing party. This motion is seldom granted.

Motion to Correct Clerical Error: If the clerk had inadvertently typed $12.5 million dollars in the judgment form, then the defense would have made and won this motion.

We spent a week researching and preparing for the hearing on the defendant's motion for a new trial. The motion was argued before Judge Conners exactly three weeks after the jury had reached its verdict. The judge took the motion under submission, which means he would think about it and send us his decision in the mail.

One week later we received the bad news. The judge granted a new trial on the issue of comparative fault.

"I can't believe it—how can a judge change what the jury decided?" I whined to Larry.

"Happens more often than you would think," he said, looking downcast as he walked to the phone to call Joe and explain what had happened.

"At least he didn't touch the $1.25 million," I said, trying to look at the positive side.

Appeal

Either party who is dissatisfied with the judgment can appeal the case to a higher court. That party files a notice of appeal within a certain time period, usually thirty days, and requests that a copy of the trial-court record (all exhibits, pleadings, court orders and a transcript of the trial testimony) be prepared and sent to the appellate court. The appealing party then files an opening brief stating the legal and factual basis for the appeal. The opposing party files a reply brief, stating why the judgment should stand, and the appealing party then files a closing brief, addressing the issues raised by the opposing party's reply brief. The appellate court can set a hearing for oral arguments from the parties, after which a decision will be made, usually in the form of a written opinion from one of the appellate justices. If either party disagrees with the appellate court decision, they may be able to appeal that decision to the state supreme court or U.S. Supreme Court.

Appeals are usually made regarding the law applied in the case as opposed to how the judge or jury weighed and decided the facts.

Larry did not appeal the judge's order granting a new trial on damages. He returned one year later and tried the case again. I had already left his employ and opened my own office. At the second trial the jury decided Joe was 15 percent at fault. The defense attorneys were still not satisfied, so they filed notice of appeal. Particularly insurance companies who do not want to pay large verdicts often do this as a settlement strategy. They can tie a case up in appeal for another year or two, and in the meantime they do not have to pay the judgment, although interest does accumulate.

After the second trial Larry was in financial trouble. His home was heavily mortgaged and he had little other income because of the time spent on Joe's case. Two months after the defense attorneys had filed their appeal, Larry negotiated with the defendants and settled the case for $750,000. Larry received reimbursement for the costs he had advanced, approximately $67,000, plus 40 percent of the balance, or $273,200. Joe received $409,800, enough to buy a modified vehicle and a specially modified home, and put some money in the bank. Joe went to work on an assembly line in a computer factory. Larry paid off his second mortgage and took a two-week vacation with his wife. I received no money from the case but did obtain a great introduction into the hardball world of big-time personal-injury litigation.

Glossary of Legal Terms

Common Legal Terms

ACCUSATION Criminal charge brought against a person, usually in the form of a criminal complaint, an indictment, information or presentment.

ACCUSED The person charged with a crime.

ACQUITTAL The verdict of a judge or jury that the defendant in a criminal case has not been found guilty beyond a reasonable doubt of the crime charged.

ACTION A dispute brought before a court for trial or settlement.

ACT OF GOD Damages caused by nature, which could not have been prevented by a person, so the person is not liable.

ACTUS REUS Latin for "criminal act."

ADJOURN To end court proceedings.

ADJUDICATION The result of a dispute brought before a court. Also called a judgment or decree.

ADMISSIBLE Evidence that can be legally admitted into court for consideration by the judge or jury.

ADMISSION A voluntary statement, usually by a party, that certain facts are true.

ADVERSARY SYSTEM The system of trial practice where each side has an opportunity to present their side of a controversy for a judge or jury to decide the truth.

AFFIDAVIT A written statement given under oath.

AFFIRMATIVE DEFENSE A legal reason that justifies the action accused of, e.g., self-defense, where a defendant is accused of assault and battery.

AFFIRMED The decision of an appellate court that the actions by the lower court, usually the trial court, are proper and will not be changed by the appellate court.

AGGRIEVED PARTY A person who has suffered injury or loss.

ALIBI Facts that prove an accused could not have committed the crime charged.

ALIMONY Monetary support paid by one spouse to the other during separation or after divorce. Called spousal support or separate maintenance in some states.

ALLEGATION Statement made in pleading that the alleging party intends to prove in court.

ALTERNATIVE DISPUTE RESOLUTION Method of resolving a dispute other than through court and trial. Mediation and arbitration are the common alternatives.

AMICUS BRIEF A document filed by an amicus curiae supporting one party's position in an appeal of a case.

AMICUS CURIAE Latin for "friend of the court." A person who voluntarily provides information to a court supporting one party's position.

ANSWER The pleading filed by the defendant responding to the allegations raised in the complaint.

APPEAL A request by the losing party to a lawsuit for a higher court to review and reverse the decision of the trial or lower court.

APPEARANCE A party voluntarily submitting themselves to the jurisdiction of a court for determination of the issues in controversy.

APPELLANT The party appealing the decision of the trial or lower court to a higher court.

APPELLATE COURT The court, usually the court of appeals or supreme court, that reviews decisions of the trial or lower court.

APPELLEE The party against whom an appellant files an appeal.

ARBITRATION An alternative dispute procedure conducted outside of the court before a neutral third party (arbitrator) for resolution of a dispute. The parties can agree if the arbitrator's decision is binding or nonbinding.

ARRAIGNMENT The hearing where the defendant in a criminal proceeding has the charges against him read and enters a plea. Sometimes called a preliminary hearing or initial appearance.

ARREST The act of taking a suspect into custody.

ASSUMPTION OF RISK Defense in personal-injury action where the plaintiff knew the risk of his actions and he proceeded anyway, and thus should not be compensated by the defendant.

ATTORNEY AT LAW A person qualified and licensed to provide legal advice and to appear in court. Same as lawyer and counselor-at-law.

ATTRACTIVE NUISANCE A dangerous condition on property that attracts children who could suffer injury.

AUTOPSY The dissection of a cadaver to determine the cause of death.

BAD FAITH A willful violation of an agreement or duty.

BAIL An amount of money set by the court that, when deposited with the court, allows a criminal defendant to be released from custody and guarantees his return to court on a specified date.

BAIL BOND The document that when properly executed allows the release of an individual in custody.

BAILIFF A court attendant who keeps order in the courtroom and has custody of the jury.

BANKRUPTCY Legal proceeding whereby a person or company that cannot pay its debts has its debts discharged after paying none or just part of its debts.

BENCH TRIAL Trial heard by a judge without a jury.

BENCH WARRANT An order issued by a judge for the arrest of an individual.

BENEFICIARY A person for whose benefit property is held in trust.

BEST EVIDENCE RULE Requires that the original of a document must be used in evidence. A copy or testimony about the document without the document present is not sufficient.

BREACH OF CONTRACT Failing to adhere to the terms of a contract without any legal excuse.

BRIEF A written statement prepared by a party to a lawsuit with the relevant facts, applicable law and reasons why the case should be decided in the party's favor.

BIND OVER Court order that person be placed in custody to answer criminal charges.

BURDEN OF PROOF The amount of proof required to win a case. In a criminal case the burden is "beyond a reasonable doubt." In a civil case the standard is "by a preponderance of the evidence."

CALENDAR The document prepared by the court calendar clerk listing the day's cases by case number, names of parties, type of case or proceeding, names of attorneys of record, and the time and courtroom where the case will be heard.

CAPITAL OFFENSE A crime punishable by death.

CAPITAL PUNISHMENT Imposition of the death penalty.

CAPTION The name of the court, parties and case number on the top of the first page of pleadings.

CASE A legal dispute, suit or action that may or may not have been filed with the court.

CASE LAW Laws based on the decision of judges in actual controversies heard by them, that were appealed by one party and decided by an appellate court, with the decisions being published to be used for reference and guidance in future cases.

CAUSE OF ACTION The facts that form the basis for a lawsuit.

CAVEAT EMPTOR Latin for "let the buyer beware." The early law of contracts, which has been replaced by the seller having various obligations of disclosure regarding the product or service sold.

CERTIORARI Appellate court order that it will accept a case from a lower court for consideration of whether the lower court's actions were proper or not.

CHAIN OF CUSTODY Showing who had possession of evidence during a crucial time period, usually from date of event to trial, to prove the item presented at the trial is the same as one from event.

CHALLENGE FOR CAUSE An attorney's objection to a juror or judge hearing a case because of some bias or prejudice against the parties or attorney or an interest in the subject matter of the case.

CHAMBERS The judge's office.

CHANGE OF VENUE Moving the location of a trial to another area where the parties will obtain a fair trial without local bias.

CHARGE TO THE JURY The action by the judge instructing the jury what law to apply to the facts.

CHIEF JUDGE The judge whose duties include administration of the court. Called presiding judge in some courts.

CIRCUIT COURT Generally courts below the U.S. Supreme Court that consider appeals from trial courts.

CIRCUMSTANTIAL EVIDENCE All evidence except eyewitness testimony.

CITATION Reference to a publication that contains legal authority. Case citation is the name of the court along with the volume and page number for location of the case cited.

CIVIL ACTION Individual or business sues another person or business who has committed a civil wrong.

CLASS ACTION A suit brought by one or more members of a large group of people on behalf of all members of the group.

CLERK OF THE COURT Court employee who maintains records of court proceedings, assists judge in administrative matters and, if assigned to an individual courtroom, administers oath to witnesses and the jury.

COMMON LAW Law established from previous cases decided by judges, as opposed to statutory law, which is passed by the state or federal legislature.

COMPARATIVE NEGLIGENCE Actions of each party are compared to each other to determine fault and the percentage of damages each is responsible for.

COMPLAINT Civil complaint is the first pleading filed by a plaintiff stating the causes of action (wrongful acts) against the defendant. Criminal complaint is the formal charges filed by the prosecution against the person believed to have committed the crime.

CONDITIONAL RELEASE Terms under which a criminal defendant is released from custody, usually providing that no laws be broken and he go to work or stay away from certain people.

CONSIDERATION Something of value given by one or both parties to the other, necessary to form a binding contract.

CONTEMPT OF COURT Showing disrespect to the court or failing to carry out a court order. Punishable by sanctions (fine) or incarceration.

CONTINGENT FEE Attorney's fees to be received only on the happening of an event, usually obtaining a settlement or favorable judgment.

CONTINUANCE Postponement of a legal proceeding to a later date or time.

CONTRACT A legally enforceable agreement between two or more competent parties.

CONTRIBUTORY NEGLIGENCE In some states if the plaintiff contributed to the cause of the accident, he cannot recover.

CONVICTION Decision by a judge or jury that a defendant is guilty of a crime.

CORONER'S INQUEST VERDICT After examination of a corpse, the coroner or in-quest jury renders verdict stating name of deceased, time and place of death, medical cause of death and whether death was by natural causes, suicide, accident or hands of another person other than by accident.

CORPUS DELECTI Latin for "body of the crime." Proof that a crime has been committed.

CORROBORATION EVIDENCE Additional evidence that supports initial evidence.

COUNSEL Term used to refer to attorneys and lawyers. Also means to advise and guide a client.

COUNTERCLAIM Also called cross-claim or cross-complaint in some courts. An allegation by a defendant that he has a claim against the plaintiff.

COURT Government branch established to resolve legal disputes.

COURT COSTS Fees paid to court in a lawsuit, e.g., filing fee, motion fee, jury fees, reporter's fee.

COURT REPORTER The person who records, word for word, testimony and other oral proceedings in court.

CRIMINAL CASE Case brought by the government against an individual accused of committing a crime.

CROSS-EXAMINATION Attorney's questioning of an adverse witness, usually a witness called by the opposing party.

DAMAGES Usually monetary compensation an injured party is entitled to in a lawsuit.

DECISION The judgment of a judge following a hearing or trial.

DECLARATORY RELIEF A judge's declaration of the rights of disputing parties.

DECREE A decision or order of the court.

DEFAULT If a defendant fails to file a response in time, the plaintiff can file a request for default and will receive a judgment for what he requested in his initial pleading served on the defendant.

DEFENDANT The person being sued in a civil case, or the person being charged with a crime in a criminal case.

DELIBERATION Jury procedure for reaching a verdict.

DEMUR A legal pleading objecting to some issue raised in the plaintiff's complaint.

DE NOVO Latin for "anew." Typically a party may request a trial de novo, which is a new trial on the same issues.

DEPOSE Questioning of a witness at a deposition.

DEPOSITION Oral testimony given under oath before a certified court reporter.

DIRECT EXAMINATION Initial questioning of a witness by the party calling them to testify.

DIRECTED VERDICT Instruction given by the judge to the jury that they must return a specific decision since one party, as a matter of law, failed to meet its burden of proof.

DISBAR To rescind a lawyer's right to practice law because of illegal or unethical conduct.

DISCOVERY Pretrial procedure for each party to obtain evidence, testimony and documents that the other party may use at trial. Usually consists of interrogatories, requests for admission, depositions and requests for production of documents.

DISMISSAL Termination of a case.

DISPOSITION Termination of a case, usually by a criminal defendant being sentenced.

DISSENT Opinion of appellate judges who disagree with the opinion of the majority of the appellate judges.

DISTRICT ATTORNEY Same as prosecutor. Government attorney who files charges and prosecutes criminals for their criminal acts.

DISTRICT COURT U.S. district courts are trial courts. Some states also call their trial courts district courts.

DIVERSION Routing a juvenile or adult offender out of the traditional criminal justice system (fine and jail) and into a rehabilitation program, e.g., drug rehabilitation, education or community service.

DOCKET A log listing the legal documents filed in a case, or a list of cases to be heard in a particular court.

DOUBLE JEOPARDY Being tried twice for the same offense. A defendant cannot be tried twice for the same crime in the same state, but he may be charged with both state and federal crimes for the same actions and tried by both, or if the first jury could not reach a decision (hung jury) or a conviction is reversed on appeal, a second trial can occur.

DUE PROCESS Guaranteed steps in legal proceedings to ensure fairness to a defendant.

EN BANC When all the judges of an appellate court sit together to hear oral arguments in a case.

ENJOIN An order, usually called an injunction, requiring a person to do or not do a specific act.

EVIDENCE Information presented by a party to help prove their allegations.

EXCLUSIONARY RULE Prevents the state from offering unconstitutionally obtained evidence against a criminal defendant.

EXEMPLARY DAMAGES Also called punitive damages, money ordered paid to make an example or to punish a defendant for wrongful conduct.

EXHIBIT Item offered by a party to the judge or jury to help prove their case.

EX PARTE One party asking for some legal action without the other party present.

EX POST FACTO Latin for "after the fact." A law that makes actions that occurred prior to the law being passed illegal. Such laws are constitutionally prohibited.

EXPUNGE Official removal of a record. Expunging a criminal record removes the record from official files and allows the defendant to represent that the event never occurred.

EXTRADITION Transfer of an accused from one state or nation to the state or nation that intends to prosecute the person for a crime.

FEDERAL QUESTION Dispute that involves the interpretation or application of the U.S. Constitution or acts of Congress. These matters are decided by federal rather than state courts.

FELONY A serious crime usually punishable by imprisonment for one year or more, as opposed to a misdemeanor, which is usually punishable by jail time for less than a year.

FILE To deliver papers, usually pleadings, to the court clerk to have them become part of the documents in a case.

FINDING The decision of a court on the factual issues.

FORUM The court or location where a dispute is heard and decided.

FRAUD Intentionally deceiving a person for the purpose of getting him to act against his interest and in favor of the person creating the fraud.

GAG ORDER Protective order by a judge to ensure a fair trial. It may prohibit parties, counsels, witnesses, law-enforcement agents and court personnel from disseminating information about a pending criminal trial to the news media. Usually used only in criminal cases.

GARNISHMENT Legally attaching a person's wages to satisfy a court order to pay money.

GOOD TIME Period credited to prisoner for periods of good behavior, which applies as a credit to reduce the total prison term.

GRAND JURY Assembly of citizens to hear or investigate allegations of criminal behavior or wrongdoing. In appropriate cases an indictment will be issued charging a person with a crime. All proceedings are conducted in secret.

HABEAS CORPUS Latin for "produce the body." A writ typically used by prisoners to challenge the constitutionality of their conviction or imprisonment.

HARMLESS ERROR An error by the trial judge but so minor so as not to have affected the rights of the parties, and therefore not sufficient to overturn the decision of the judge or jury.

HEARING Procedure for receiving and evaluating evidence on a matter in controversy.

HEARSAY A statement by a witness about something that he did not see firsthand, but rather heard about from someone else.

HEARSAY RULE Rule of evidence that, unless there is an exception, is not admissible at trial.

HOLDING Decision of a court, often used by other courts in deciding similar matters.

HOSTILE WITNESS A witness called by a party who is antagonistic to the party calling him. Usually the calling party can use leading questions with hostile witnesses.

HUNG JURY A jury that is unable to reach a verdict.

IMMUNITY Guarantee by the government to not bring criminal charges against a party, usually in exchange for the party agreeing to testify against others.

IMPEACHMENT OF A WITNESS Attacking the credibility of a witness by evidence or testimony of other witnesses.

IMPLIED CONTRACT An unwritten or unspoken contract based on the circumstances.

INADMISSIBLE Evidence that is not allowed at a hearing or trial.

IN CAMERA Latin for "in chambers." A hearing held in the judge's chambers rather than in open court, for privacy or security reasons.

INDICTMENT The formal charges by a grand jury that sufficient evidence exists against a person to justify a trial.

INDIGENT A person whose income and assets fall below a certain level, qualifying him for representation by a public defender.

INFERIOR COURT Courts of limited jurisdiction.

IN FORMA PAUPERIS Latin for "in the manner of a pauper." Because of limited income or assets, a person may qualify for waiver of court fees and can sue "in forma pauperis."

INFORMATION Formal accusation by a prosecutor charging a defendant with a crime. An alternative to a grand-jury indictment.

INFRACTION Minor violation of law.

INJUNCTION Court order prohibiting or requiring certain acts.

IN PRO PER Person representing himself in a legal proceeding. In criminal cases, if the court finds the defendant is mentally competent, he has the right to represent himself.

INSTRUCTIONS Directions given by a judge to a jury regarding how to proceed with deliberations and what law to apply to the facts.

INTERROGATORIES Written questions from one party to another, which must be answered in writing and under oath. Part of the discovery process.

INTESTATE Dying without a will.

INTESTATE SUCCESSION State laws that determine who receives property of a deceased who died without a will.

IRREVOCABLE TRUST Trust that cannot be revoked by the person creating it.

ISSUE A disputed point between parties to a lawsuit.

JUDGE Government employee who decides lawsuits brought to court. The terms "judge" and "presiding judge" are usually used in trial courts, "judge" and "chief judge" in intermediate courts of appeal and "justice" and "chief justice" usually in courts of last resort.

JUDGMENT The final decision in a lawsuit.

JUDGMENT PROOF A person without sufficient funds to pay a judgment.

JUDICIAL ECONOMY Efficient use of the court's time.

JUDICIAL NOTICE Court's acceptance of the existence of something as a matter of law or fact without the necessity of formal proof of that matter.

JURISDICTION A court's authority to hear a particular case.

JUROR A person chosen to serve on a jury.

JURY A group of people selected according to law who hear facts of a case and decide which party's case is more believable.

JURY PANEL Group of people from which a jury is selected.

JURY VIEW Jury travels outside the courtroom to view the scene of an event that occurred in a case or some other relevant evidence, like a building or vehicle, that cannot be brought into the courtroom. Judge, clerk, reporter, bailiff, attorneys and jury all attend. Court is in session during view.

JUSTICE A judge on the appellate level.

LAWSUIT Legal proceeding wherein the plaintiff claims that the defendant breached some obligation or duty that caused the plaintiff harm and for which the defendant should be held legally accountable.

LAY WITNESS A witness other than an expert witness.

LEADING QUESTION Question phrased in such a manner that it suggests the answer.

LIABLE Finding that a party is legally responsible to another party.

LIBEL Written or printed matter that injures another's reputation.

LIEN A legal hold on property for security for a debt.

LIQUIDATED DAMAGES Amount agreed to by parties to a contract as the damages if the contract is breached.

LITIGANT Party to a lawsuit, e.g., plaintiff or defendant.

LITIGATION The process of filing suit in court and having the court determine the outcome of a controversy.

LIVING TRUST Trust set up during the lifetime of the person creating it. Also known as an inter vivos trust.

MANSLAUGHTER The unlawful killing of a person without premeditation.

MEDIATION Process whereby disputing parties have a neutral third party (mediator) help them resolve their dispute.

MENS REA Latin for "guilty mind." Required to find criminal responsibility.

MERITS Issues of legal substance upon which a case is decided.

MISDEMEANOR Crime usually punishable by less than one year in jail.

MISTRIAL Trial that, because of error or misconduct or jury's inability to reach a decision, does not resolve the case. The case usually starts over at a later date with a new jury.

MOOT CASE A case not based on existing facts or rights wherein the decision is legally meaningless.

MOTION A request to the court for an order.

MURDER The unlawful killing of one human being by another with malice aforethought.

NEGLIGENCE Failure to exercise ordinary care in one's actions.

NOLO CONTENDERE Latin for "no contest." Plea entered by criminal defendant that he does not dispute the charges, but he does not admit them. Has same effect as guilty plea in a criminal case, but may not be considered as an admission of guilt in a civil case.

OBJECTION Disagreeing with the properness of a court proceeding or evidence offered by an opposing party.

OF COUNSEL Attorney who assists but is not fully responsible for the case.

OFFER OF PROOF Showing to a judge the substance and relevancy of evidence before he rules on other party's objection that the evidence is irrelevant.

OPINION A written explanation of a decision by a judge.

ORAL ARGUMENT Lawyers summarizing their position and answering judge's questions.

ORDER Decision by a judge directing or forbidding certain action.

PAROLE Supervised release of a prisoner with conditions attached.

PARTIES People involved in a legal proceeding, e.g., plaintiff and defendant.

PEREMPTORY CHALLENGE Attorney's rejection of a potential juror with no need to state a reason.

PERJURY Making a false statement under oath.

PETIT JURY The jurors who decide a civil or criminal case, also called a trial jury.

PETITIONER Person filing papers with the court asking for specified action.

PLAIN ERROR Obvious error in trial court proceedings requiring an appellate court to reverse and grant a new trial.

PLAINTIFF Person who initiates lawsuit, usually by filing a complaint.

PLEA Accused's response to criminal charges.

PLEA BARGAIN Agreement between prosecution and criminal defendant to resolve a case.

PLEADING Legal documents filed by the parties to a lawsuit, e.g., complaint, answer or demur.

POLLING THE JURY Procedure whereby each juror is asked in open court if he agrees with the verdict.

PRECEDENT Law applied in a previously decided case that is used to help decide a current case.

PREJUDICIAL ERROR Mistake by judge that justifies appellate court's reversal of his decision.

PRELIMINARY HEARING Procedure where judge decides if sufficient evidence exists to justify trying a criminal defendant for the crime charged.

PREPONDERANCE OF THE EVIDENCE Standard of proof where there is more evidence in favor than against a factual issue.

PRESENTENCE INVESTIGATION Usually conducted by the probation department to gain background information about a guilty defendant to determine the appropriate sentence.

PRESUMPTION A rule of law that, if certain facts exist, the judge or jury can conclude other facts.

PRETRIAL CONFERENCE Meeting between attorneys and judge prior to trial to make the trial more efficient by narrowing the issues to be tried and discussing procedures during trial.

PRIMA-FACIE CASE The minimum facts that must exist to create a legal case.

PROBABLE CAUSE Sufficient facts to believe an individual has committed a crime.

PROBATION Conditional release of a criminal defendant.

PRO BONO PUBLICO Latin for "for the good of the public." When an attorney takes a case, usually free of charge, to benefit a person with limited finances or the public in general.

PRO SE Latin for "for oneself." Refers to person who represents himself in court without an attorney. Alternative term is "in pro per."

PROSECUTOR Government attorney who tries criminal cases, also known as district attorney.

PUBLIC DEFENDER Government attorney who defends indigent criminal defendants.

QUASH To void a legal document.

QUASI-JUDICIAL STAFF Court personnel who hear certain types of cases, e.g., traffic, family law or support issues. Sometimes called referees, commissioners or hearing officers.

REASONABLE DOUBT Uncertainty about one's guilt.

REBUTTAL Contrary evidence.

RECORD A written account of court proceedings.

RECUSAL Disqualification of a judge for prejudice or for having an interest in the subject of the dispute.

RE-DIRECT EXAMINATION Questioning of a party's own witness following cross-examination by the opposing party.

REMAND Appellate court sending case back to lower court for further action.

RES JUDICATA Latin for "a thing decided." A matter once decided by a court cannot be raised again by either party.

REVERSE Action by an appellate court setting aside the decision of a lower court.

REVOCABLE TRUST Trust that the creator can change or terminate during his lifetime.

SANCTION Punishment (usually a monetary fine) by a judge of a party or attorney for improper conduct in a legal proceeding.

SEARCH WARRANT Judge's order that police may search a specific location for specific evidence.

SENTENCE A guilty defendant's punishment ordered by the court.

SEQUESTER Court order that a jury is not to have contact with people or media sources during trial or deliberations.

SERVE Properly giving a legal document to an opposing party, usually by personally handing it to them.

SETTLEMENT Resolution of a dispute, either between the parties, with the aid of attorneys, or with the assistance of a judge.

SETTLOR Person who creates a trust, also called trustor or grantor.

SIDEBAR Discussion between judge and attorneys, usually at the side of the judge's bench, done quietly so jurors and parties do not hear.

SLANDER Defamatory spoken words that harm someone's reputation.

SPECIAL APPEARANCE Attorney appearing for a party for a limited purpose, as opposed to a general appearance where the attorney agrees to represent the party for the entire case.

SPECIAL DAMAGES Costs of medical treatment, loss of wages and other monetary expenses caused by the other party's actions. Also called economic damages.

SPECIFIC PERFORMANCE Court order requiring a party to do what they promised to do.

STANDING The legal right to initiate a lawsuit.

STARE DECISIS Applying legal decisions from prior cases to substantially similar current cases.

STATUTE Law created by legislature. Also called code.

STATUTE OF LIMITATION Time period within which a plaintiff must file suit.

STAY Suspension of a legal proceeding or order.

STIPULATION Agreement between parties on a particular legal issue, thus saving time by not requiring the formal introduction of evidence to prove the particular issue.

STRIKE Remove from the court record improper question or answer or evidence.

SUA SPONTE Latin for "of itself." A court acting on its own motion without waiting for one of the parties to make the motion.

SUBPOENA Written court order for a person to appear at a legal proceeding.

SUBPOENA DUCES TECUM Written court order for person to appear and produce specified documents at a legal proceeding.

SUBSTANTIVE LAW Law dealing with rights, duties and liabilities as opposed to procedural law, which is law dealing with method of asserting rights.

SUMMARY JUDGMENT Court decision that one party wins, based on information and evidence offered in writing, prior to trial.

SUMMONS Legal document notifying a party of a lawsuit and the time within which they must file a response.

TEMPORARY RESTRAINING ORDER Immediate order that prohibits a person from certain conduct or actions until the time of a hearing.

TESTIMONY Oral evidence from a witness.

TORT A civil wrong or breach of a legal duty.

TRANSCRIPT The official record of a hearing or trial.

TRUST A legal instrument used to hold and manage property. Person who creates the trust is the trustor, grantor or settlor, person who manages the property is the trustee, and the person who receives the benefit of the trust is the beneficiary.

TRUSTEE Person who manages property placed in a trust.

UNDUE INFLUENCE Influencing another so that his or her decisions or actions are not from free will but rather the result of the undue influence. Basis to void actions taken because of the undue influence, e.g., creation of a will.

UPHOLD The decision of an appellate court not to reverse a lower-court decision.

VACATE To set aside a previous decision.

VENIRE Panel of citizens called for jury service.

VENUE The proper geographically located court to hear a case.

VERDICT Decision of a jury or a judge.

VOIR DIRE Latin for "speak the truth." Procedure for questioning prospective jurors to determine their ability to be fair and impartial.

WARRANT An order signed by a judge or magistrate directing specific action.

WEIGHT OF EVIDENCE Amount of evidence in favor of one position or another.

WITNESS A person who testifies under oath.

WRIT An order of the court requiring a specific act.

WRIT OF CERTIORARI A U.S. Supreme Court order to a lower court to deliver the records of a case that it will hear on appeal.

Abbreviations and Acronyms

AJ Associate judge or justice.

BFP Bona fide purchaser—one who acted in good faith and without knowledge of outstanding rights of others when acquiring property.

CI A confidential informant.

DA District attorney.

DEPO Short for deposition.

DWI Driving while intoxicated.

EEOC Equal Employment Opportunity Commission.

ET AL Latin for "and others."

FOIA Freedom of Information Act.

IN PRO PER Short for In Propria Persona, Latin meaning "for oneself." A person representing himself in a legal proceeding.

JD Juris Doctor. Degree awarded by most law schools. Some still award an LLB.

LLB Legum Baccalaureus (Bachelor of Law). Degree awarded by some law schools. Most award a JD.

MO Modus operandi—method of operation.

NGI Not guilty by reason of insanity.

OR Own recognizance—criminal defendant released on his own responsibility to return at a later date. No bail required.

PD Public defender.

PJ Presiding judge.

RICO The Federal Racketeering Influenced and Corrupt Organization statute enacted in 1970 to provide prosecutors with a tool that cuts into the economic base of organized crime. The statute imposes severe criminal penalties and provides the government with significant civil enforcement powers when offenses are committed by infiltrating and controlling enterprises. Many states have passed what are called "little RICO" statutes.

SDT Subpoena Duces Tecum.

TRO Temporary restraining order.

UCC Uniform Commercial Code.

CERT Certiorari—the U.S. Supreme Court must grant certiorari to hear a case.

Common Legal Slang

BODY DUMP Body of person killed at one place and dumped at another location.

BOILERPLATE Standard form or template used in a legal matter.

CLIENT CONTROL Client who is willing to accept advice of attorney.

COP A PLEA Defendant deciding to plead guilty to a lesser charge or to the stated charge in exchange for a lighter sentence.

DEEP POCKET A defendant with lots of money.

GRISS CALENDAR The criminal calendar usually called first thing in the morning in most courts.

LATENT PRINTS Fingerprints found at the scene of a crime.

ODDI "Other dude did it" defense raised by one accused of a crime.

PLEAD THE SHEET Prosecution's hard-line position that the criminal defendant must plead guilty to all charges listed on the criminal complaint. No room for plea bargaining.

PRO BONO Short for "pro bono publico." When an attorney takes a case for free.

RACK TWELVE Bring in a jury panel. Usually said after settlement efforts fail and one side wants to start a trial and let a jury decide the issues in controversy.

RED HERRING An issue with no legal merit, raised by one party to distract attention from the relevant issues.

RIP Restitution, injury, punishment. Prosecutors RIP a file—consult with the victim before they make a plea-bargain offer.

ROLLOVER When one accused of a crime makes a deal with the police or district attorney to testify against another defendant in exchange for being charged with a lesser crime or receiving a reduced sentence.

TEN PRINTS Fingerprints taken from a known person. Also called ink prints.

WHALE Used to describe a case that the prosecutor cannot possibly lose. Even if the prosecutor didn't show up for the trial, the defendant would still be convicted. Prosecutors sometimes draw a picture of a whale on the file, just to brighten up the defense attorney's day.

WOBBLER A crime that can be charged by the district attorney either as a misdemeanor or a felony.

Research Resources

The Federal Court System

For information on the U.S. Supreme Court, for copies of recent opinions, to visit the court or for general information:

Public Information Officer, Supreme Court of the United States
Washington, DC 20543, Telephone: (202) 479-3211
www.findlaw.com, www.law.cornell.edu

For information on other federal courts:

Public Information Officer, Administrative Office of United States Courts
One Columbus Circle, NE, Washington, DC 20544
Telephone: (202) 273-0107, www.uscourts.gov

For a wide variety of information on criminal and juvenile justice:

National Criminal Justice Reference Service
P.O. Box 6000, Rockville, MD 20849-6000
Telephone: (800) 851-3420, www.ncjrs.org

For other federal court information and Web site links:

The Federal Judicial Center
One Columbus Circle, NE, Washington, DC 20002
Telephone: (202) 273-4160, www.fjc.gov

The State Court System

For information on the state court system including court administration, sentencing, court technology, alternative dispute resolution and trends:

National Center for State Courts
300 Newport Avenue, Williamsburg, VA 23185
Telephone: (757) 253-2000, www.ncsc.dni.us

For information on a specific state's court system contact, depending on the state:

> State Court Administrative Office, Administrative Office of the Court or Office of the State Court Administrator, usually located where the state supreme court is located, which is usually the state capitol.

For information on a local court, contact that court (different names in different states):

> Trial Court Administrator, Clerk of the Court or Court Executive Officer

Finding the Law in a Law Library

Some public libraries have the state code and general legal reference books. The reference librarian can assist you. Your best bet for detailed information is a law library. Many courthouses have law libraries open to the public. They typically carry the state's codes, state and federal reporters (appellate court decisions with the facts and law of the case) and books on specific topics. Law librarians will assist you in locating particular books, but don't expect them to do research for you. An increasing number of law libraries have computers for research, either on CDs or on-line. Law schools have law libraries often open to the public. Large law offices have law libraries and if requested they may allow you to use their books.

Walking into a law library can be an overwhelming and humbling experience. You may be looking for general information, a statute on a specific subject or a case dealing with a particular legal topic. Once you know the categories of books in the library, it's relatively easy to locate what you are interested in.

Legal Encyclopedias

This is a great way to begin reading about a legal topic or just to scan for ideas. Legal encyclopedias are organized alphabetically by topic, e.g., "arson," "murder," "will contest."

For a general overview of American law, look at:

> American Jurisprudence 2d edition (called Am.Jur.2d), and
> Corpus Juris Secundum.

For a more in-depth look at selected topics on state or federal law, look at:

American Law Reports

For an overview of the law in a specific state, the most populous states have their own encyclopedias, e.g.:

California Jurisprudence

New York Jurisprudence

Texas Jurisprudence

Treatises

These books usually cover a specific legal topic in depth and are written by a recognized authority in the field. For example:

Collier on Bankruptcy

Couch on Insurance

Nimmer on Copyrights

Statutes/Codes

Statutes or codes are laws passed by Congress or a state's legislature and written into books called "code books." These books contain the laws of the U.S. and states and are organized by topic, e.g., civil procedure, crimes and evidence. Some books contain only the text of the statute, while others are annotated and contain explanatory information about the statutes and references to court decisions that have interpreted the statutes. For example:

United States Code Annotated

Your state's code annotated

Case Reporters

Case reporters are books with case law—cases presented to and ruled on by trial judges and then appealed by one or both parties to the intermediate appellate court or supreme court, which renders an opinion as to the propriety of the trial judge's actions.

Each state has case reporters (sometimes just called "reporters") for its appellate (state appellate reports) and supreme courts (state reports), as does the U.S. Court of Appeals (Federal Reporter) and U.S. Supreme Court (choice of three: U.S. Supreme Court Reports; Supreme Court Reporter; Supreme Court Reports, Lawyer's Edition).

Case books make interesting reading since they tell the facts of the case, how the trial judge decided and how the appellate court decided.

Proof of Facts

To determine what must be proved to win a civil or criminal case, look at:

American Jurisprudence Proof of Facts

Law Reviews

Law students and professors have their articles published in their school's law review. These articles tend to be the author's ideas about how the law on a particular topic should evolve, as opposed to the current state of the law. Look at:

Harvard Law Review

Law review for law schools in your state

Legal Journals

Legal journals, most published by bar associations, contain articles on recent developments in legal topics and topics of current interest. Look at:

American Bar Association Journal

Your state's bar association journal

Digests

Digests contain short statements of the law on various topics that are assigned a key number for ease of locating the same topic discussed in other cases. The digests are organized by federal and state cases.

Form Books

If you are interested in a particular legal form, i.e., a complaint or answer or subpoena, look at:

American Jurisprudence Legal Forms

or state-specific formbooks, e.g.:

California Forms of Pleading and Practice

Illinois Forms Business and Practice

New Jersey Forms—Legal and Business

Practice Manuals

If you are interested in how an attorney would handle a particular type of case, look at a practice manual for that subject, e.g.:

Defense of Narcotics Cases

Michigan Probate

Prosecution and Defense of Criminal Conspiracy Cases

If you get serious about legal research, *Legal Research, How to Find and Understand the Law* by Stephen Elias and Susan Levinkind, published by Nolo Press, will show you the way.

Internet Resources

For legal subjects, law schools, legal organizations, law firms and lawyers, federal and state laws and cases, legal news and more:

www.law.com

www.findlaw.com

For U.S. Supreme Court cases, U.S. Codes and links to other legal sites:

www.law.cornell.edu

For current news on legal topics:

www.ljx.com

For information and transcripts of testimony on current or recent high profile trials:

www.courttv.com

For a search engine for law-related topics:

www.lawcrawler.com

For a long list of self-help legal books for the nonlawyer:

www.nolo.com

For more legal Web sites than you can ever visit:

Law on the Net by James Evans, published by Nolo Press, Berkeley, California, lists over two thousand law-related sites, including federal law, state law, international law, law schools, libraries and research, the legal profession, publications, discussion groups and legal topics A to Z.

Legal Organizations

American Bar Association, 750 N. Lake Shore Drive, Chicago, IL 60611, (312) 988-5000, (800) 285-2221, www.abanet.org

National District Attorney's Association, 99 Canal CN Plaza, Suite 510, Alexandria, VA 22314, (703) 549-9222, www.ndaa-apri.org

Helps prosecutors with trials. Have various publications on criminal prosecution available to the public.

National Association of Criminal Defense Lawyers, 1627 K St. NW, 12th Fl, Washington, DC 20006, (202) 872-8688, www.criminaljustice.org
Lawyers interested in the defense of criminal cases.

American College of Trial Lawyers, 8001 Irvine Center Drive, Suite 960, Irvine, CA 92618, (949) 727-3194, www.actl.com
An honorary legal association; membership by invitation only.

Association of Trial Lawyers of America, 1050 31st St. NW, Washington, DC 20007, (800) 424-2725, www.atlanet.org
Litigation and practice support organization for trial lawyers.

Judges' Education:

The National Judicial College, Judicial College Building 358, University of Nevada, Reno, Reno, NV 89557, (800) 255-8343, www@judges.org

Use of Social-Science Research in Jury Selection and Case Presentation:

National Jury Project, 285 West Broadway, New York, NY 10013, (212) 219-8962, www.njp.com
Offices in New York, California and Minnesota

Reference Books

A History of The American Bar. Charles Warren. Howard Fertig, 1966.

American Civil Procedure. Geoffrey C. Hazard, Jr. and Michele Taruffo. New Haven: Yale University Press, 1993.

American Legal History. Kermit L. Hall, William M. Wiecek and Paul Finkelman. New York: Oxford University Press, 1991.

An Introduction to Legal Systems. Duncan M. Derrett, editor. New York: Frederick A. Praeger, 1968.

Criminal Law. Wayne R. LaFave and Austin W. Scott, 2d ed. West Publishing Co., 1986.

Everybody's Guide to the Law. Melvin M. Belli, Sr. and Allen P. Wilkinson. Harcourt Brace Jovanovich, 1986.

Federal Crime and Its Enforcement. Norman Abrams and Sara S. Beale. West Publishing Co., 1993.

Fundamentals of American Law. Alan B. Morrison, editor. New York: Oxford University Press, 1996.

Fundamentals of Trial Technique. Thomas A. Mavet, Donald Casswell, and Gordon P. MacDonald. Little, Brown, 1984.

Introduction to Anglo-American Law. Hugh Evander Willis. Indiana University, 1926.

Origins of the Common Law. Arthur R. Hogue. Indianapolis: Liberty Press, 1966.

Search Warrant Law Deskbook. John M. Burkoff. Clark Boardman Callaghan.

The Code of Hammurabi, King of Babylon. Robert Francis Harper. Chicago: The University of Chicago Press, 1904.

The Digest of Justinian, 4 Volumes. Alan Watson, editor. University of Pennsylvania Press, 1985.

The Edicts of Asoka. N.A. Nikam and Richard McKeon, editors. Chicago: The University of Chicago Press, 1959.

The Jury in America. John Guinther. New York: Facts On File Publications, 1988.

Abuse of process, 177
Accessories, 75
Accomplices, 74-75
Actual legal controversies, 5
Administrative law, 206
Admiralty law, 206
Adoptions, 201-202
Adversary system, 5
Advocates, 16-17
Air and space law, 206
Alimony, 200
Alternative dispute resolutions (ADR),
    53-54, 216
"Ambulance chasers," defined, 25
Annulments, 198-199
Antitrust law, 192
Appeals, 170-171, 247-248
Appellate law, 206
Application of law, judges, 13
Arbitration, 54
Arraignment, 135-137
Arrest, 114-126
    warrant, 115-120
Arson, 70
Assault, 176
Attorney fees, 194, 212

Bail, 132-134
Bailiffs, 34-37
Bankruptcy, 195-196
"Bar," defined, 15
Battery, 176
Bench trials, 216
Bench warrants, 125
Bigamy, 72
Bill of Rights, 4
Brandishing a weapon, 73

Bribery, 74
Burglary, 70
Business law, 186-189
Business records, searches of, 109-110

Carjacking, 66
Case law, 13
Challenges, 151-152
Child custody, 200-201
Civil law, 175-207
Civil trials. *See also* specific aspect of trial
    sequence, 210, 225
Class-action lawsuits, 184
Clerk of the courts, 42
Closing arguments, 241-243
Code of Hammurabi, 2
Codes, 13
Commercial law, 191-192
Common law, 4-8
Common-law marriages, 198
Compensatory damages, 193
Computers, searches of, 107
Confessions, 126-129
Consent, search, 98-99
Consequential damages, 193
Conservatorships, 204
Conspiracy, 60
Constitutional law, 13
Contracts, 185-186
Controlled substance offenses, 73
Copyrights, 191
Corporations, 186-187
Corpus delicti, 60
Costs, 194
Counselors, 16-17
Court reporters, 39-40
Courtroom, 15

bailiffs, 34-37
clerk of the courts, 42
clerks, 37-39
court reporters, 39-40
family-court mediators, 42-43
filing clerks, 42
interpreters, 40-41
jury commissioners, 43-44
law clerks, 41
law librarians, 44-45
personnel, 34-46
probation officers, 45-46
research attorneys, 41-42
Courtroom clerks, 37-39
Courtroom interpreters, 40-41
Crimes, 58-76. *See also* specific crime
corpus delicti, 60
elements, 59-60
Criminals, 50-51
Criminal trials, 130-174. *See also* specific
aspect of trial sequence, 148

Damages, 192-194. *See also* specific damage
Dangerous animals, 183-184
Death penalty, 152-153, 167-168
Debtor-creditor laws, 194-195
Defamation, 177-178
Defendants, 51-53
case, 239-240
Defense, 159-160
Defenses, 76-82
Definitions, 249-264
Discovery, 139-140, 214-216
Disturbing the peace, 72
Divorces, 199
Driving under the influence, 73
Due process, 4-5
Durable power of attorney, 203-204

Edicts of Emperor Asoka, 2
Emotional distress
intentional, 177
negligent, 180

Employment discrimination, 187-188
Environmental law, 205
Estate planning, 203-205
Evidence. *See also* search and seizure
gathering, 138
introducing, 240
Examinations, 154-158
Exclusionary rule, search and seizure,
113-114
Expert witnesses, 46-47
Extortion, 69

False imprisonment, 62, 176-177
Family laws, 197-202
Family-court mediators, 42-43
Federal court system, 9-11
Federal crimes, 74
Filing clerks, 42
Forgery, 69
Form of question, 231-232
Fraud, 179

Gambling, 72
Garbage, searches of, 109
Glossary, 249-264
Grand juries, 47-48
Grand theft, 68
Guardianships, 204

Henry II, 7
History of legal system, 1-13
Homicide, 63

Illegal weapons, 70
Immigration law, 205-206
In pro pers, 54
Incest, 72
Insurance law, 206-207
Intellectual property law, 189-191
Intentional misconduct, 176-179.
See specific type
Interference with relations, 179
International law, 206

Intestate distributions, 203
Invasion of privacy, 178
Investigations, 211-212

Judges, 28-34
  application of law, 13
  discipline, 31
  duties, 30
  education, 29
  removal, 31
  rent-a-judge, 54
  role, 5-6
  selection, 28-29
Judgments, 246
Juries, 47-50, 147-150, 153, 162-165
  deliberations, 244-245
  grand juries, 47-48
  instructions, 243-244
  modern, evolution of, 7
  petit juries, 48
  selection, 224-229
Jurisdiction, 12
Jury commissioners, 43-44
Justinian Code, 2
Juvenile proceedings, 171-174

Kidnapping, 62

Labor law, 192
Landlord-tenant laws, 196-197
Law clerks, 27, 41
Law firms, 21-23
  law clerks, 27
  legal secretaries, 27
  paralegals, 27
  personnel, 26-28
  private investigators, 28
  receptionists, 26-27
Law librarians, 44-45
Lawyers, 14-21
  advocates, 16-17
  "ambulance chasers," defined, 25
  behavior, 15-16

corporate attorneys, 20-21
counselors, 16-17
duties, 15-16
law firms, 20-21
litigators, 16-17
notebooks, 24-25
personalities, 25-26
prosecutors, 17-20
public defenders, 17-20
research attorneys, 41-42
role, 6
sole practitioners, 23-24
tools, 24-25
Legal secretaries, 27
Legal terms, 249-264
Liability
  product, 184
  strict, 182-184
Libel, 177-178
Limited-liability companies, 187
Liquidated damages, 193
Litigators, 16-17
Living wills, 204
Loitering, 71

Magna Carta, 4
Mail, searches of, 106-107
Malicious mischief, 72
Malicious prosecution, 177
Malpractice, 181
Manslaughter, 65-66
Marital property, 199-200
Maritime law, 206
Marriages, 198
Mayhem, 63
Mediation, 53-54
Military law, 10-11
Minors, crimes involving, 73
Miranda warnings, 128-129
Mistrial, 165
Motions, 240-241, 246-247
Multiple offenses, 75

Multiple prosecutions, 75-76
Murder, 64-65

Name changes, 202
Negligence, 179-182
Nominal damages, 192
Notebooks
  lawyers, 24-25
Nuisances, 197

Objections, 158-159
Obscenity, 71
Opening statements, 229-230
Origin of legal system, 1-13

Pandering, 71
Paralegals, 27
Partnerships, 186
Patents, 189-190
Paternity, 202
People, searches of, 100-102
Perjury, 74
Personal injury, 175-184. *See also* specific
  type
Personal property conversion, 178-179
Petit juries, 48
Petty theft, 69
Pimping, 71
Places, searches of, 102-106
Plaintiffs, 51
  case, 232-239
Plain view seizure, 97-98
Plea bargaining, 143
Precedent, 5
Preliminary hearings, 137-138
Premarital agreements, 197-198
Pretrial conferences, 222-224
Private investigators, 28
Probate, 203
Probation, 170
Probation officers, 45-46
Product liability, 184

Property damage, 175-184. *See also* specific
  type
Prosecutors, 17-20
Prostitution, 71
Public defenders, 17-20
Punishments, 82-84
Punitive damages, 193

Rape, 63
Real property laws, 196-197
Receiving stolen property, 69
Receptionists, 26-27
Rent-a-judge, 54
Research attorneys, 41-42
Research resources, 265-271
Riot, 72
Robbery, 66
Rout, 72
Rules of evidence, 231

Search and seizure, 85-114
  business records, searches of, 109-110
  computers, searches of, 107
  consent, 98-99
  exclusionary rule, 113-114
  exigent circumstances, 99
  garbage, searches of, 109
  mail, searches of, 106-107
  people, searches of, 100-102
  places, searches of, 102-106
  plain view, 97-98
  private parties, 112
  surveillance methods, 110-112
  telephone, searches of, 107
  vehicles, searches of, 107-108
  warrants, 88-97
Sentencing, 168-170
Separations, 199
Settlement conferences, 220-222
Sex offenses, 67
Sexual harassment, 188-189
Slander, 177-178
Sole practitioners, 23-24

Sole proprietorships, 186
Solicitation, 60
Stalking, 66-67
State court system, 11-12
Statutory law, 13
Strict liability, 182-184
Structure of legal system, 1-13
Surveillance methods, 110-112

Taxation law, 205
Telephone, searches of, 107
Ten Commandments, 2
Theft, 67
Tools
  lawyers, 24-25
Tort law, 175-184
Trade secrets, 190
Trademarks, 190-191
Trespass to land, 178
Trial by jury, 6-7
Trials. *See* specific type
Trusts, 204

Ultrahazardous activities, 183
U.S. Constitution, 4

Unlawful assembly, 72

Vagrancy, 71
Vehicles, searches of, 107-108
Venue, 13, 142
Verdicts, 245-246
Victims, 51
Voir dire, 150-151

Warrants
  arrest, 115-120
  bench, 125
  exceptions, 97-100
  "knock-and-announce," 94-95
  search, 88-97
Western Law, 2-3
William the Conqueror, 7
Wills, 203
Witnesses, 144-145
  expert, 46-47
Workers' compensation, 187
Written laws, first, 2
Wrongful birth, 182
Wrongful death, 181-182
Wrongful termination, 189